McCAFFERTY

KING OF THE ROAD

As told to Don Talbot

BOOLARONG PRESS

First published in 1995 by Boolarong Press
With McCafferty's Management Pty Ltd, P.O. Box 643, Toowoomba, 4350.

Copyright © McCafferty's Management Pty Ltd

National Library of Australia
Cataloguing-in-Publication data

   McCafferty, king of the road.

     Includes index.
     ISBN 0 646 23461 7.

     1. McCafferty's Express Coaches – History. 2. Tour bus
     lines – Queensland – History. 3. Bus lines – Queensland –
     History. I. Talbot, Don, 1933-. II. McCafferty's
     Management.

388.322065943

BOOLARONG PRESS
35 Hamilton Road, Moorooka, Brisbane, QLD 4105.
Design and phototypesetting by
Ocean Graphics Pty Ltd, Gold Coast, QLD.
Printed and bound by Watson Ferguson Company, Brisbane.

Contents

Introduction

This story of motorised coach travel in Australia stretches back 55 years to an event in Toowoomba, Queensland, when a young man with vision sat under a tree and planned a coach network to serve every major centre in Australia.

Across the road waiting for passengers was his first bus, a small green and cream 27 h.p. Reo with 35 polished seats. It was his pride and joy and over the years, with hard work and perseverance, he saw the fleet increase to 105 luxury coaches and a staff of 600 across Australia.

This book tells of how Jack McCafferty and McCafferty's – Australia's National Coachline – have survived against the odds to become what is now regarded as a national icon with an annual turnover of $50 million. This is no mean feat when takings on the first day's operation totalled only $5!

Open the pages and enjoy reading about the battles, the wins and the losses, and about the people who make up Australia's coach industry. They are a great crew. It's a remarkable journey and I hope you enjoy the ride.

Jack McCafferty in the Board Room.

About the author

Working as a writer and journalist in Australia I get some fascinating assignments, but none as interesting or as rewarding as what is written in this book.

It is the result of many months of travel to different parts of Australia to interview people associated with the coach industry, and with McCafferty's in particular.

It is the story of Jack McCafferty and the company he created and which has prospered and expanded into every state and territory of Australia and across the waters overseas.

I could not have written this book without the assistance of Mr Jack McCafferty and his family, and the enthusiastic co-operation of staff and former staff of McCafferty's. Everywhere I went doors opened and stories tumbled out – it appears that everyone I met had something to say about McCafferty's.

In 1940, Jack McCafferty sat under a tree at Picnic Point, Toowoomba, alongside his first bus and dreamt of providing a public transport service to connect cities, towns and remote communities across Australia. Today, his dream is a reality and McCafferty's are a national icon. This is his story.

Don Talbot
Toowoomba
November 1994

Acknowledgements

Special thanks to newspapers including *The Chronicle* (Toowoomba) for granting permission to reproduce a number of press photographs in this book. Other photographs have been provided by present and former staff and fellow travellers and friends including Mr Ron Douglas of Toowoomba.

Chapter 1

Newspapers, milk and marriage

(1914-1939)

'Whatever I have done I could never have done on my own, without the full support of my wife and family. If you haven't got that support then you get distracted along the way, and my wife has always let me run the business and she has looked after the house.'

JACK McCAFFERTY

Today, our family company – McCafferty's – is worth on paper more than $15 million. 'That's a hell of a lot' you say – but remember it was a lot of hard work that got us there and I believe it's time I put pen to paper to outline what has happened in the coach industry in Australia along the way and to tell you of the days when I didn't have a cent in my pocket.

I wasn't born with a silver spoon in my mouth and it was a real struggle to survive during the Great Depression of the 1930s.

I came into the world at Breakfast Creek, Brisbane, on March 11, 1914, the son of railway engine driver James (Jim) Gregory McCafferty and Martha Jean McCafferty (née Cherry), formerly of Oakey, Queensland.

My grandfather had also been in transportation. He operated a bullock wagon from Ipswich to Drayton on the Darling Downs and was close on 100 when he threw in the towel.

Our family left our rented house at Breakfast Creek and moved to Warwick in 1919, when I was five years old. I also had one sister Vera, who is now deceased.

I attended classes at Warwick East State School until I moved to Toowoomba and went to Wilsonton State School and later attended St Mary's Christian Brothers College, Warwick. I also spent some

2nd HEAT.

1. James Purtell .. .. ..   Scratch.
2. John Doyle .. ..   1 Yard.
3. Eddie Brennan .. ..   2 Yards.
4. Jack Frawley .. .. ..   3 Yards.
5. Ted Bacon .. ..   3 Yards.
6. Leslie Dillon .. .. ..   4 Yards.
7. Jack McCafferty .. ..   4 Yards.
8. Colin Oldham .. .. ..   5 Yards.

1st ....

2nd ....

3rd ....

Time:

Extract from Christian Brothers' College, Warwick, annual sports program, September 6, 1923.

years at Warwick High School, where I was terrified of speaking in public, and on Fridays, when students were required to speak out in class, I was usually absent.

After my grandfather died in Toowoomba, I lived with my aunt Adelaide at grandfather's house, in Gowrie Road, which was later renamed Bridge Street.

At 13, I returned to Warwick and got my first job selling newspapers and magazines on the platform at Warwick Railway Station. It was my first sortie into merchandising and dealing with the public and people fascinated me.

In those days we handled the main Sydney newspapers as well as the *Daily Mail*, *The Truth*, and *The Patriot* . . . I used to read all the railway timetables and the railway appendix with all the rules for railway workers, in fact anything in print I could get my hands on because in those days there was no radio or TV.

At weekends, I delivered meat to homes for a Warwick butcher and carried the meat in a basket fixed to the handlebars of a heavy delivery bicycle. My pay was four shillings a week. It was hard work but I loved calling on people in their homes and seeing how they lived.

Aunt Adelaide McCafferty

I was always active and looking for something to do, and if ever I had an hour or so to spend I would poke around the Warwick Railway Station offering to do odd jobs. At times I helped mailman Mick O'Brien sort out bags of mail and take them in a horse-drawn spring cart from the station to the Warwick Post Office.

During the Great Depression, I joined the ranks of the unemployed. The Government was sending unemployed men to search for gold. They were given a shovel, a bucket and a special pass to search for gold in the outback and up Mt Morgan way.

I had never heard of anyone striking gold. I think it was just an excuse to get the young people out of the cities during the Depression.

However, although I had joined the queue for equipment and passes, I later had second thoughts. It was then I decided that trying to do something in Toowoomba might be a better proposition than searching for the elusive gold, so I turned in my special pass, bucket and shovel and returned to my aunt's farm.

There was no work but my aunt had a few dairy cows. I persuaded her to allow me to go out with the horse and cart in Toowoomba and see if I could sell milk in the early morning.

It was a time when there were no refrigerators, very few ice chests, and no pasteurised milk. People depended on fresh milk.

I used to get up very early in the morning and help milk the cows. Then it was off down the street with the horse and cart. On the first day I sold six and a half gallons (29.54 litres) of milk – that's 52 pints at tuppence (two cents) a pint , and a penny for half a pint. A lot of people could only afford half a pint. I used to carry pint measures on the cart to measure out a half pint, a pint and a quart. I would run into each house to deliver the milk. Sometimes it was guesswork, but most times people got more than the required measure. As business increased I went to Albert Ellis and ordered a proper milk cart made with rubber tyres, instead of iron, at a cost of £17 ($34), so that all my customers would hear in the early hours of the morning was the 'clippety-clop' of the horse. 'Girlie' knew every stop along the route and I reckon that I had the fastest milk cart in the west.

I changed horses and the newcomer in the shafts was 'Darkie'. He was like a trotter and used to go like the clappers, but he soon recognised the houses where our customers lived and would stop and wait while deliveries were made.

There was keen competition among the milk vendors and some of them were not happy because I was getting out of bed earlier and providing a better service.

I got belted up a couple of times by my competitors. Sometimes they would wait until I was away from the cart delivering milk to a house and then they would put a whip to the horse, particularly when I hadn't locked the wheel.

At other times, they would creep up on the cart in the dark, open the tap and let the milk run away on the ground. You could lose a lot of milk on the gravel roads before you realised what had been done.

I soon had too many customers for the amount of milk we could get from our cows and I decided to use some money borrowed from an uncle to buy a small truck. It was a Superior K Chevrolet utility and I drove it to other dairy farms to purchase milk. Farmers around Westbrook couldn't get rid of their milk anywhere else and I would offer them 4d a gallon. They were pleased to off-load it because even the cheese factory couldn't take deliveries and it would be poured away. In Toowoomba I was selling it for one shilling and fourpence a gallon.

By 1939, I was selling 250 gallons a day. Each day's work would start at 2 a.m. Sometimes I would come home straight from a dance and go out on the milk run without going to bed.

I would be going home when other milkmen were starting their run and I made sure that my customers always had fresh milk for breakfast. There were two deliveries every day.

Money was being saved and by now I had a utility – the best milk-delivery utility in Toowoomba – a Plymouth coupe.

There were about a dozen milkmen in Toowoomba to serve a population of about 25,000. You had to have a licence to sell milk, and inspectors used to make checks.

I concentrated on the Newtown area. I would start serving one customer, and if she was satisfied she would tell her neighbours. I called myself Silverwood Dairy (I took the name from Silverwood Dam at Warwick) and in no time at all I would be delivering milk to every house in the street.

It used to be good milk. What annoys me today is that there are so many different types of milk; they extract all the fat and cream and then charge you more for the product. I can't believe they can do this.

Eventually I realised that my milk business was working on borrowed time. Pasteurisation was coming and I could see the warm milk business being threatened. I sold out to a chap named Richards and I got a good price for it too. I had been going through a bad patch and a crisis had developed when I got ill with mumps and couldn't find anyone to take over the run. I was glad when it was sold and I could try something new and my wife, Lorna, was fully behind me as she explains here:

> *'He wanted to get out of the milk run. It's typical of Jack. He has a wonderful mind for progress. Our solicitor Mr Bernays was*

Jack McCafferty's mind flashed back to his days as a milkman when he took over the reins of this replica of his original milk cart in 1980. The cart is now on display in the Cobb & Co Museum in Toowoomba.

cleaning out his papers years later when he came across an
application which Jack had written to his company asking for a job.
"If I had known then what I know now I would have employed
you," he said.'

For a short time, I worked at Toowoomba's first pasteurised milk
factory in Dent Street, but my vision went beyond watching bottles
on the production line.

I had set my mind on running a hotel, and this could have
happened if I had found the right place at the time. But this was not
to be and again I know that my wife was pleased, and she
expressed it this way:

> 'Jack always had it inside him to run a hotel because his
> grandfather had operated the Charlton Hotel. My mother hated
> hotels and wouldn't want to see me inside one.'

I met Lorna Myrle Schultz, of Millmerran, at a dance in
Cambooya, and we seemed to hit it off straight away. I didn't waste
time and we were married in 1939. We drove to Melbourne in my
Chevrolet car and looked around to see if we could buy a hotel.
However, we couldn't find anything of interest and returned to
Toowoomba to examine other ventures. Lorna and I had both had
difficult upbringings and this is how she saw our first meeting:

> 'When I met Jack at the dance, I realised that we were both loners.
> My two sisters had dragged me out to Cambooya one night and
> Jack and I danced and talked. I found that we had so much in
> common. Jack had had a very hard life in his early years, and mine
> had also been difficult.
>
> Now we were friends there was the problem of religion – Jack's
> family were Catholics and my family were strong Lutherans. In those
> days, they would stand outside each other's church but not go in —
> but when a reception was held, with food and drink, everyone was
> there!
>
> It was in 1939 and people were getting uneasy about the war. Jack
> went down to Brisbane to tell an uncle, who was a doctor, about our
> intended marriage. When the doctor heard that I was a Lutheran and
> not Catholic, he advised Jack to look elsewhere for a bride.
>
> It was sad in those days for anyone involved in a mixed marriage.
> Earlier Jack had gone with another girl, but had been told to 'get out'
> because he was a Catholic and she wasn't.
>
> It was terrible but we had so much in common and we persevered.
> Jack's grandparents came from the same area as mine – Kingsthorpe,
> Gowrie Junction and Charlton. We felt the same way about so many

things and it wasn't long before we were married – I think he wanted someone to look after him.

I was country born and bred. My grandfather lived at Kingsthorpe, just behind Kingsthorpe Station. He had 14 children, and all those uncles and aunts were on properties.

After my father died, when I was very young, my mother sold the property at Millmerran, and we had a shop for a while in Millmerran town. I was the fourth girl of six children and the youngest were twins, a girl and the only boy.

I went to school at Millmerran, and later when my mother moved to Toowoomba I stayed at various places. When I was 14, my mother remarried and lived in the Clifton district.

I didn't really get on with my stepfather's two sons. Their family had remarkable wheat fields and they also used to grow sugar melons. We would make holes in the melons with a knife trying to find the ones which were ripe.'

Chapter 2

Getting my first bus

(1940-1945)

'The total first week's takings from my bus run amounted to £21 ($42). From this I had to pay for petrol, wear and tear on the bus and manage to live on the rest.'

JACK McCAFFERTY

It was then that I decided to buy a bus run and I found one that had been established for about 15 years. I purchased the Picnic Point-Rangeville service from Humbert Bourke and began running it on April Fool's Day 1940. It is a date that is etched in my mind – and if things hadn't gone right with that bus run this story wouldn't have been written.

I paid £2,300 for the 27 h.p. Reo 35-seater that was being used on the service. It was very modern, painted green and cream, and was

McCafferty's first bus, which began operating in Toowoomba in 1940.

the first 'forward control' bus in Toowoomba. The engine was inside the body and the driver sat at the side of the engine, which had a bright aluminium cover. On the other side of the engine space was provided for bags and luggage and the seats had deep rubber cushions. The body was built by Watt Bros, Brisbane.

The fellow who drove for the previous owner had developed a reputation as a 'woman chaser'. The women he liked rarely paid for their fares and when I took over they would hop on and say, 'I'll pay you when I come back'. Of course, most times they never did until I changed the system by introducing bus tickets and making passengers buy them from the start.

I charged passengers 7d a single from the Western Hotel stand, Russell and Ruthven Streets (alongside the present Commonwealth Bank), to Picnic Point, 5d to Rangeville and 3d to John Street. People used to walk half a mile to save money and to just pay the threepenny fare. The other drivers got crooked on me, but I considered that the only way to run the business was by issuing tickets.

My wife and I with daughter Kay, who was just beginning to walk, were living at 166 Jellicoe Street, Toowoomba.

The house had a garage large enough to accommodate the 'new bus' and I was proud of our first timetable, which ran like clockwork.

The first run departed Picnic Point at 8 a.m. and ran along Rowbotham – South – Mackenzie – Perth – Kitchener – James – Suffolk – Ipswich – John – Herries – Hume – Margaret – Ruthven – Bowen – and Neil Streets to the corner of Russell and Ruthven Streets, adjoining the Commonwealth Bank.

This was the official stand for various services going to the General Hospital and Drayton – Tourist Road and St Vincent's Hospital – Middle Ridge Golf Links – Ruthven Street South – Hume Street South – Picnic Point – Rangeville and Stuart Street.

The return service at 8.40 a.m. usually took Miss Irvine, the school teacher, to the Rangeville school. On the way past the Toowoomba Post Office, one of the Post Office staff would be waiting in the street to put on one or two bags of mail. I think I was paid about two shillings a day for taking the mail out and bringing it in at 9.30 a.m. from the Rangeville Post Office attached to Ted Hayes' store.

The run operated every hour from 10 a.m. onwards to Picnic Point and returned at half past every hour from Picnic Point. The last service was 5.40 p.m. out – 10 minutes after the shops closed.

9

On Tuesdays, Thursdays and Saturdays, services were extended from Picnic Point down Rowbotham Street to Alderley Street and then along High Street to resume regular services. For many homes in this area it was their only public transport and, as these roads were only gravel, the bus could not operate in very wet periods.

Families living on this route included Eric Lister (Corio Hatchery), Sid Hargens, Connors, McLeods, Schultz, Sheriff, Hartman, Nuss, Bowtell, Olsen, Leadbetter, Batterbee (jeweller), Freda Ott, Marshalls, Cornicks, Bushells, Starkeys, Parsons, Cummings, Waterson, Davis, Theis and Court. There were also the Gibbs, Kanes, Lawrences, Krugers, Stockleys, Bourkes, Tames, Sunters, Patons, Robinsons, Gibsons, Myra Doyles, McNamaras, Camerons, Rippingale, Hamwoods, Leggatts, Philps, Fallons and Horans.

On the first day, I mixed with other bus operators for the first time and I could feel they were not over enthusiastic about a much younger bus owner joining their ranks.

All the bus drivers used to wear three-quarter length dust-coats and we always looked smart in our ironed, starched dust-coats and especially when we wore white ones.

Drivers in Toowoomba at that time included Stan Parbutt (Maranoa – St Vincent's Hospital run), Wally Cousins (Hume Street South), Reg Paroz (Middle Ridge), George Wingett (Stuart Street South), George Manteit (General Hospital and Drayton) and Stan Yesberg (Ruthven Street South).

At the finish of the first day's operation I counted the money in the bag – I used to wear it over my shoulder – and the takings amounted to £2.10s, equal to $5 in today's decimal currency. Petrol cost about two shillings (20c) a gallon and I would use about seven gallons a day. The cheapest petrol I ever purchased was one shilling and eightpence (17c) a gallon (4.54 litres). Wages for a bus driver varied between £4 ($8) and £5 ($10) a week for any length of hours.

Most buses used to run to the picture theatres in Toowoomba every Wednesday night and for matinee and night performances on Saturdays, but after I started I ran every night including Sunday. This was because, not long after I took over Picnic Point run, the number of potential passengers had mushroomed with the arrival of about 300 members of the First Australian Army Engineers established at Picnic Point. They also took over the Picnic Point Kiosk as their headquarters.

They took over the whole of the Picnic Point area and these chaps used to go downtown to the dances and the theatres every night. There were three main picture theatres, the Empire, Strand

and Princess (later called Coronet), while other films were screened at the Town Hall Theatre and at Newtown. Popular dance halls were the Trades Hall, Trocadero, Memorial Hall, the Holy Name Hall (where you paid one shilling admission to dance to Erin O'Loughlan's Orchestra), Drayton Hall, Philharmonic Hall (Jack Caves Band) and the Paragon Dance Hall, upstairs near the old White Horse Hotel. Sometimes it would be 1.30 in the morning before I got home and I often worked from 6 a.m. to midnight.

In those days many of the passengers were girls going to work and they would go home on the bus for lunch and return to work again each afternoon.

The total first week's takings from my bus run amounted to £21 ($42). From this I had to pay for petrol, wear and tear on the bus and manage to live on the rest. I kept on that way for a while and Lorna used to wash the bus in the long, dark evenings when it was parked alongside our house in John Street, while she was also tending the children. In the winter, she had to wash the ice off the windscreen, and she quickly found that cold water got the ice off better than hot water.

During the war years it was difficult, because you could not get parts, tyres or fuel. You also had to cope with the black-out and learn to drive without using lights at night. When the bus run finished for the day Lorna and I would still be working. She remembers that time very well:

> '*Jack would work on the bus late at night. I was pregnant at the time and I'd stand on a box to clean the bus. The engine had an aluminium cover over it and I used to use Phenyle to get the grease off. Jack would often drive off when the bus was still wet through, hoping that the floor would be dry before he picked up his first passenger.*
>
> *There was a lot of gossip and envy about our business, but if you are busy in your life and you know you are doing the right thing then you haven't time to concern yourselves with such practices.*
>
> *Jack never had time for gossip.'*

Not long after I had taken over the run, the Second World War (1939-45) began in earnest. I tried to enlist but was rejected from joining the forces because I was in a reserved occupation in a protected industry and had to keep the wheels rolling. There was a lot of rationing that was necessary for the war effort and you couldn't buy petrol, tyres, meat, tea, butter, sugar, clothing and other essential items without coupons.

The State Transport Department controlled all licensed bus routes for Queensland and each licence was valid for three years with fees of 10% of turnover payable monthly.

Petrol and tyres were severely restricted and coupons had to be obtained for each month's usage of fuel. To buy a new tyre you had to obtain a special permit from the Superintendent of Traffic.

The Transport Department was controlled by the local police service, because under the State Transport Act it was not possible to operate a service in opposition to the Railway.

On special occasions permits would be granted and the charge was one penny per passenger per mile for the whole return journey. These permits would only be issued if the Railway Department did not have the steam locomotives available because of the war effort of moving troops and warfare materials, plus the shortage of manpower.

Operating a bus was a big change from driving the milk cart; for one thing it was easier and also in wet weather it was drier.

But life itself was not particularly easy, although Lorna went along with it all right and raised our family of four sons and two daughters.

It was very difficult because there was not much money, and I remember some days when up till midday I would be lucky to have taken 10s ($1) in fares.

But within six years I had managed to increase my weekly takings from that £21 ($42) in the first week to £92 ($184).

I was the first bus proprietor in Toowoomba to allow concession fares to pensioners on all services. McCafferty's eventually had eight town buses painted in a distinctive livery with orange top and black from half-way down.

The buses would be packed on cinema nights and again on Sundays, when families went to church and to the cemetery. The fare was just sixpence from Bridge Street right out to the Drayton cemetery. There were no designated bus stops, buses picked up wherever they were hailed.

When the film *Gone with the Wind* came to town, it was about five hours long and we weren't used to that. It was after midnight when the patrons finally came out. Right across the world the film, which featured Clark Gable and Vivien Leigh, was an outstanding success.

During my lifetime in the bus industry I have employed hundreds of drivers – some very good and some not so good. At the start of the Picnic Point run it was very hard to get a relief driver as all able-bodied men had been called up in the services. One chap I used to employ was a big fellow with flat feet (the army didn't want these types). We used to call him 'Paddles'. I remember once he was driving the new 'White' bus – it was during wet weather. On occasions like this, because the road wasn't sealed, we would omit going around Alderley Street. However, he decided to take the new bus around and the next thing I got a message saying the bus was bogged in Alderley Street. When I went to see it I discovered my new bus lying on its side in a deep washout. I wasn't impressed and a little later the driver was no longer working for me. He got the usual McCafferty's treatment for this – 'Look for another job'.

During the war, tight restrictions were placed on home lighting to prevent any form of light that could be seen by the enemy at night. I had to use covers over the bus headlights that allowed only a small amount of light to show on the road (a slit about 16cm by 4cm). This made it very difficult for drivers on foggy nights as the few street lights that were installed were not allowed to be lit.

Sections of Toowoomba were divided into squares that were controlled by Air Raid Wardens. Some of these fellows, who were mostly semi-retired, would get carried away with their responsibility and if a tiny speck of light showed through maybe a hole in the blind, they would be on to you like a ton of bricks. Every resident had to dig a trench to protect the family in the event of an air raid.

Occasionally the air raid sirens would go off for practice but of course we didn't know if it was a real air raid until the all clear had sounded. Fortunately there were no raids on Toowoomba. When the hospital ship, *Centaur* was sunk by the Japanese outside Brisbane hundreds perished and we were not told about it for days after.

The *Courier Mail*, which was being printed in Brisbane as a broadsheet, was only allowed about eight pages a day, while in Toowoomba *The Chronicle* was reduced to only four pages. News could not be released unless authorised by the Defence Department.

In the early days before the army moved in, Picnic Point Kiosk was run by the Mathison sisters, and well I remember the morning and afternoon teas they used to provide me with. For some years the army used the kiosk and it was not available to the public until about 1946, when it was released and the Council appointed a lessee to run it. I believe the first lessee was Bob Starkey and his family who used to live close to Picnic Point in Rowbotham Street.

It was while sitting under the trees at Picnic Point, waiting for the appointed moment of departure, that I would daydream about making the Picnic Point look-out a decent tourist attraction, getting

Jack McCafferty in the Mayor's office.

more visitors to Toowoomba and expanding my business. I was always a dreamer and perhaps a bit of a pioneer. I would watch Reg Ansett's Pioneer touring charabancs arrive at Picnic Point and I would think that could be me one day.

After several years of operation and lessee changes (one lessee was Ray Shackleton), the City Council built a much larger kiosk at Picnic Point, which was successfully run by the well-known Bob Weis and his family.

When Bob's lease was up he was unsuccessful with his tender and I believe Toowoomba was the loser, because I was certain Bob Weis was the man who had the vision to develop this tourist attraction to Toowoomba's advantage.

I was the Mayor of Toowoomba at this time and most members of the council wanted to give Bob the lease, but in those days councils were compelled to accept the lowest or highest tender.

'The Mountain Goat' and passengers enjoying a picnic at Somerset Dam in 1946.

The Rangeville area in the early days of taking over the Picnic Point bus run was very sparsely occupied and there were plenty of empty paddocks. Some properties were actually sold publicly by the city council because people couldn't pay their rates.

Rangeville Store, on the corner of High and South Streets, was run by Ted Hayes and his wife. The Rangeville School only had an enrolment of about 80 or 90 pupils. Mr McGladrigan was the headteacher and Alan Marsh his assistant. I was on the school committee for some years and the committee used to arrange concerts and dances in the original school. They were well supported and helped school funds considerably. Mr Mallon followed Bill Sugars as headteacher and he remained there for many years. During my terms as Mayor of Toowoomba (1958-1967), many of the new sub-division streets opened up in the Rangeville area and I named them after residents of the area.

After I'd taken over Picnic Point run, an air base was established at Oakey and I gained the contract to take personnel out there in sometimes three bus-loads and bring them back into Toowoomba every day.

Chapter 3

A time to expand

The Picnic Point run was going well and now I was looking at expanding the business. My main competitor was the Maranoa and St Vincent's bus run. It was operated by the Beaumont family of Ipswich and their driver Stan Parbutt used to deliberately delay his service so as to come down just ahead of my bus and clean up all the passengers at Herries and Mary Street.

They hated McCafferty's and I knew they would not sell to me so I got an agent in Brisbane, Ross Harrison, of Harrison and Bothwell, to successfully negotiate the purchase. This gave me two services in the same area.

The next step was to buy a new bus. Getting a chassis was far from easy after the war but I managed to buy a new White chassis, a left-hand drive, but it was the only type available. The next problem was getting a body built on it. Again the shortage of bodybuilders and materials, plus the fact that there was a rush to build new buses by other operators, caused considerable delay.

Watt Bros of Brisbane were the builders and it nearly drove me crazy because it took nearly 12 months to complete the body for the 39-seater, which I named 'The Challenger'.

'The Challenger', McCafferty's first new bus – a 1944 White with bodywork by Watts of Brisbane.

Meanwhile, the body on the Reo began to fall to pieces, so I bought a new Lend Lease Chevrolet chassis and I got Bill Becker Body Building of Russell Street, Toowoomba, to lift the body off the Reo chassis and put it on to the Chevrolet chassis. The rest of the Reo was later sold for secondhand parts.

The main purpose of this exercise was to get it done in a minimum of time with as little body modification as possible. The result was a unique bus with the whole of the Chevrolet engine and bonnet inside the coach body and I drove it from the middle of the coach – but it overcame my problems.

I needed yet another bus to add to the fleet to keep up with expansion plans and so I bought a new KS5 International chassis and asked Bill Becker to put a 36-seater body on it. Leather seat trimming was not available so the seats were moulded in Masonite. They were all right if you didn't have to sit too long.

Buses in Toowoomba in those early days had some unusual nicknames. There was 'Golden Dream', 'Blondie', 'Leaping Lena', 'Blue Bird', 'Excelsior' , 'Suicide' and 'Pigeon'.

During this period I got help from George Rowbotham, one of Toowoomba's early bus drivers. If there was a breakdown, then George was the one who came along to assist. I would help him, particularly at Toowoomba Show time, in providing his service with a relief driver from time to time. None of the other operators would lend me a spare bus – they hoped I would give up and walk away from the bus business, but they underestimated my determination.

To his credit George only had one accident in 50 years' driving – a collision with a horse and sulky in the early 1920s. In 1994, George, aged 93, and I, at 80, both featured in a special article in *The Chronicle*, Toowoomba, about the early days of bus travel. I've included some of George Rowbotham's comments here as a tribute to his support to me during difficult times.

'We travelled on horse-drawn buses, carrying 10 to 12 passengers, in the days when it was threepence to ride from Fairholme College to town, and a penny for children. There used to be four horse cabs outside the Bank of New South Wales, and on the horse buses they used to put a dipper of corn into the nosebag to add to the chaff and give the horse a bit of get up and go.

Horse-drawn bus drivers included Jack Olsen, Alan Miles, Dave Yesberg and Johnny Teys. Motorised buses took over from the horses after World War 1 in about 1919, but there were no self-starters, batteries or generators, just a magneto, and in wet weather they could be hard to start. The only way you could start a Ford in

*The Holberton Street bus pictured
in Toowoomba in the early 1930s.*

*frosty weather was to jack the back wheel up. It was a ton of fun in
those days.*

*My first Model T Fords and an International bus had solid
rubber tyres. The bus had calico blinds for the windows and
kerosene sulky lamps for headlights. Some people wanted the blinds
up and some wanted them down, and it could get quite draughty.
You had a hell of a job lighting the tail-light with the westerly wind
blowing.*

*The first coach builder in Toowoomba was Jim Lucy who in later
years used to restore old cars. He was one of the few fellows that
could make mudguards for Model T Fords.*

*I gave up driving in 1972 and gave the business to my son
Maurice. It was sold to Hagan's in 1979.*

*Toowoomba's biggest day for buses was when St Vincent's
Hospital opened in November 1922. They were flat out ferrying
visitors between Toowoomba Railway Station and the hospital.*

*In 1926 I was in the Magistrates Court for leaving my bus at an
intersection while I went to get a haircut. I was fined two shillings
and sixpence.*

*There were no bus stops and we picked up passengers wherever
they hailed the bus.*

*During the 1930s, Toowoomba had about 17 bus operators. They
included George Manteit, who had the most streamlined
International machine, and a man called Crow who ran the St
Vincent's Hospital bus. Others included Ray Tomkys, Dave
Yesberg, the Bowman boys, Arthur Longford on the Gowrie run,*

Wally Cousins, George Wingett, an operator called Naumann, whose bus was called the Bluebird of Happiness; Pat Cafferkey, Jack Olsen, who had a 'Black Maria' bus; Alan Miles, Bill Fett, Charlie Mossetter, Alf Collins and Geoff McLaughlin.'

Moving closer to the operations – with room to expand

It was while we were living at John Street that Tony, Rodney and Gail were born, and our other children – Ken and Neil – were born after the family finally moved to 4 Turnbull Street in 1950.

The army remained at Picnic Point for about four years, and when war ended in 1945 I looked further afield and had taken over the opposition to gain the St Vincent's Hospital bus run from Dick Beaumont. I also bought the Gowrie Road run from Dudley Andrews. The Gowrie Road bus service ran from the Town Hall via Ruthven Street, then Russell, Mort, Norwood, West and Bridge Streets to the Holberton Street corner. This purchase enabled me to complete an ambition that I had held for some time, to operate buses from the west side of Toowoomba to the east side. After a lot of opposition from the bureaucracy I got it operating. People could now travel direct from the western side of the town to St Vincent's Hospital and Picnic Point, and the service used to operate every night until after the pictures.

I had purchased a Dodge bus from Dick Beaumont and when that was sold it became a caravan.

In 1944, I had bought that new left-hand-drive White 42-passenger vehicle and followed this purchase by a succession of ex-US Army Studebaker buses. Then, from 1947 until 1953, we purchased no fewer than 17 Bedford buses, with the later models classified at 36hp.

A number of secondhand buses also joined the stable in that period, including a Ford with side seats, which was later sold as a horse float, and an International 23-seater, which was later sold as a caravan.

My early personal transport began with a Willys utility in 1944, followed by a Rugby tourer in 1945, a Buick in 1946, and then a succession of Chevrolet sedans and a station-wagon. My first Holden came on the scene in 1949, followed by Chevrolets in 1950 and 1952, and a blue Plymouth sedan that arrived in 1954.

I now had a staff of six but still did all the paperwork late at night. However, I found that I had to employ an accountant to look after the garage.

It was then that I began my own advertising campaign for the Picnic Point service using a photograph of a 44-seater bus and offering safe, comfortable travel daily on the Picnic Point route. The following is an example of one of McCafferty's early press advertisements:

> *'On Sunday afternoon, the bus passes St Vincent's Hospital, Whinstanes College and Tourist Road. Sunday afternoon attractions at Picnic Point include the City Band in a select musical program; Dick Turner, radio vocalist, in popular songs; Merv Beeh, the King of the Accordion Keyboard; and a delightful program of recorded music (favourite dance combinations and dance bands on the public address system).'*

Long hours had become an established part of my life, and I was the first to run a through bus service from Picnic Point to St Vincent's Hospital and Gowrie Road.

Chapter 4

Co-ordinating with the railway

(1946-1955)

'If you handle the public correctly, it can result in the customer repeating to hundreds of others about the good service they receive from your staff. However, if you say something wrong, then you could possibly lose a customer; so the moral is to remember the old adage, "THE CUSTOMER IS ALWAYS RIGHT", even though you may have doubts about it.'

JACK McCAFFERTY

From that modest beginning in 1940, on the Picnic Point route, I acquired in 1946 a licence to operate a service between Toowoomba and Helidon, co-ordinating with the passenger-train service between Helidon and Brisbane.

The big 44-passenger Mack bus purchased from Arnold Riley, Casino, NSW, in about 1946. The bus, which had all aluminium panels, was used on the coach-rail co-ordinated run between Toowoomba and Helidon.

This service was very important to the city of Toowoomba, as Toowoomba was regarded as the gateway to the Darling Downs, perched on top of a steep escarpment overlooking a fairly flat, fertile valley extending to Brisbane and the coast.

The Warrego Highway takes a direct route of 19km from Toowoomba to Helidon, whereas the railway travels a circuitous route of 50km down a range interspersed with tunnels. In 1946 there was heavy passenger traffic between Toowoomba and Brisbane, and by changing from train to coach at Helidon on the return journey travellers could cut at least an hour off their journey.

A limited service was also approved by the Transport Department for Greyhound to operate a restricted through service from Toowoomba to Brisbane and return. First of all they used a seven-seater car and then gradually increased the service to 20-seater and 25-seater buses with extra services each day.

The co-ordinated run had operated before the Second World War, but then the licence had been cancelled to conserve petrol.

Before I took it over, the service had recommenced and was being operated from Toowoomba by the Red and Gold Garage managed by Bill Robinson. The office was at Eight Double Eight Taxis at 255 Margaret Street, next-door to Harders and McQuades-Palmers Garage. It was just across the road from where Village Fair stands today.

I needed finance to operate the co-ordinated run and I turned to my relatives for help. I had two uncles who were both doctors and who had money. One had married into the noted O'Brien flour-milling family of Toowoomba, and the other fellow (Sid McCafferty) was a doctor who specialised in women's diseases.

I borrowed money from Sid to purchase the business and he arranged my bank loan. Later, when the business was running successfully, he turned up in Toowoomba, and after examining the books and seeing that the business was making a profit said he was taking it over and that I could 'walk away'.

I couldn't believe it. Apparently I had signed a blank form of attorney when we were discussing getting a bank loan and my "helpful" uncle had typed in his own wording after I had returned home.

Although my finances were stretched to the limit, I had to go to court and eventually I was able to retain the business. But the battle left me devastated; my health had run down and I spent some time in hospital receiving treatment for a duodenal ulcer.

I took over the co-ordinated service in 1946 with a 26-passenger charabanc-style Ford with doors along the side for each row of seats. It was like a toast-rack but was a good performer on the Range, with plenty of power.

Of course, the road from Helidon to Toowoomba was not all bitumen in those days and the Range Road had a very steep gradient. Down near Helidon Spa the road was unsealed and we used to drive over a lightly running creek with no bridge. At times we could not get through if water in the creek was too high. Likewise, the very old and low-level Sheepstation Creek Bridge, just near the Helidon Railway Station, was not negotiable at times of heavy rain.

Helidon was a very important refreshment stop for passenger trains. Miss Beanland was the manageress of the refreshment rooms and the pies baked on the premises by Merv Fossey attained the reputation as the best in Australia. Merv Fossey later began running a shop at Marlborough in Central Queensland.

During the busiest periods, during the Carnival of Flowers and holidays, we would have up to 12 buses waiting at Helidon to meet the train. The bus fare in those days was only the equivalent of 25 cents for adults, single, or you could buy a co-ordinated ticket for Toowoomba to Brisbane for about the equivalent of $1.10 adult single.

Family picnic at Somerset Dam in 1946. Jack McCafferty is on the left with sons Rodney and Tony, Mrs Lorna McCafferty, Dick Eversen, Susan Eversen, Mrs May Eversen, Kay McCafferty, Mrs Norm Miller and baby.

In the workshop, Ray George proved to be a great mechanic. He recalls those early days when one of our coaches had roll-down blinds instead of windows along the sides!

> *'When I started at McCafferty's in 1946, there were eight buses: a White WA18, a Reo with Mack motor, three American Studebakers with Syd Wood bodies, a Chev, and a Ford charabanc which had doors all along the side with transverse seats. There was also a Ford which we called the* **Pigeon** *. . . it had no windows, just roll-down blinds along the sides.*
>
> *My first job was to fit a new engine block in the White, the old one had cracked through overheating. The price of an engine block then was £200.*
>
> *George Crostwaith, who was a mechanic, was checking one of the Studebakers for a rattle in the motor and revving it up when one of the con rods let go and came straight out through the side of the engine block. It bounced off the brick wall and finished over near the loading ramp where people were waiting to catch a bus. Being short of buses as usual, we stuffed some rag in the hole in the block and took the bus down to Helidon to pick up passengers off the train. The bus didn't pull so well but made the trip back O.K.'*

The first new Highway Holiday coach, a Bedford chassis and body built by Shuttlewood at Toowong, Brisbane in 1950.

The Highway Holiday coach at the kiosk at Echo Point, Katoomba, NSW.

A tour group in the late 1940s with the silhouette of the driver – Jack McCafferty at the wheel of an ex-army bus refitted for tour work.

Among our early drivers was Mick Manteit, who's now 80 and living in retirement in Toowoomba. He remembers times when pay was low and there were long hours behind the wheel:

'I first drove buses for the West Toowoomba Bus Service before the Second World War. Then, I went into the army and after service in New Guinea finished up in Ordnance handling motor vehicle spare parts at Harristown, Toowoomba.

After being discharged in Brisbane, I came home from the army on the Thursday on the train and Bill Goddard, who had the Harlaxton Bus Service, met me and I started driving for him a few days later.

He later sold out and I met Jack at the Red and Gold taxi and bus depot, and he asked me what I was doing. When I told him the situation, he just pointed to a bus standing in the depot and said, 'Take it out to Cooby Dam'. I had to find my way there and that's how my career with Jack started. I remained there for the next 20 years.

When I began with Jack in 1947 my pay was four pounds 16 shillings a week and I tell you our wages went up very slowly.

It was while Jack had a depot across the road from the Toowoomba Post Office that Jack introduced the 16-day holiday to Sydney.

I drove one of the company's ex-US Army Studebakers, and the passengers who were mainly Toowoomba and Brisbane people helped us lift the luggage up on to the rack on the roof. Can you imagine passengers doing that today?

The trip took us along the New England Highway to Stanthorpe, Glen Innes overnight, Armidale, Tamworth, Maitland and Newcastle and back up the coast to Taree, Grafton, Lismore and Brisbane.

It was so successful that Jack went on to organise trips to the Blue Mountains, which included day trips to Katoomba, Wentworth Falls and the Jenolan Caves.

General Motors in 1949 began building the most up-to-date bus then available – a Comair 27-passenger Bedford. Over the years, Jack purchased about 12 of these buses, which were fitted with forward-controls.

We met some marvellous people on the trips and they used to send the drivers Christmas cards.

We wore either a white or grey three-quarter length dust-coat, with blue trousers and blue shirt.

We had a radio on board that used to squeak and squawk but the main entertainment was singalongs, and there was always someone who could vamp on the piano when we reached the hotel for the night.

One good thing was that there were only McCafferty's and Pioneer coaches touring on the road. Our passengers were in one party for 16 days and everyone got to know everybody else. With Pioneer there would be passengers from Victoria, New South Wales and Queensland and they were constantly changing along the route.

I remember occasions on Sundays at Bernly Hotel, Potts Point, when Pioneer passengers would have a free day and be completely lost. I would encourage them to travel with us to Circular Quay and we would go out on the Harbour Show Boat. They got on well with our group and we all looked after them.

If there were special trips I would love to be involved. I took groups of marching girls to Newcastle, football clubs to Melbourne and Adelaide, bowls clubs around the country. I drove out to Roma and picked up Roma bowlers to go to Lismore for the weekend, and then I took the Toowoomba Band to Tanunda in South Australia.

On one occasion I had this Studebaker in the Blue Mountains. The engine was steaming and boiling and I was losing power fast. Eventually, I drove into a garage at Katoomba and they discovered that the engine was taking in water in the cylinders and they put on a new head gasket.

Without the gasket I wouldn't have made it down that dangerous, narrow road to the Jenolan Caves.

On the way home the gasket blew again and I was late into Maitland for lunch and I had to pay the waitresses overtime. I struggled on to Tamworth on four cylinders and instead of getting in at 6 p.m. it was more like 9 p.m. I had 20 passengers on board and the trip was a real headache

Another gasket was placed in position on the following day but just after I got home it blew again and this time the cylinder head had to be shaved.

On another occasion I was coming up a range in a Bedford when I lost power and pressed my foot on the accelerator but nothing happened. Then I looked closely and the accelerator linkage under the floorboards had come adrift. There was no way I could fix it properly so I went out and got a piece of wire off a fence and attached one end to the carburettor and I worked it by hand.

I rang Toowoomba, and said "I'm coming home on a wing and a prayer."

I ran out of hands sometimes. I had to change gear with the same hand working the carburettor, while the other hand kept the bus on the road.'

The media had become very important in our operations and we were using radio as well as print. I established a good rapport with people such as Dick Eversen, who was at Toowoomba's sole commercial radio station 4GR. Now aged 83, Dick is in retirement at the Gold Coast and he had this to say about his role with McCafferty's:

'When I was working in Toowoomba as a 4GR announcer in 1940 I would go and see Jack McCafferty about advertising. We had an excellent business relationship and became very good friends and our friendship continues today.

At one stage, I conducted a coach party to the Blue Mountains and it was most successful.

Later, I became part-owner of the commercial radio station at Charleville and I used to travel there by train. Whenever I came back through Toowoomba on the Western Mail, Jack would take me home for a breakfast of bacon and eggs.

I've been associated with Jack McCafferty for more than 50 years. He's a man with above average knowledge and business qualities and a wonderful father to his family of two girls and four boys.

Jack's character is full of initiative and enterprise and he has the ability to overcome obstacles as well as the drive to succeed.

He's involving himself in something that he knows very well. He has stayed with the one thing he knows best and has made a success of it. The camaraderie which he enjoys with his staff is truly amazing.'

Another man who speaks very highly of our company's approach to business and advertising is former radio announcer and advertising executive Jim Fagg, now living in retirement in Toowoomba. He has known our family for 60 years and again he provided an important service that he mentions here:

'I came to Toowoomba from Brisbane in 1946 and joined the only commercial radio station then in Toowoomba – 4GR.

It was in the old 4GR premises in the Alexandra Building, opposite Burstows building in Ruthven Street, that Jack and I formed a firm friendship which endures today.

Jack McCafferty used to sponsor half-hour programs of drama and music.

He ran 'Eight aces in popular music' from 1946-48 and he particularly liked promoting popular music and music by bands. He sponsored Smokey Dawson's 'Ride Tenderfoot' on 4GR every week for years.

He would approve 50-word (30-second) commercials to be dropped into programs throughout the day.

Jack was always very receptive to promotional ideas and used to publicise his day tours around Toowoomba, as well as McCafferty's half-day tours, tours to the coast and highway holidays. There was also ample publicity for the 14-day trips to Sydney and Katoomba in the Blue Mountains, and other tours taking travellers to the Red Centre, Alice Springs and Darwin, and around Australia.'

By the time World War II had ended in 1945 we were looking for someone to help with the mechanical side of the buses. I checked the local market and picked out a mechanic, Ron Goodenough, and asked him to come along for an interview:

'I was approached by McCafferty's in about 1945, when they required a mechanic. McCafferty's were then operating from the Red and Gold building in Margaret Street. When I went to look at the workshop at the back it turned out to be a 20ft x 10ft car garage. You couldn't get a bus inside and there was no inspection pit.

I went back to my old job and told another mechanic, Ray George, that there was a vacancy at McCafferty's and they were offering £10 ($20) a week. 'Lead me to it,' replied Ray, and he started with McCafferty's in December 1946. In his early years, Ray George had operated a garage at Helidon in the Lockyer Valley.'

It wasn't until August 1953 that Ron Goodenough joined the company, some time after we'd moved to larger premises alongside the Strand Theatre, with a back entrance into Church Street.

Most buses during the 1940s were worn out. The army released some secondhand Studebaker buses with 27 seats and I bought about four of them from the US Army. New Lend Lease chassis for

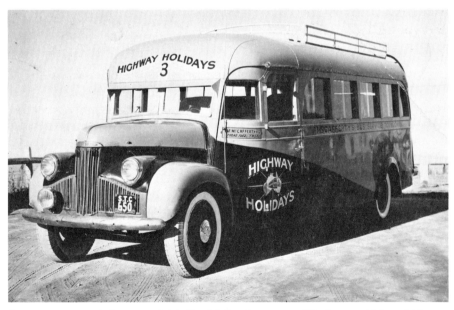

Luggage was carried on top of this Studebaker bus, an ex-US Army vehicle, which was used on McCafferty's tours in the 1950s.

trucks and buses were released by the army for sale to the public and most of these chassis were either International, Chevrolet or Ford.

I was now using two Studebaker buses, purchased from an army disposal sale, to provide extra service and comfort to passengers on the co-ordinated coach and rail run between Toowoomba and Brisbane. The service, which had operated three times a day, was now increased to four.

Back in 1947, we had moved into premises next to the Strand Theatre and that became the Co-ordinated Terminal. The front office was occupied by Wylie Smith and Company and we used the rear portion off Church Street.

Passengers had to alight from the buses and walk through Smith's machinery section to Margaret Street, where taxis would be waiting, right opposite the Post Office. If you needed a quick meal, then you would join the queue at Barney Hudson's hot pie cart in front of the Strand Theatre.

The adult single fare from Toowoomba to Helidon was four shillings, and it cost 11 shillings to travel from Toowoomba to Brisbane by bus and train. A Saturday/Sunday return fare could be purchased for 11 shillings and threepence.

After the opening of the Co-ordinated Terminal in Toowoomba in 1947 and looking ahead – I could see I needed larger premises – I purchased two old boarding houses around the corner at 28-30 Neil Street for £27,000. On land that had been formerly owned by the O'Brien family I began building Toowoomba's first Atlantic petrol service station (later to become Esso), and became a sub-agent for Holden.

However, the project was delayed because the occupants of the boarding houses were reluctant to move out and I had to get a court order. The building work also took longer than expected because we didn't have the cash to employ large numbers of building workers. Many of the staff were concerned over the cash-flow problem and the following comment came from one of our early employees:

> *'The money tree was getting a bit shaky and the limbs were starting to droop a bit. Some of the workmen on the project were a bit like bushrangers – Mrs Kelly wouldn't let young Ned play with them. By the time they had finished Jack had bugger all.'*

I have always strived to treat people fairly and I get annoyed when they are disadvantaged through no fault of their own. Ron Goodenough remembers one such occasion:

The early 1950s and the corner of Russell and Neil Streets, Toowoomba, showing the two houses that had to be removed to make way for McCafferty's terminal, which was officially opened on November 25, 1956.

'I will always remember the day a certain bus arrived in Toowoomba from Helidon. I was checking the fault book half an hour later when I noticed that a couple with two children from the bus were still sitting on a seat at the terminal. They were looking really worried.

I asked at the office about the couple, and the woman on the counter said, "I don't know why they are still waiting there."

Jack McCafferty apparently overhead us and he walked past the counter and went straight up to the couple.

The next minute he was taking them to a nearby snack bar and they were having a feed.

The man said they were on their way from New South Wales to work for a company near Roma in south-west Queensland. They were supposed to have been met in Toowoomba, but no one had turned up and they were penniless.

Jack came back to the office, gave the family tickets to get to Roma, and then phoned the company and told them what he thought of them.'

By 1948, I was working every day of the year, and I was enjoying the big new left-hand-drive 43-seater White bus named 'The Challenger'.

'Come to Picnic Point – Toowoomba's Turret Top – 2240 feet above sea level. Fresh, Invigorating Mountain Air' extolled the press advertisements. Travellers were encouraged to spend the whole day at Picnic Point. Sunday afternoon entertainment included the RSL and Municipal Band and the 'Wizard of the Accordion' Merv Beeh. The cafe was open every day with home-made cakes and scones, which were 'electrically cooked on the premises' and hot water was available.

My advertisements also asked readers to tune to 4GR radio station every Friday at 6.15 p.m. for the 'Smokey Dawson Home Folks' session, and 8 p.m. every Saturday for a 30-minute live artist show. I had decided that advertising on commercial radio was an excellent way to reinforce my newspaper advertisements.

In August 1948 my company purchased its fourth Bedford bus from Eagers, Toowoomba, for £2135.15s.4d. In those days it was not so easy to organise accommodation on the road as it is now. Mick Manteit has this to say:

> *'Drivers used to run into difficulties with accommodation and places being booked out in the early days.*
>
> *Whenever I rang up head office Jack would always reply, 'Oh, you can sort it out'.*
>
> *It got so bad at times that I would have passengers scattered in accommodation all over town. One time I was so disgusted that I wrote a letter to Jack sacking myself and saying that I had had enough and I was on my way home.*

Early model Bedford bus, 1948.

When I woke up the next morning, I thought it was a long way to walk home so I just carried on driving. When I returned to Toowoomba Jack never said a word.

The people who went on the buses were all wonderful people but we had some really tight schedules on very bad roads.

I'd leave Brisbane at 8 a.m. and get to Toowoomba to head down the New England Highway. At 11 a.m. I would be racing to Warwick for midday lunch and I had to reach the hotel before lunch hour finished, otherwise I would have to pay the girls overtime to serve at the tables.

Once lunch was over, I'd race to Tenterfield and I had to arrive at the Police Station before 4 p.m. to get a permit to travel interstate. Then it was another race to get to Glen Innes in time for the evening meal. Quite often we would arrive late and the manager would say, "Bring them into the dining room and we'll sort out the rooms later".'

Appreciation of through Toowoomba city services

Among the many letters I received in 1948 was one from Mr J.E. Bates, who was Secretary of the Newtown Progress Association. It read:

'At the last meeting of the above association it was directed that I write you, commending you on the efficiency and service you are giving the public with your "through" bus service from Gowrie Rd to Picnic Point.

'In expressing our appreciation we would like to add that it would be Toowoomba's gain if there was more of this efficiency and service right throughout the bus routes.'

During the Queensland railway strike in the late 1940s we were running buses out to country towns to meet the Sydney train. Ray George recalls those days:

'There were big loads of people and tons of luggage which was carried on racks on the roof and on the back of the bus. On one trip to Roma the luggage on the rear platform of the Mack was strapped on with big leather straps through all the suitcase handles. However, some of the suitcases swung around and dragged on the ground. When we got to Roma all that was left were three big straps and about 19 suitcase handles. Looking at the insurance claims they must have been the best dressed passengers we ever carried.

Coming from Wallangarra there would often be more passengers than we anticipated so there would be people sitting right down the aisle on their luggage. No one complained, they were all just happy to get there.'

Three early model Bedfords showing destinations in the Toowoomba area.

Long-distance tours to such places as Central Australia and Ayers Rock – using Fisherman's Bend Bedford OBs fitted with 'ultra-luxurious' seats – came in 1950, and the Gold Coast service began with a minibus from Toowoomba to Tweed Heads with a weekend service in the late 1950s.

Special trips in September 1950, operating out of our depot opposite the Post Office in Margaret Street, Toowoomba, included a trip to the Warwick Races (20/- return), and punters were also catered for at Gatton, Esk and Oakey Races.

There was also a full-day tour to Queen Mary Falls, Killarney, via Allora and Warwick (adults 20/-, children 14/-); half-day tour to Cooby Creek via Mt Kynoch, afternoon tea available (adults 6/6, children 4/-); half-day tour to Oakey and Jondaryan (adults 12/-, children 8/-); Catholic Ball, Oakey (6/- return); full-day tour to Stanley River Dam, Somerset, via Hampton and Esk (Adults 20/-, children 14/-); half-day tour to Heifer Creek via Drayton, Ascot, West Haldon, Grantham and Helidon, afternoon tea available (adults 12/-, children 8/-); and a half-day tour to Pittsworth via Westbrook and Wyreema (adults 12/-, children 8/-). 'The Washpool' picnic area near the Helidon Spa was a very popular picnic and swimming attraction.

I had just eight buses in 1950 and it was then that I decided that there weren't sufficient returns in local town runs and it would be

Excursion group at Mt Kynoch, Toowoomba, in 1950.

better to concentrate on long-distance tours, charter work and day trips. I maintained some inner city bus runs, but sold these later when the private family car starting making inroads into bus travel in 1950-52.

In April the following year, I purchased Bedford Bus No. 12, also from Eagers, Toowoomba, at a cost of £2207.5s.4d, and the insurance bill for that vehicle totalled £44.7s.5d

Towards the end of the 1940s, the major rail strike that lasted for several weeks saw McCafferty's running services to Wallangarra, Dalby, Roma and Goondiwindi. At a time when many roads were not much better than stock routes, Wallangarra was a very important rail link with Sydney.

The pride of our fleet for tours was a new coach built by Shuttlewood in Brisbane. It was a very modern touring coach with luxury seats, ample luggage space and plenty of body style.

This was the start of the Highway Holiday tours in 1950. It was the beginning of a new era for coach travel in Australia. Our first trips were down to Sydney, the Blue Mountains and Jenolan Caves with a three-night stopover at the Lapstone Hill Hotel – which had been the Rest and Recuperation Centre for the Royal Australian Air Force during the Second World War and by now had been handed back to the public. We had stayed at the Lapstone Hill Hotel when we ran our first tour from Toowoomba to the Blue Mountains and the Jenolan Caves in 1948.

It was a luxurious hotel with views over the golf course. Later on we used to do tours to the Barossa Valley, the Melbourne Cup and

An early postcard of the Lapstone Hotel in the Blue Mountains.

Getting new Bedfords purchased through Eagers, Toowoomba, in 1952. Reg Andrews (workshop foreman, Eagers) is on the left, with Jack McCafferty and Jack Coates, Manager, Eagers.

shorter one-day trips around South-East Queensland. Before each tour left we had to obtain a permit from the Police Station and we were taxed one halfpenny a passenger a mile and we had to make the payment before we turned a wheel. Otherwise we could face a heavy fine.

Highway Holidays owe a lot to Shuttlewood's first touring coach specifically built for extended tours.

Motor bodybuilder F.H. Shuttlewood was located in Sylvan Road, Toowong.

He was the first Queensland coachbuilder to make and fit aircraft-type reclining seats to a coach. Each green leather seat was fitted with a passenger-operated lever and ratchet, and was adjustable to seven different positions by a fingertip control in the arm rest.

The Shuttlewood 21-passenger coach, which was mounted on a Bedford chassis, also featured a specially insulated roof, non-glare glass in all windows, individual electric fans, a built-in radio and individually controlled reading lights set over each pair of seats.

The Brisbane Sunday newspaper *The Truth* on July 16, 1950, gave space for a report on the new coach. It stated in part:

> *'A special test was made last week of the insulated roof, and in the test proved to be unaffected by transmitted heat, although it had stood in the sun, with all doors and windows closed, for several hours......... The non-glare windows, although they appear green from the outside, give the same advantages as clear glass, from inside the coach.'*

Chapter 5

Blue Mountains tours and Redex trials

'Jack never thinks of himself as wealthy. He didn't have a new car until the late 1970s, and when the family talked him into buying a unit on the Gold Coast he said he didn't need it. He felt it would be big-noting himself.'

WENDY McCAFFERTY

A statue featuring two figures, titled 'Jack and Lorna,' stands in the back garden of a home at Withcott, just below the Toowoomba range.

It was taken from our home in Turnbull Street, Toowoomba, where it once formed part of a fountain on a fish pond. When my family demolished our old house, the statue of a boy and girl had developed cracks at the base and was going to be bulldozed away.

We gave it to Coral Probst (née Tame), who had admired the figures when she was a young girl, and it now has pride of place at her home in Shorelands Drive, where she lives with her husband Alf, who drives for our company.

Both Coral and Alf have enjoyed a long association with our family and company.

When Coral left school in November, 1951, she went to work for me at the premises at 159 Margaret Street, alongside the Strand Theatre. Many years later she recalled:

'I was the only girl on the staff and I got involved in doing everything. I did all the bookwork, the accounts, including the weekly rent from the drivers of the Red and Gold taxis.

We had a manual switchboard and we'd take calls for taxis as well as bookings for buses.

As a young girl, I lived in a house which backed on to the McCafferty's home block and I grew up with the older McCafferty children, Kay and Tony.

I was seven years old when I saw the sea for the first time, and that was when I went with the McCaffertys on a holiday to Coolangatta.

I believe Jack McCafferty was impressed with my ability because he told me that he would give me a job when I finished school.

My brothers used to tease me and say, "Oh, yes the only job you'll get will be greasing buses."

When I started work on November 26, 1951, I was the only girl in the office until Kay McCafferty left high school and she joined the company when we moved round the corner into Neil Street.

A lot of staff pitched in and helped to put down a concrete slab for the company's new service station.

On the Saturday of the Toowoomba Carnival of Flowers, it was my job to get up very early and work out which way visiting coaches would drive around Toowoomba taking tourists to see the prize-winning gardens. I typed out the instructions on wax stencils which were placed on an old Gestetner duplicating machine and made copies for dozens of coach drivers. Drivers coming into town would all call at the depot first to pick up a route plan before heading off around the city. My husband Alf remembers the first Carnival of Flowers procession, which travelled northwards along Ruthven Street, in the opposite direction to what it does now.

Our office was also selling tickets for the co-ordinated coach and rail service to Brisbane and there were only about half a dozen

A double-decker bought from the Sydney Transport Commission in the early 1950s.

services going out each day. Double-deckers were being used as well as ordinary coaches and passenger numbers on the school bus runs were increasing.

There was a lot of fun among the staff. We used to have impromptu parties when we finished work on a Friday night, and Mr Mac didn't know about them. We'd pool a small amount of money and someone would go down the street to buy chips and there would be just a few bottles of beer, enough for a couple of glasses each at the most, and then we'd climb upstairs on a double-decker bus at the depot to enjoy the evening.

We were like one big happy family. There were only about eight drivers, and you knew them all and their families. The drivers included Fred Nichols, Jim Fyfe, Jim McKay, Mick Manteit, Jacky Bale and Andy Anderson, who was also a taxi driver. Ray George, the mechanic, was also there and he was the longest-serving employee.

On one occasion, Tony McCafferty had been working late and he came out and saw there was a party on upstairs in the double-decker, so he hopped into the driving seat, started the engine and took off down the road. We went along Margaret Street and when we looked behind there was a police car following. We were trying to hide our drinks, but then the police turned off at the top of the Range and Tony turned round and took us back to Neil Street.'

Today, Tony as General Manager is at the helm of the company. His mother believes that if he had not become part of McCafferty's management team he could have gone in perhaps a very different direction:

'Tony could have been anything, but he has stayed with his father. They wanted him to be business manager for Coles, he could have gone into photography, and he could have been an Airforce pilot, but he missed out on joining the RAAF by one day when he finished school.

He was very disappointed about that. He used to have model planes and loved flying.

He organised our coaches, and he is progressive in his mind.

Sometimes, Tony and Jack clash but they can't do without each other. Jack might be slowing down a bit, and Tony can see something in a different light that he believes should be done and they get into each other a little bit and sometimes we wonder who is going to win.

Tony first married Wendy and then Joy. Tony and Joy's children are Nicholas and Tara. Tony's first son, John, is getting interested in the coach workshop in Toowoomba and this is great.

> *We discuss company business at home; we've always talked about it because for Jack the business is his life. He's an avid newspaper reader, and whenever we are away the papers just mount up until he returns and he starts going through them. Life has not been easy and they used to call me the "Iron Lady" – but I have to keep up with Jack because he is highly motivated.'*

In the 1950s there was often a cash-flow problem and sometimes we had to take drastic measures to keep expenditure down to a minimum. Ray George recalls those difficult times:

> 'When we moved down to Neil Street and had the service station, things were tough at times and I can recall the boss many times saying, "Can we hold out till the end of the month without buying stock and fuel?"
>
> Coral Probst, who ran the office and looked after the pay, often had to wait at the bank to get clearance from the manager to cash a cheque for the pay.
>
> One time Jack told me there were three secondhand buses for sale in Melbourne which he would like to buy for only £1,500, but the bank wouldn't give him the money. I offered to lend him the money if he would let me have one bus.
>
> However, he said he didn't mind me dealing in cars but didn't want me to be dealing in buses for myself. This was the closest I got to having any financial interest in McCafferty's.'

Taking part in three Round Australia Redex Trials in 1953, 1954 and 1955 broadened my outlook and I realised there was a huge part of Australia just waiting for tourists.

In the first year, I was in a Chevrolet sedan with my mechanic Ray George as co-driver; the second year in a Holden with a policeman, Tom Leonard, and a journalist, Peter Richardson, who was with *The Chronicle*; and on the third trial I was in another Holden with Toowoomba businessman John McKinney.

The first Redex Trial in 1953 took about 260 cars on 12 days of furious driving from Sydney to Townsville, west to Darwin, then through Central Australia to Adelaide and Melbourne and back to Sydney. It opened up my eyes to the opportunities of travel in the outback and I couldn't wait to expand further. We were pleased that we had completed the whole course and finished about 25th.

There were more than 200 entries in the second Redex Trial in 1954, including 'Granny' Brown in a 1930s Rolls-Royce. The elderly lady managed to complete the '54 and '55 events with a sign on the back of the Rolls-Royce proclaiming 'this car does eight miles to the gallon'.

Jack McCafferty handles an 8mm camera to capture a very clean Redex car before it heads off for the round Australia trial.

Chief Mechanic Ray George (left) and Jack McCafferty with McCafferty's Redex Trial entry in 1954.

Our best performance was on the third trip. We finished in the first 12, but the way in which the judges allocated the points didn't favour the early model Holdens.

In this trial, the route included Toowoomba and the send-off was held at the Queens Park Kiosk.

Driving at speed along the unsealed road from Townsville to Mt Isa was travelling 'in dust all the way'. Today, coaches travel the route on bitumen all the way.

There was one rallying episode from the West that stays in my mind: The 90-mile plain in Western Australia was another experience of the second race. The heat of the day made vehicle differentials white-hot driving over the sand.

Then there were certain wily citizens of Broome, who decided to have a lark with the Redex teams and they changed directional signs on the salt-pan roads.

In the 1955 Redex, while driving with John McKinney (co-driver) and Peter Richardson (navigator), we battled the heat and dust over a route that was 10,500 miles long.

Our Holden No. 50 started in Sydney with 181 other entrants and the trial took us on a three-week endurance test along some of the roughest roads in Australia.

Other entries from southern Queensland included Toowoomba racing driver Arthur Griffiths, and Sam Hecker, of Maryborough.

I told the media that I expected to take things quietly on the Sydney to Cairns section of the trial. I thought that if our car was still in good condition there, we would be in a better position to push the car hard on the long Northern Territory and Western Australian bad stretches. Peter Richardson was reporting for Toowoomba's daily newspaper and extracts from his stories that appeared in *The Chronicle* make interesting reading:

> 'The overall average speed for the 267 hours of driving time in the trial is about 39 mph. This may not seem high on first thought, but when the numerous horror sections and the need for low speeds through built-up areas are considered, it is apparent that cars will have to be thrashed mercilessly for days on end if their drivers are to have a chance of finishing "in the money".'
>
> We had a smooth, uneventful run from Toowoomba, covering the 500 miles to Newcastle in 11 hours' running time.
>
> The car ran sweetly, although the gross weight of 31 cwt. caused bottoming on sudden dips. We will have to off-load everything not absolutely essential before starting on Sunday.'

At Mataranka Homestead, Northern Territory, during the 1955 Redex Trial. John McKinney (McKinney's Toowoomba) and Peter Richardson (The Chronicle, Toowoomba) are pictured enjoying the cool waters (first left and third from the left), while Jack McCafferty, with the cap, studies the map.

When the cars left Sydney they were farewelled by a crowd of more than 100,000 people. The public took to their hearts the exploits of the drivers including one man who first threw sticks of gelignite from his car and then, as this press report reveals, changed from throwing gelignite to something less hazardous:

> 'One of the most popular drivers was last year's winner, "Gelignite" Jack Murray, a Bondi garage proprietor, who is driving this year with his brother, Ray. Their car is last year's winning "Grey Ghost" Ford.

McCafferty's 1955 Redex car travelling at speed.

> *As he drove off, Jack Murray tossed dozens of balloons into the crowd — somewhat less explosive than the gelignite he threw out several times during last year's trial.'*

By the time the cars had reached Port Hedland, only 72 of the original 176 cars were still in the race. By Melbourne the figure was down to 64 and we were among the minority who actually completed the course.

At the time when it was the Coronation Year in Britain, McCafferty's Bus Services were running a fleet of 14 taxis, which were available at the Toowoomba Railway Station and General Hospital, and three new Bedford buses that had been added to the already modern Bedford fleet.

The buses were available for charter and two trips were announced to take Toowoomba residents to travel on Queensland's second air-conditioned train, the new Sunlander between Toowoomba and Helidon.

On Saturday and Sunday, May 30 and 31, 1953, adults paid five shillings (50c) and children half a crown (25c) to travel on the train from Toowoomba Station to Helidon and return to Toowoomba by bus.

At that time the co-ordinated rail and road fares from Toowoomba to Brisbane were: first class £1/1/10 single and second class 15/2 single. 'Up' fare only, Helidon to Toowoomba, 3/- single. The co-ordinated service now featured the latest stainless steel rail cars and modern motor coaches.

Our eldest son, Tony, was just 12 years old when he began serving petrol at the bowsers of McCafferty's 24-hour petrol station. I used to watch him and think that one day he would be General Manager, but he needed to be shown the ropes.

In those days we had on display a large map of Queensland and ambitions to open up outback routes.

Today, Tony is our company's General Manager and on the wall of his office is a map of the world, taken from space. There's also a map of Australia showing all the main roads.

Outside his office windows on the terminal concourse, coaches fill up with passengers and freight as one day follows another.

We had gradually sold all our town runs and moved further afield. I had bought the Warwick-Allora run from Jack Rigney, but now my vision was firmly focused on long-distance coach travel.

'Metro Star' coach used on the Toowoomba-Helidon co-ordinated route in 1971.

Tony McCafferty and his wife, Joy.

The Picnic Point service was sold to Bert Truss, the Tourist Road service to Bill Chittick and the Gowrie Road service to Dudley Andrews.

In the High Court the various state transport authorities were being challenged for a ruling on free trade between states as set out in Section 92 of the Commonwealth Constitution.

The result was a freeing-up of interstate transport operations. No longer did coach operators have to comply with each state's transport requirements. If we were operating interstate we were free to operate without any restrictions.

This was the era when Reg Ansett commenced Pioneer Coach Tours, covering all Australian states.

I was now concentrating on interstate runs and the co-ordinated road-rail service. I have found a terrific sense of humour among coach drivers over the years. One of the occasions is recalled by Ron Crossley, at the time he was employed as a carpenter:

> *'We were working on the terminal in Neil Street when Harry Robbins drove in with a bus on the co-ordinated run. Mr Mac was there and he said, "How many on the co-ordinated Harry?"*
>
> *"Twenty – ten for me and ten for you Mr Mac," Harry answered in a joking manner.'*

Special paintwork on a Bedford coach for a visit to Toowoomba by the Queen in 1954.

The old depot in Toowoomba under construction in 1955. Part of this section of the original building was used at the workshop in Taylor Street in 1979.

We expanded again in Toowoomba in 1953, when a fleet of taxis came under McCafferty's banner.

The Neil Street site was undergoing great changes and there was an important ceremony in 1955 with the official opening of our first major terminal and Toowoomba's first Atlantic 24-hour service station. The service station was to continue in business until about 1970, the year I gave up being a full-time bus driver.

We had a Holden sub-dealership, maintained a taxi fleet that had two-way radio communication, and promoted the co-ordinated and tourist bus services.

The official opening ceremony was performed by the then Queensland Transport Minister John (Jack) E. Duggan. My daughter Kay and Coral Probst were among the first employees at the new terminal. Public relations man Roger Fair was MC for the function.

Kay can remember when the female members of our staff did all sorts of tasks:

> *'Coral was doing most of the office work, while I acted as what was commonly called in those days a 'Girl Friday', running messages and doing all the odd jobs. We came to work wearing pink nylon dresses and cardigans and thought we were very smart.'*

We have much to thank our children for and my wife often sings their praises:

> *'As for Kay, she was a wonderful girl. She was in high school, learning dancing, studying and when Jack and I had to go to functions, she would just take over.*
> *We could never repay any of our children.'*

Our Inter-City Coach Terminal in Toowoomba was not only the nerve centre of our operations but provided a regional terminal facility for other coach companies, among them Pioneer, Skennars, Intertour and Border Coaches.

On a ledge inside my office today is a small scale model of a McCafferty's coach presented by a Toowoomba taxi driver, Graham Ziser of Garden City Cabs. Other model coaches, with three-colour McCafferty's decals, became commercially available to enthusiasts in 1993. They were advertised in a model magazine at $45.50 apiece.

The Redex Trials had certainly changed my vision of Australia. I saw the need to open up more opportunities for people in the outback – and I was going to do it come hell or high water. But first

McCAFFERTY
Service Centre

ASSOCIATE DEALER FOR

HOLDEN

AUSTRALIA'S OWN CAR

Confidential Terms

Trade-ins Arranged

Holden, with 30 m.p.g. economy, 6 cylinder power, 21 h.p. performance, offers value beyond comparison. Comfort . . . appearance . . . low running costs, combine to make Holden first choice of the great majority.

CALL AT THE NEW McCAFFERTY SERVICE CENTRE FOR A DEMONSTRATION DRIVE

28-30 NEIL STREET, TOOWOOMBA

The first Holden and McCafferty's takes up the challenge.

there was something else that I had to get out of my system and that delayed expansion of the coach industry across the country.

I was always active in community affairs, and before 1955 I was on the Rangeville State School committee, a member of the Toowoomba Tourist Association and keenly interested in local affairs. Now, I thought it was the right time to try for a seat on the Toowoomba City Council.

I was already a member of the Australian Labour Party, and when I got the highest vote of the eight ALP candidates at the 1955 council elections I was elected as an alderman – third in a field of 28 candidates. Three years later I was elected Mayor by 4,500 votes, and served nine years (1958-1967).

In the run-up to the first election, I joined J.E. 'Jack' Duggan, former Leader of the State Parliamentary Labour Party, in leading the Toowoomba Labour Day procession. About 100 trade unionists marched in the first procession of its kind in the city for nine years. Among the placards carried were those that read, 'Keep Out The Tories', 'No Interference With Trade Union Affairs', 'Restore Full Price Control', and 'Restoration of Margins'.

The marchers were followed by eight floats sponsored by trade unions; eight teams of marching girls, basketball girls, Toowoomba

Jack and Lorna McCafferty, when Jack was Mayor.

City Amateur Wheelers, amateur athletes, two ambulance cars, one fire brigade unit, and a variety of trade displays.

In one of my press interviews before being elected Mayor, I said that I wished to correct an impression that I was in favour of a 'wide open' policy with regard to Sunday sport.

I said my policy was to 'make it legal' for such sports as were then being played on Sundays to be carried on in future. There was no possibility of the council allowing such things as horse racing or trotting to be conducted on Sundays.

My loyalties were now divided between my public duties and the coach industry. The availability of International Lend Lease chassis enabled General Motors to produce their first luxury 27-passenger Comair Bedford bus (OB model, 25 horsepower) at their Fisherman's Bend Plant in Melbourne, and they built hundreds of them. Later on they produced a larger 33-passenger Bedford bus – the SB model, 36 horsepower. At one stage, McCafferty's had a fleet of 11 of these Bedfords, painted orange and black. At the time they were regarded as 'very modern with plenty of room'.

Handling the mechanical side of the Bedfords was Ron Goodenough, who worked with McCafferty's from August 1953 to August 1975:

> *'I remember the company taking delivery of their first SB Bedford. It was Number 6 and it arrived from Victoria on the Friday night and was booked out on the Saturday morning by a local football club, who wanted to travel to Brisbane and back to Toowoomba.*
>
> *On the Monday morning, the cleaner came into the workshop and said, "Ron, you'd better have a look at this bus." It was a shambles, they had used the backs of the seats to open their beer bottles and they had had girls in with spiked shoes and of course Jack had an obsession with spike shoes. He had brought the matter up at the Toowoomba City Council about this kind of shoe marking bitumen footpaths.*
>
> *Girls had been hopping across the seats and their heels had gone through the cushions. What a mess those fellows had made inside that bus. I told the cleaner to leave it and I called Mr McCafferty. He rang the secretary and the manager of the club and they came down and inspected the damage. The manager was shocked but then the secretary said to Mr Mac: "Oh, it's only a bus anyway."*
>
> *Did that stir the boss up.*
>
> *"For your information this bus would cost a lot more than your house – that's if you've got one," Mr Mac replied. He was furious. He told the officials that their club was barred and its players would never be allowed on board to attend matches again.'*

That was in the days before there were signs inside our coaches such as those that are very necessary today. Among the common signs now are ones which state 'Persons found damaging any part of this vehicle will render themselves liable to prosecution'. There is also another saying 'No Food, Drink or Alcohol to be carried on this vehicle', and a more recent addition: 'Smoking Prohibited by State and Federal Regulations'. When the latter sign was introduced it was supported by 'No Smoking' stickers on passengers' windows.

Maintenance on the Bedfords in an emergency was a far cry from today's practices. Ray George remembers:

> *'The boss and I went to Sydney and bought an SB bus from John A. Gilbert to use on the Armidale to Brisbane service. Coming home through The Summit near Stanthorpe the engine gave an almighty bang so I pulled up straight away.*
>
> *As this model Bedford had a bad habit of breaking exhaust valves we tipped this was the problem. I had very few tools with me, only a screwdriver and pliers. However, the sump was very easy to remove with a screwdriver and still retain the oil in it. I did this and then with one of the windscreen blind rods I poked up through the piston and managed to get the broken valve head to drop down through the hole it had punched in the piston. With the sump back on we continued on to Toowoomba using about four gallons of oil and clouds of smoke but arrived home with no further delay. It shows how lucky you can be.*
>
> *Another time we bought an SB bus from Hardy Amby at Narrandera and the same thing happened just out of Grong Grong. This time we were not so lucky and the whole top of the piston had collapsed so we had to get Hardy Amby with his tow truck to tow us back to Narrandera, where he treated us to a sumptuous dinner of fish and chips and we carried out repairs next day.'*

Chapter 6

Selling Holdens and servicing buses

(1956-1960)

'We had a few problems with the first workshop which was in Neil Street, Toowoomba. There was an inspection pit but it was hard to get a whole bus into the workshop and half of it would be left sticking outside the back door. We had to turn each vehicle around to complete the maintenance.'

DENNIS DENSLEY

Coral Probst did a lot of typing in our office. Among her work were some of the company's early advertisements, including the following one on behalf of McCafferty's Service Centre in Neil Street in September 1957:

'Your Friendly Holden Associate Dealer. Safe and Dependable Used Cars at keenest prices. Buy wisely and well . . . buy a sound used vehicle from McCafferty's Service Centre who guarantee a good deal and complete satisfaction.'

At the same time a 1955 Ford Zephyr sedan, with radio and new paintwork, was being offered for £850, a 1955 air-ride model Holden £650, a Ford Popular utility 'an economical unit for the tradesman, was £350, a 1954 Chevrolet sedan £1,300, a 1952 Commer with a 6 cwt. payload £475, and a 'cheap coupe' in the form of a 1939 Austin 10 utility £95. It was the days when motorists could do a lot of maintenance with their own tool kits.

The company's emergency recovery vehicle, in those early days, was a Bedford truck fitted with air compressors and all necessary equipment and tools as well as a Ringfeder coupling. This unit was ready at all times to set off for anywhere in the State to handle a

Inside McCafferty's Taylor Street workshop, Toowoomba.

major breakdown or similar emergency. The unit, which was used in the pioneering days of coach travel, is still operating and doing yardwork at the Toowoomba workshop.

Emergencies still happen and it is not uncommon for our Workshop Manager, Dennis Densley, to receive a phone call during the night from a driver needing mechanical advice. This is how he sees his role:

> *'I often get very early calls. We keep a record of other companies across Australia which can assist with repair work. However, we advise coach drivers with a problem to check-out local knowledge because things change so quickly.*
>
> *I joined McCafferty's 26 years ago and worked alongside Ron Goodenough until Ron retired.*
>
> *In the early days, there was a great assortment of coaches from Bedfords and Hinos to Scania and AEC, Albion and Leyland double-deckers purchased in Sydney. The Hinos were the first to be fitted with toilets.*
>
> *Airbag suspension was hard on suspension and parts in those early days, but the Hinos had introduced that type of suspension to the coach industry in Australia.*
>
> *Over the years, the best coach model for maintenance has been the Landseer, a Denning coach which is no longer made. It featured improved bodywork far ahead of other coaches.'*

Ted Rolls, General Manager of Denning, and Jack McCafferty (1989).

I felt that Denning coaches changed direction when they were taken over by JRA (Jaguar Rover Australia), and the effect was noticeable early in the 1990s. JRA had also taken over Austral.

The Toowoomba workshop has 18 mechanics and three apprentices, while there are five mechanics at the Brisbane workshop. We also employ three spare parts people and five trade assistants doing such tasks as lubrication.

At any one time there's over $1 million of spare parts on hand for coach and car fleet maintenance.

The workshops have a strict program to ensure that every vehicle is serviced in a seven to 14-day period, and it takes two mechanics 12 hours minimum to service a large coach. If the vehicle needs a brake reline, then it takes longer.

A computer print-out shows which coaches are required for maintenance and a chart on the wall plots their course through the workshop. Close at hand are manual records of the fleet, which includes more than 100 Denning coaches, and one 20-seater Toyota Coaster that is based at Alice Springs, together with a 23-seater Nissan.

To assist maintenance and prevent misunderstandings, coach drivers print their names as well as adding their signatures to fault lists, which are often faxed into the workshops from outside terminals.

If there's a problem, then the office can contact the driver who filled in the report. Our mechanics take a pride in maintaining the fleet on the road. Dennis Densley keeps a close eye on each coach as it runs up the kilometres:

> *'It is hard to put an estimate on the life of a modern coach. We prolong the life by using good products such as Castrol oils and grease. As long as the chassis and body are in good order, then a coach can continue working. However, when a whole new body is needed, the economics of purchasing one may not be worthwhile.'*

Probably, for our company, the main choice for new coaches is now down to two major body and chassis builders in Australia – Austral Denning and Motor Coach Australia.

McCafferty's have adopted a policy, when ordering new coaches, of specifying as many non-electronic parts on the engines as possible.

This is for ease of maintenance and more importantly, ease of repair should a coach break down outside a major city.

I leave the running of our company's workshop at Toowoomba to Dennis and this is how he see operations:

> *'Our workshop is equipped to carry out all work except tasks such as trimming, radiator repairs, crankshaft grinding and alternator overhauls, which are sub-contracted.*
>
> *The company's maintenance program at the workshop is simple, but effective. Each vehicle is directed to one of six inspection pits.*
>
> *Then follows an inspection of tyre tread, test of cooling system, belt tension check, brake adjustment and lining check, wheel-bearing play and noise check, clutch-free travel and clutch-brake check, inspection of body and external lights, airbag suspension parts; universal joints and tailshaft splines are also inspected while all dash switches and gauges are checked for operation and accuracy. After king pins, tie rod ends and drag links are checked, the fault book is inspected for any driver or customer complaints and the vehicle is test run and necessary repairs are listed on a yellow check sheet.*
>
> *The next major service comes up once a month, or every 20,000km. This is far more involved and the check sheet lists about 100 items ranging from a simple check to see if the toilet light is working to checking the steering box and gearbox.'*

An early photograph of Dennis Densley (centre) and his workshop staff.

McCafferty's trained staff do their own engine overhauls and change engines when performance demands.

Refurbishment and body and panel repairs are sub-let to a number of experienced Denning body repair firms.

In the early days it was fairly easy to obtain a licence to drive a coach – or an 'omnibus' as they were officially called. What happened when Alf Probst went to get his licence in about 1960 is related here:

> 'Ray George and I took an SB Bedford up to the Toowoomba Police Station, and the policeman told me to get into the driving seat. I drove down Herries Street, along Mackenzie Street and then back along Margaret Street. Coming down Margaret Street the officer told me to change into second gear. There was a crash and a bang, but I got it in. He said I needed a bit more practice but I would get my licence.
>
> I went on to do charter work driving Commer nine-passenger vans, and a VW nine-passenger, which travelled to the Gold Coast when the highway was a two-lane road and we carried luggage on the roof-rack.

> *There were also tours to Darwin and Alice Springs and we formed a great team with me driving and my wife Coral as the "hostie".*
>
> *One of the worst trips was when we were heading for Kynuna during a very bad storm. Jack McCafferty was on board and when the police said the road ahead was too boggy, we pulled up at the Blue Heeler Hotel, Kynuna.*
>
> *We all headed into the pub and some time later we couldn't locate Mr Mac. Eventually, we found that he had taken a room at the back of the hotel and was having a good sleep.*
>
> *When we set off again, Clive Fletcher was driving, and I was resting in the back. The bus started swinging from one side to the other and suddenly everything stopped. The alternator had packed up in the middle of nowhere and there was no-one on board who could fix it. Then, along came a vehicle and it stopped and Jack McCafferty went over and found out that he actually knew the driver, who was an auto-electrician from Dalby. We couldn't believe it and that fellow got us out of a very difficult situation.'*

One good turn deserves another. On an earlier occasion, while waiting at the Kynuna Blue Heeler Hotel, a chap came in and shouted out "Is Jack McCafferty about?". He found me and said he was returning to Ipswich in his car, after attending a friend's funeral out west, and had run short of money. I gave him $50 and he was grateful for it and he did pay it back. It was this same chap – the auto electrician – who came along later and fixed the alternator on the coach. Otherwise we could have stayed there for days.

Sometime our drivers are taken advantage of after they have tried to help members of the public. Alf Probst recalls one such occasion when he was driving a Metrolink coach late one cold winter's night heading back to Toowoomba from Ipswich:

> *'At Ipswich, there was a bloke who was pretty drunk and I took pity on him because it was so cold and told him to get to the back of the bus and have a sleep.*
>
> *Many kilometres further along the road, I was coming into Withcott when a girl, who had been sitting at the back, came forward and said, "Excuse me driver, there's a fellow whose drinking in the back of the bus and he's been harassing me throughout the journey."*
>
> *I was appalled. I stopped the bus, walked down the aisle, grabbed the offender by the back of his coat and hauled him off the coach. Once out on the footpath he suddenly sobered up, but I shut the door and drove off up the Range to Toowoomba.*

> *I have great admiration for Jack McCafferty. Jack has carved out the business. Mr Mac has foresight, and he keeps abreast of everything going on in the world.*
>
> *I admire him for his ability to have a go at something. Sometimes it doesn't work and other times it really takes off.'*

Another stalwart, who was responsible for our company's progress over the years, is Ray George. He started as a mechanic in 1946 and up to his retirement some 10 years ago he held many positions as a tour driver, co-ordinator and 'jack of all trades'. He was manager in Toowoomba and at the Gold Coast.

Ray George and I used to go down to Victoria and scout around for secondhand school buses for resale in Queensland, when the Government opened up many country school runs. During this period we would have driven about 40 buses up to Toowoomba. We also used to drive the new General Motors Comair Bedford buses up from the factory.

In the 1960s, our company bought double-deckers from the Chullora Bus Works in Sydney. They were selling off their Leyland, Albion and AEC double-deckers for £500 to £600. Ray George and Tony McCafferty flew to Sydney at speed. They drove the coaches back at 35mph.

Quite often the double-deckers attracted attention as they were driven through country towns for the first time. An occasion when one of the double-deckers never made it to Toowoomba is remembered by Tony McCafferty:

> *'Two fellows approached us when we'd stopped for a break at Armidale and asked me if they could buy one of the double-deckers.*
>
> *I thought they were joking so I doubled the price we'd paid. I was amazed when one of the men produced a cheque book and handed over the money. Instead of returning to Toowoomba, Ray had to travel back to Sydney to pick up another bus.*
>
> *Then there was the time when we had a problem to get three secondhand buses home from Sydney, but only had one set of trade plates.*
>
> *It was a Saturday and we couldn't obtain a permit to travel, so we drove all three buses cautiously towards Toowoomba with one trade plate on the first vehicle, and the other on the back of the third vehicle.*
>
> *At Coonabarabran, we stopped for refreshments and returned to our buses to see two police officers inspecting them.*
>
> *"Can we see your permit?", one of the officers asked and, while I was thinking what to say, there was the sound of two cars colliding just down the street. The police officers took off for the*

> accident in a hurry, and we three coach drivers leapt into our
> vehicles and headed for Toowoomba. Well, the police never told us
> to remain stationary.'

We needed the double-deckers for school bus runs and special
excursions.

Up till 1980, McCafferty's ran an extensive school bus service
from small settlements in the Lockyer Valley, just east of
Toowoomba. Students from centres such as Helidon, Blanchview,
Withcott and Murphy's Creek travelled to and from Toowoomba
on Bedford and Hino buses. The Hinos eventually became the first
long-distance coaches.

One of the drivers who started with McCafferty's on Bedfords is
Wally Emerson. He remembers the days when he drove double-
deckers on school runs to Murphys Creek and Helidon and
transported students between St Ursula's and Downlands College:

> 'It was quite a feat to drive a double-decker with pre-selected gears
> up the Toowoomba Range. The only time you might get booked for
> speeding was when you were travelling down the Range and got to
> the straight stretch near the bottom, but even then it would be
> difficult as those buses had a top speed of only 30 to 40 miles
> an hour.'

Eventually, we found that too much equipment was tied up with
these metropolitan-type buses and they were pensioned off.

Our working and home life revolved around the coach industry.
There were some complaints from our partners. Wendy McCafferty
had this to say:

> 'One night we went to the Travelodge Restaurant in Toowoomba
> for dinner. I noted that the table was set parallel to the traffic in
> Margaret Street. Tony and Jack sat there throughout the meal
> checking out coaches, passenger numbers and timetables. I told
> them, "I'm never coming here to dinner with you again."
>
> Then, on another occasion, Tony and I were on holiday at Kirra
> and Tony sat out on the veranda counting coaches and passengers.
> I gave up and went to the beach.
>
> Some companies pay people big money to do serious research and
> it doesn't come off. Jack McCafferty has his finger on the pulse. He
> can sum up things quickly and he is a visionary. He likes being the
> first to do something. Then he will move to something else.'

Among the more unusual stories that circulate about me is one
that really is true. In my early days after I bought a unit at Hi-Surf,

The scene at the Commonwealth Aircraft Factory at Fisherman's Bend, Melbourne, with the Mayor (centre), his son Tony (left) and Mr H.G. Richardson, Sales Superintendent of the CAF. McCafferty's were taking delivery of their fourth new 41-passenger bus. The four buses were purchased at a cost of £25,000 and the 1050-mile trip was completed in three days.

Surfers Paradise, on the Gold Coast, I would often head there for the weekend and position myself at the window with a pair of binoculars. I was able to check passenger numbers on passing coaches, and not only those coaches belonging to my own company.

On one occasion, I found another pair of binoculars was also focused on the coaches.

Rival coach operator Jim Kirkland (Managing Director of Kirklands, a Lismore-based company) had a unit at Golden Gate across the road and he was doing the same thing.

It is great to be able to get away from the office once in a while and to sit in the unit and watch the sea and the boats on the Nerang River. I know I was against buying the unit in the first place, but I admit it has been well worthwhile.

When back in Toowoomba in the early days, I found it useful to collect the mail myself from the old Margaret Street Post Office, which is made of attractive Helidon sandstone. I could have sent a junior, but to reach the Post Office I had to walk past the Greyhound depot and I could keep an eye on their operations. You always need to check out the competition. I wasn't necessarily looking for anything bad, but if they had a new idea it might be something we could incorporate in our company. I often feel that companies that never look at their competitors come to a sticky end.

Sometimes I would drive along the road and park near Queens Park and count how many passengers were travelling on the 'Skinny dog'. At one stage I went out and bought 1000 shares in Australian Coachlines (formerly Greyhound), so that I could receive their annual reports and other information. I think I paid 20 cents a share. They are now worth around 7.5 cents – a loss on paper but it was money well spent.

Once back in the office I also insisted on being the first to look at the mail. This ensured that any problems were seen and attended to and not swept into the wastepaper basket.

There was always a lot of good humour among staff and passengers particularly during and after tours. Former driver Clive Fletcher recalls:

> *'We were about to leave Longreach at 7 a.m. and this Dutchman came down and said, "I think I had a snake in bed with me last night. I got up through the night and must have hit the switch on the electric blanket and didn't know. When I awoke I lay very, very still. Something in that bed was very warm and I swore it was a snake".'*

Clive's wife, Joyce, who often accompanied her husband on the long trips, helped sort out problems while her husband concentrated on the driving:

> *'Clive and I found that if you haven't got your coach sorted out in the first 24 hours you're in trouble because you upset other people. You have to do things so carefully not to upset people.*

The Bank of New South Wales (which later became Westpac) celebrated its centenary in Toowoomba in 1960. Manager Merv Parrott is on the right alongside Jack McCafferty and other bank officials.

There was one woman who was constantly crying. When we were ready to leave the hotel, she and her husband had both sent their breakfast back to be warmed-up and the man said his wife was sick and had a headache.

That delayed our departure and when we arrived at Winton they were doing up the hotel and some rooms didn't have toilets.

Clive and I happened to be in one of these rooms alongside these people. The woman howled in bed for an hour and I knocked on the door and found that she was crying because she might have to get up in the night and go down the corridor to the toilet. I took her on a trip down the corridor and showed her that the lights would be left on all night but she was still upset.

I guess that when you are an adult but you carry on like a child then you must be treated like a child. It only takes one person to upset the whole coach-load.

I knocked on her door again and I gave her my torch. "Now you will be able to see your way and if you want someone to go to the toilet with you just knock on my wall," I said.

You wouldn't believe the change. She really smartened up and the next morning she was on the coach and there was no more trouble, in fact she was the only passenger who helped us get the barbecue ready.

Then, on another tour there was a woman who got sick and wouldn't eat or drink.

When we arrived at Ayers Rock we had to help her out of the coach. I got a cup of tea and took it to her room, but she just turned her back on me.

Later, the motel owners tried to serve her with a cup of tea and she did the same to them. My husband went and got the nursing sister and again the woman gave her the cold treatment. Then the nursing sister spoke very sternly to the woman and told her that she was all on her own. Whatever happened no blame could be attached to the motel or the coach company because staff had been doing their best for her.

"We can't fly you out at night so it's up to you," she said. "If anything goes wrong you only have yourself to blame – I'll see you at breakfast in the morning."

She was there and she smartened up.'

Repairs in the outback can be simple or damned difficult. Ray George tells of one such incident:

'Harry Robbins took a load of volunteer workers out to Wave Hill Station to do some building for the Aboriginal people there. He rang from Winton on his way out and said "the diff on the Hino's stuffed, mate". I took another Hino out overnight to Winton and

next morning we transferred his load on to the other bus and sent
them on their way.

*In the meantime Harry had pulled the old diff out and had it on
the ground in 100 pieces. He said in his usual dry humour, "She's
all there mate, just needs a bit of adjustment". The whole thing was
an absolute mess. However, the crown wheel and pinion had about
half of each tooth left, so with new bearings and steel to make a
saddle for the pinion bearing, and grinding the jagged edges off the
teeth, I managed to assemble the diff and fit it back into the bus by
midnight. Then after a couple of beers out of the fridge I set off
towards Longreach and to my amazement the diff was quiet as a
mouse. Arrived at Longreach about 3 a.m. so had a camp till 6 a.m.
then rang the boss to say that I felt if I took it steady, I would get
home O.K.*

*He said, "We need a bus at Clermont to do the run into Rocky,
can you be there by 1 p.m. to load?" As we do the difficult
immediately, the impossible takes a little longer. I did the service
from Clermont on time and they then turned it straight round to go
back to Clermont and I took it on the inland run the next day to
Toowoomba.'*

There were some great days and daring trips. On one occasion
driver Wally Emerson took a little Mitsubishi mini-bus to Perth. He
passed one of McCafferty's big Hino coaches and the driver of that
vehicle, which dwarfed the mini-bus, thought he was seeing
things.

Before he left our coach company in 1984 to concentrate on
music, Wally did several trips to Perth across the Nullarbor and
remembers them with nostalgia:

*'There was no CB or other radio communication on board the
coaches and the driver and passengers had to find their own method
of entertainment.*

*We used to have singalongs with popular songs such as "Roll
out the barrel". We would put different words to nursery rhymes.*

*One of the popular competitions was to select one of the coach
wheels before we started the trip and draw numbers in chalk around
the tyre. The winner was the person whose selected number was
closest to the ground when the coach next stopped.*

*We would also get passengers to write down the last three digits
of the numberplate of cars going by; the driver would call out as he
was going along like bingo.*

*We had talent quests on board on long tours, and there was
plenty of yarn telling.*

Tony and I had small motorbikes which we stored underneath in the luggage bin. Whenever we arrived in a town and had a day free then we took off on the bikes to explore the place.'

Another memorable trip for Wally was while travelling back to Toowoomba from Rockhampton with the municipal band:

'I picked up the bandsmen on Easter Sunday. They had to be in Gladstone on the Monday to play for the arrival of yachts in the Brisbane to Gladstone race.

After marching up the main street of Gladstone and giving a performance, they went to the Gladstone Band Hall where they were served a few beers and a lot of mud crabs. The grateful locals handed out more beer and mud crabs as they boarded the coach. Tea was at Maryborough – for those who still had room in their stomachs – and it was while I was driving through Indooroopilly in Brisbane that a voice called out that two of the men should have been dropped off at Redcliffe.

I turned the coach around and eventually got home in Toowoomba at 5 a.m. Jan Emerson and Wendy McCafferty cleaned the coach out and I had a few hours sleep before taking off for Perth at 10 a.m.

I am now President of the Toowoomba Municipal Band, a role which Jack McCafferty had when he was Mayor of Toowoomba.

I learnt some business strengths from McCafferty's. These included how to deal with people, the day-to-day running of a business and marketing techniques.'

Organising meals in the outback was often difficult because of long distances and the constant need to maintain schedules. Among the many experiences of Ron Goodenough was this one:

'On a trip across the Nullarbor our group was accompanied by Jack and Lorna McCafferty and we'd stopped at a hotel and beers were on the bar.

Suddenly Jack turned round and asked, "Where's everybody?"

I told him that they had all gone into the dining room after a waitress had announced, "Your dinner's ready."

The 40 passengers were tucking into a scrumptious roast dinner.

I said to Jack, "This isn't our meal stop. We've got another 112 miles to go to Eucla, I don't think this meal was intended for us."

Then, an irate publican arrived and said, "Are you the driver of this coach?" When I answered "Yes", he blew the tripe out of me.

The publican said the meal we'd just eaten had been intended for passengers travelling on a Pioneer coach across the Nullarbor. There was no way he could ask his cooks to provide another roast dinner because if he did they would walk out. He said it was hard to get good cooks and, when you got them, you had to treat them with kid gloves.

After he had gone, Mrs Mac said to her husband,"Jack, you should have taken over that conversation." He replied: "Oh, Ron handled it better than me because he was very patient with that man. I would have lost my temper. We would never have got service here again, whereas now we can return because Ron's apologised".'

At times, the actions of some passengers prove extremely trying. On one occasion, Ron was returning from Western Australia and while crossing the Nullarbor had ordered meals using the Flying Doctor radio service.

The coach pulled in to one venue where meals had been ordered for 43 people. Lorna and I were among them but when we sat down to eat there were four empty chairs.

The missing passengers were still sitting on the coach.

Ron went out to them and said, 'We're all waiting to eat, aren't you coming?' They replied, 'We're not eating at this place because there are pigs roaming around.'

Ron pointed out that what they thought were pigs were really bandicoots. However, they still refused to eat and we had to pay for those extra four meals.

When the coach got to Ceduna, Ron drove it into a service station and gave the passengers a break of 20 minutes for drinks and a toilet stop. However, when we were ready to leave, the same four passengers were missing.

They were sitting in the service station restaurant having a meal and taking their time. Everyone was late getting back to Whyalla that night because of four selfish people.

Break-downs in the outback call for fast action if schedules are to be maintained and passengers kept sheltered from the heat. Ray George tells of one of these occasions when things didn't go quite according to plan:

'Coach No. 28, with Bill Hooper as driver, broke down at Balladonia on the western end of the Nullarbor on a tour to Perth. I caught a plane out of Brisbane at 6 a.m. and arrived at Perth at midday.

An Airwork Beechcraft Baron was waiting to fly me back to Balladonia. We picked up Rod McCafferty at Norseman, where he had organised a bus to bring the passengers into the motel at Norseman.

We took off again and the pilot gave me the map and said look out for where the telegraph line crosses the highway and that will be Balladonia homestead. When I did see this I told the pilot and he immediately banked and came down on to the airstrip. As the plane was taxiing from the end of the strip we noticed a lot of water across the strip. As it was too late to take off we ploughed into the water and the plane bogged down and tipped on to its nose. The port side propeller dug in and hit a tree root and bent the tips of the prop.

We climbed out and the pilot asked a fellow on a truck, who came from the homestead, if he had an axe and a hammer to straighten the prop. I was glad that I wasn't going back to Perth with him. I got the bus repaired and we went on to Kalgoorlie where the passengers were booked into a motel. The proprietor abused Bill for being late for dinner and said he should have let him know. However, Rod McCafferty had rung him from Norseman but he wouldn't accept a reverse charge call. We didn't use that motel any more.'

A broken windscreen can be a real hazard as Clive Fletcher well remembers:

'Keeping to the schedule is always a problem in the outback. On one trip out from Toowoomba we did a windscreen on the first night going into Mitchell, and the co-driver, Stan Neale, rang up for a spare to be flown to Mt Isa. He also contacted a panel beater but he was too busy and he agreed to let us use his tools if we could get the new windscreen. When it arrived the curved windscreen had been packed in a crate. The panel beater took one look at it and said, "I bet that thing's broken when you get it out. The only way to send a windscreen by air is to wrap it in paper – then they take good care of it."

It was shattered on the curve, but we put it in and fixed the break with masking tape.

We've had some great trips and sometimes had to get people out of bed to serve us fuel. At one place we couldn't get our passengers – a group of Christian Brothers – out of a coach house and we were hopelessly behind schedule. It was 1.30 a.m. when we awoke a garage owner at Tennant Creek seeking fuel and he was not too impressed.

Then, just a few miles out of Tennant Creek, Stan Neale showed me the temperature gauge, which had gone up as far as it would go. We stopped and had a look and I first thought we'd done a fan belt. Then I found that the fan nuts had fallen off and had dropped down in the guard. There was a mark on the radiator so we started to take the radiator out.

Among our passengers was a man called Jack Pobar, who was nicknamed the "Toowoomba Swaggie". He was a great character with an endless stream of poetry and stories. He entertained the passengers while we lit a fire and got a billy boiling.

It was after daylight when the first car came along and there were two young blokes on board, but they couldn't have cared less. Then a second vehicle came along with an elderly couple from Townsville who were going around Australia in a ute. The woman stayed with the coach and Stan and I went back to the service station at Tennant Creek where the bloke said, "Oh, no. Not you again."

We told him what was wrong and he agreed to help. We bought some food for the passengers, and then a council truck came along with water and filled up all the containers on the coach and once the radiator was fixed we were able to travel on to Alice Springs.'

Most passengers are great people but occasionally our drivers strike the opposite. Ron Goodenough recalls one such person:

'You get some whingers and the worst one I ever struck was a woman going to Perth. She started on me at Goondiwindi complaining about the meal. We lunched at the best hotel in the town and all the other patrons were thrilled. When we got to Dubbo that night she went crook about facilities at a Travelodge Motel.

The next day we reached Broken Hill, where two motels and the pub were booked for accommodation and the woman was booked into the top pub in town.

When she insisted that the lock be changed on the door the obliging publican changed it.

Then, when the party arrived at Whyalla, the motel couldn't take everybody, and we used the second-best hotel and the woman was among the passengers booked there.

I carried her luggage up to the room which she was to share with another woman and she ticked me off all the time.

However, when I returned to pick up her bags from the room the next morning, she had turned into a real pussy cat.

She never said another word all the way to Perth. The other woman who had shared her room had told her off and explained that the driver was doing everything he could to make the trip pleasant. He had already said that once we arrived at a motel or hotel the proprietor took over and there was nothing the driver could do about sleeping arrangements.

It turned out that the woman with all the complaints was married but was travelling to Perth with someone else's husband. Apparently the sleeping arrangements had not been to her satisfaction.

When you have a legitimate complaint Jack McCafferty always listens, providing what you say is the truth.

Jack requires mechanics to be conscientious and meticulous, and I recommended Dennis Densley to take over from me when I left. Dennis is still there today.

When a fellow once told me that McCafferty's didn't pay their bills, I saw red. "Do they owe you money?" I asked. "No they don't," the man replied.

"Well, then you're talking a load of rubbish," I said.

At one time I was 2,000 miles from Toowoomba when I ran into trouble, and I wanted something done on the bus but didn't have the money. I went to a firm and said I've got a problem with the radio in the bus. I'm from McCafferty's, Toowoomba, Queensland, but I haven't got any money with me. Can you help?

The proprietor looked at me and replied, "McCafferty's eh? Yes, that's all right, we'll fix it."

On another occasion, I was in Dubbo and I walked into a business and got a brand-new cylinder head, a full set of valves and springs and all the gaskets and then sat up all night doing a valve grind by the roadside. Once again I didn't have the money but it was no problem. I just said, 'McCafferty's, Toowoomba, Queensland', and showed them my identification.'

Our eldest son Tony was born in Toowoomba and went to boarding school at the prestigious Downlands College before working his way up through the ranks of the company.

On finishing school in 1960 he joined the business full-time as a lube attendant at McCafferty's Service Centre and handled

Jack celebrates his birthday in 1960 with his wife Lorna, Gail (aged 10), Ken (7) and Neil (5).

vehicles on the driveway. We had Atlantic petrol initially, and when the first Esso petrol was dispensed on the Darling Downs it was used to fill the petrol tank of the Mayor's car in March 1962.

Tony got his bus driver's licence earlier than usual for such an occupation. The very first coach he drove was a 12-passenger Commer mini-bus on a charter trip from Toowoomba to Mackay. It was carrying a bevy of young ladies who were members of a vigoro team. They won the Queensland championship and it proved a great trip.

In 1961, we were advertising: 'Gold Coast bus excursion. Weekend return fare £2, single 25 shillings.' Then there was the 'Special Sunday Excursion £1 return (Plus tax if applicable – seats must be booked for the day before departure).'

The 1960s found us still operating under the restrictive Queensland Transport Act but it was now easier to obtain permits for special trips with the freeing-up of petrol and tyres. Better bus chassis were also becoming available.

Roads continued to be a problem and as a result of their rough conditions and the limited horsepower of our buses it took us three days to do a tour to Sydney from Brisbane.

Chapter 7

Death threats and the working man

(1961-1966)

'People today are more highly educated, but then they won't put up with things like we did. You have to use your own common sense and native intelligence. I still feel that a lot of academics are hopeless.'

LORNA McCAFFERTY

Jack McCafferty pictured in his mayoral robes in 1958.

I received two death threats while active with Toowoomba City Council.

The first, written by an anonymous voter in 1961, was not taken too seriously. The writer threatened to kill me if I defeated an opponent in the Council elections.

The second threat was more serious. A telephone caller to my home threatened to cut my throat. I had a police guard until the man was caught.

At this time I was continuing to do my own form of market research to see from just where we could attract potential customers. Ron Goodenough has this to say about those days:

> 'Early in the piece, Jack McCafferty realised that the working man was probably his best customer.
>
> On returning from a tour to the Bunya Mountains the driver, Mick Manteit, was so mad about complaints over prices and the bad trip that he'd had that he slammed the bus door vigorously and the glass flew out of the offside window across the floor and out of the other door.
>
> McCafferty's had a contract with the Tourist Bureau to run trips to the Bunya Mountains but the cost of £2.14 was too expensive for the family man. Jack decided to charge £1 a head, and on the first Sunday picnic day tour of the Bunyas they had to put on three coaches to carry 99 passengers.
>
> They ran that tour to the Bunyas over several weeks and each time they had full loads.'

When I was the Mayor in 1962, I pressed for the establishment of an all-weather road to the Bunya Mountains.

On one day, 80 passengers had travelled in two buses from Toowoomba to the Bunya Mountains, a distance of about 72 miles. Because of the rough, narrow road up the range, great care was needed to avoid a collision on some of the sharp bends.

While improvements had been made to the Bunya Mountains road over the previous year, there was still a need for improvement on the road up the range.

After the experience of increased loadings on the Bunya trips, I decided to run a cheap tour to Lismore through Woodenbong as a day return for £1.10.

Following the success of the Highway Holidays, I continued on expanding in Touring Australia Tours including many Round Australia Tours, which at times used to fill three coaches. This was only made possible with the introduction of more powerful

The Mayor and Mayoress of Toowoomba.

coaches with airbag suspension instead of leaf steel springs and more comfortable riding.

I bought my first Air Ride Coach in 1967. It was a 42-passenger Hino Air Ride fully imported from Japan. Many more Hino coaches were added to the fleet over the years.

Most of the bodies were built by Freighters Body Works in Adelaide. One I remember well was named 'The Moonraker' because of its modern style. At this time we had numerous tours running all over Australia. Tour drivers in those days included my son Tony, Clive Fletcher, Murray Jackson, Fred Nichols, Mick Manteit, Steve Cooper and Gary Barnes.

Passengers liked the airbag suspension on the Hino coaches and McCafferty's bought another Hino (No. 12) and took the Toowoomba Municipal Band to South Australia for a contest in the Barossa Valley.

When we attempted to get the coach off the ferry after crossing the Murray River late at night, the coach wouldn't climb up the steep bank and the driver had to ask the passengers to alight. Ron Goodenough was adamant that the gear ratio on the automatic Hino was not suitable for climbing steep hills.

While the band was busy in the Barossa, I went with Ron to see the company in Adelaide that had marketed the coach. I saw the general manager and Ron went into the workshop where he saw a similar coach being prepared. Ron, who was never one to hold back an opinion, continues the story:

'*A company in Victoria had ordered that particular model coach to run tours to the Snowy Mountains. I told the foreman of that company that if the coach was the same as McCafferty's No. 12, he could forget it.*

Did that create a stir. I was called over the loudspeaker to go immediately to the main office. The general manager of the company told me that I had been making ridiculous statements in their workshop.

I told him that it was he who was wrong. I claimed that the coach wouldn't even get up Anzac Hill in Alice Springs, if it was full of passengers, and on the Toowoomba Range, drivers couldn't stop because if they did the vehicle was too highly geared to ascend the remainder of the Range.

After Jack and I had left the company, they went back to the drawing board and changed the gear ratios and the coach became a great success.'

There are no prizes for working out who gets the title of the Worst Passenger, but if McCafferty's had such an award it would surely go to a visitor to Toowoomba's annual Carnival of Flowers. Tony McCafferty was there:

'*On returning a group of passengers to the train at Helidon, one of our coach drivers was confronted by a middle-aged man who had done nothing but complain throughout the journey.*

"I've had a lot to whinge about today haven't I?" the man said.

"Yes, to tell the truth you're the worst whinger I've ever had on my coach," the driver replied.

"Well, to tell you the truth I am never happy unless I am whingeing, so I must have really had a good day." He then put his hand in his pocket and gave the driver a tip.'

The annual Carnival of Flowers is always great for business and in the early days the trains arriving at Helidon played a major role. It was a time when all hands and all coaches – the fast and the slow – were needed, as Ray George recalls:

'*Carnival of Flowers week in Toowoomba was probably the busiest of the year. On the Saturday of the procession we would meet the trains at Helidon to bring the people up to the Carnival. In the early days, the railway ran two trains from Brisbane. The first one was a special and there would be about 360 people on board. Then, the regular train arrived 30 minutes later, quite often with just as many passengers. The Helidon Railway Station was a hive of activity with buses stretching right out to the road. I would have to round up all the local buses I could get to help us out and quite a few which normally only did local town runs would have problems getting up the Toowoomba Range. They would then do a tour of the gardens in the afternoon and take the passengers back to Helidon to catch the train. It was such a relief to sit back that night and think that another Carnival Saturday was over. We could coast for the rest of the week.'*

I regarded the Helidon Railway Station as the 'gateway to Toowoomba' and I called for a facelift to the facilities in 1962.

In 16 years the Helidon station facilities had not received any improvement and yet the station had become an important terminal. Since the new diesel rail car had been introduced to the co-ordinated service 12 months earlier, passenger traffic had increased to 65,312, an increase of 14,074 over the previous 12 months.

One of the highlights of early 1963 was a visit to Queensland by the Queen and Prince Philip.

Lorna, as Mayoress of Toowoomba, chose a graceful gown for a dinner party held at Government House, Brisbane. I'm not good on describing dresses but the media noted that she was wearing a formal gown of shimmering French brocade in aqua and silver tonings. It had a high neckline in front and a low V-neckline at the back. The gown also featured two French roses on the nipped-in waistline, and a bell skirt. A chiffon drape of aqua, attached to one shoulder, fell gracefully down the back. The Mayoress completed her outfit with full-length white gloves and silver accessories. Well that was how the newspapers described it – but not exactly as it happened, as Lorna explains:

'In those days it was hats and gloves and being written up in the social columns and you never wore the same dress twice.

Jack was very good and he wasn't mean. When I suggested making my own clothes, he said, "What are dressmakers for?"

And as for hats there was Eunice Becker of Bon Marche Salon in an arcade off Ruthven Street, Toowoomba. My dressmaker was Mrs Bernice Hamer (née Olsen). She had a business above Hopkins Jewellers.

She made my dress for the Queen's visit. However, everything did not go as planned, and when I arrived in Brisbane and got dressed for the big occasion, I found that my silver shoes had been left behind at our home in Toowoomba. The manager of Lennons Hotel scouted around among his staff to get me shoes to match my silver dress, but the nearest they could come up with was a pair of bone-coloured ones. I never did have the courage to tell my dressmaker, who wanted to know all about the Queen, and was thrilled that I had sat at the Queen's table wearing a dress made in Toowoomba.

We felt very honoured to be invited. There were two tables with only 25 persons at each. I sat directly opposite the Queen, and Jack was at the other table with Prince Philip, the Duke of Edinburgh. My partner was Professor Sir Fred Schonell, and Jack's partner was Lady Tooth.'

Lorna fitted in well as Mayoress and she quickly learnt the art of making speeches and the need to have a wardrobe of clothes. But it was not all straightforward, as she states here:

'It wasn't easy for me in the Mayoralty period. It wasn't easy for me at all. I wasn't good at making speeches and yet I was asked to open flower shows and musicales and sometimes I opened functions while standing on the back of a truck.

Support came from women around me whose husbands were prominent people and they all lived in Toowoomba. They included Lady Ellen Chalk, Lady Hilda Swartz, Mrs Beatrice Duggan and Mrs 'Cush' Anderson. They were wonderful friends and they helped me so much.

There was another person, Mrs Arch Kerr, who gained an award for her charitable work. She was always encouraging Jack and I.

The Mayor makes a point during a Red Cross appeal in Toowoomba.

We took our work very seriously. It's different today. Wives today do their own thing in business or something else.

In those days dress was all important and I remember my friend Hilda Swartz being very embarrassed on one occasion when she arrived at a function with a very wide skirt, but without the hoop arrangement to keep the skirt pushed out. She spent the night walking around with her dress bunched up.'

It was the decade of the Beatles, the war in Vietnam and political assassinations, and also a time for increasing and improving services by coach companies.

People began to use services like McCafferty's more and more. For the first time there was a real alternative to taking the car – buses had been improved and were now popularly called coaches.

I was proud of our coaches and couldn't stand vandalism of any kind.

In 1963, when I was Mayor of Toowoomba, I said that if I had my way, vandals who destroyed property, such as street signs, would be whipped. It looked as though whipping would be the only deterrent.

Opening S.A. Best's Toowoomba premises in Bell Street when Jack McCafferty was Mayor. Pictured, left to right: C. W. Theaker, J. W. S. Branthwaite, A. O. Meakin, C. P. Theaker (Chairman of Directors), Alderman Jack McCafferty, D. P. Theaker and W. A. Turnbull.

It's no good fining them or sending them to jail. Legislation should be introduced so that courts could hand out whippings to these louts and bodgies.

Later, the Toowoomba Trades and Labour Council carried a resolution condemning my attitude as being against the principles of the whole Labour movement.

In the workshop we were having a few difficulties with the Bedfords, according to Ron Goodenough:

> *'One of the problems with the Bedfords was that they were always changing models and so many spare parts had to be ordered that other dealers came to McCafferty's when their own spares ran out.*
>
> *The gearboxes caused a lot of trouble. Coaches used to jump out of gear and it was a problem getting matched gears. I used to send the gears, which had sometimes 'jumped out' after only about 1,000 miles, to a Brisbane engineering firm and they back-cut them so that they would lock together. They were then re-sold all over the country by McCafferty's – because they worked.'*

Some instructions given to McCafferty's about the Comair buses in 1963 make interesting reading.

Our company was taking delivery of two Comairs from Bus Sales Pty Ltd, South Melbourne. The letter added the following instructions:

> *'Both vehicles will be ready for check-out shortly after 10 a.m. and apart from petrol, you will find that they will be completely serviced.*
>
> *It should be possible, unless you have other calls to make, to leave Melbourne by midday. As with any other vehicle, the first 200 miles should be taken quietly and I feel that you should provide about six hours for the run to Albury. It is suggested that arrangements be made with Preston Motors, Albury, to do an oil change on your arrival if possible, so that you could have a clear run the following day.'*

When Tony McCafferty went to Darwin and Alice Springs with a Comair, the roads weren't the best. They were narrow and unsealed for many miles and played havoc with tyres.

I was now paying our mechanic six shillings an hour to help with maintenance and McCafferty's were selling secondhand buses as a sideline.

School buses were being used extensively in Queensland and McCafferty's staff would travel to Melbourne to buy secondhand buses at auction. Over the years, we brought 200 of them to

The company's first Comair in 1963.

Toowoomba. The buses were mainly snub-nosed Bedfords, which could carry 25 passengers, and there was a ready market for them in Queensland.

Among the drivers who travelled south to pick up secondhand Bedfords was Clive Fletcher, who remembers his initial task:

> *'I got my first job from Jack in 1963, when I went to Melbourne to bring back secondhand buses. Ray George, Jack, myself and another driver went first to Oakey and then flew to Brisbane, Sydney and across to Melbourne.*
>
> *How did I come to get my licence? Well, the Church of Christ in Toowoomba needed a bus to collect children for Sunday School and to take people to family camps at Caloundra over the long weekend in January. Jack McCafferty made a Bedford available as long as the church provided the driver and paid for the petrol. The church driver had given up and I volunteered to take his place. I didn't realise that it would land me in a full-time job and from Bedfords I moved to a Ford charabanc and then to Comairs and later buses. I stayed with McCafferty's full-time until 1985, and then continued as a casual driver for seven or eight years. My wife, Joyce, and I often talk about McCafferty's. We enjoyed our time there and we feel we played a part in the company and if we had the opportunity we would both do the same thing again.'*

There was a strong work ethic in those times as Clive's wife Joyce recalls:

> *'We came out of the war years when people worked for what we called 'love money'. I helped Clive on the buses and I also worked*

Taking delivery of a new Comair bus from General Motors, Fisherman's Bend, Melbourne, in 1963. Jack McCafferty is at the wheel with Tony looking on.

> *for a jeweller. We would work back at night. We gave our time to the firm and if by the end of the year the firm had done good then we got a bonus. We didn't look for dollars – it was a different generation.*
>
> *When we toured the Centre it was great. Every morning there was this beautiful sun coming up. The outback is a really beautiful place but I have heard people say, "Why spend money to go out there and see nothing".'*

My son Tony had moved to larger 41-passenger coaches. In 1963 he made our company's first long-distance trip to Alice Springs with a full complement of passengers. He drove a six-cylinder petrol-engined Bedford SB3 coach all the way to Alice Springs to open up a new coach route to the Red Heart of Australia. Tony returned home to Toowoomba and after two weeks went out on the same route again.

When warning lights come on inside a coach it can be a false alarm, but then as Clive Fletcher says here sometimes it's genuine and people react in different ways:

> *'When things go wrong on a coach some people really 'drop their bundle'. We were driving a Denning coach in the Northern*

Territory when a warning light came on showing that the water level was very low. I stopped the coach at a place which had a garage, toilets and telephone box and found out that a pipe from one cylinder head to another was leaking. Some of the passengers were really shaken because we had stopped unexpectedly in the outback. They were worried that they would never get home. The garage didn't have a replacement hose, so I went out and got some copper pipe off a wreck and attached it to the hose and secured it with pieces of wire. I rang Toowoomba and they advised me to travel on to Darwin and then see if I could get a new hose fitted. We continued on our way and the copper pipe held until we got back to Toowoomba.

I believe that McCafferty's have progressed because of the kindness they give to people. Jack McCafferty has always looked after the families of the drivers and outsiders too. There are not too many people in the world like him. There are so many little ways in which he has helped. I know a group of Christian Brothers were given a free trip. I also remember a woman who paid a lot to go on a trip around Australia, and when she turned up at McCafferty's counter to enquire about another smaller trip, she was handed a free ticket.'

The Toowoomba Sports Ground Trust in 1963. Seated, the Mayor Alderman Jack McCafferty, E. S. Brown (Chairman), J. E. Duggan MLA. Standing: E. J. Llewelyn, J. Voght, G. W. Allen (Secretary), K. G. Jefferies and D. F. Thompson MBE.

By 1963, faster rail services were running between Toowoomba and Brisbane, following the quadruplication of the railway lines between Roma Street and Corinda.

Just before Christmas, an additional fast 2000 Class Rail Motor was introduced on the line. School children going on holidays and travelling by rail were told to obtain a vacation form from their head teacher to qualify for special rail concession fares.

Students, 16 years of age and over, paid only 9/7 rail fare, plus 4s bus fare, from Toowoomba to Brisbane, and students under 16 paid only 6/5 rail fare, plus 2s bus fare. Many purchased their rail tickets beforehand at the Toowoomba Railway Station to save congestion at Helidon.

Chapter 8

Mayoralty first,
Canberra maybe

'I was working as the Mayor's secretary in January 1961 when an Oakey farmer came in and presented Alderman McCafferty with the biggest melon he'd ever grown. The farmer, Mr J.A. Jull, said it weighed 52^1/$_4$ lb, and he thought the Mayor would like to have it.

Jack saw a photo opportunity and the melon and I made page one in the Toowoomba Chronicle on Saturday, January 28, 1961.'

CORAL PROBST

I was in the middle of a debate in 1964 on whether films should be screened on Sundays.

Applications from the Downs Drive-In Theatre and the Empire Theatre Pty Ltd, in Toowoomba, to carry out the screenings were approved by the City Council. The drive-in had installed 500 speakers, one for each car.

Council decreed that films had to be suitable for general exhibition and must not be screened before 8.30 p.m. This was despite a strong protest from the Toowoomba Ministers' Fraternal. The ministers pointed out that the Council had a responsibility involving the 'moral and spiritual welfare of the citizens of this city, both young and old'.

I had been elected Mayor with 13,225 votes. My only competitor, Jack Cossart, polled 8,973 and there were 629 informal votes.

When I took over as Mayor from Alderman M.J.R. "Curly" Anderson MLA in 1958, I scotched any move to reduce the mayoral allowance of £800 annually.

I said that the £800 would hardly keep myself and my wife in clothes. During the next three years we would have to take part in two major centenary celebrations, Queensland (1959) and Toowoomba (1960).

Lorna and I often shared duties but she didn't always appreciate my sense of humour as she says here:

> 'Jack's got a photographic memory, he can remember dates. When he opened the Aero Club in Toowoomba he amazed officials by rattling off dates without looking at any notes.
>
> I remember I had to officially open a Christmas festival at the YMCA in the Laurel Bank Hall and I went to great efforts to get details about dates and all about Christmas written down.
>
> Jack was also invited to go along and he said, "Let me see your notes."
>
> He read them and handed them back. When the proceedings began, the organiser said, "We welcome the Mayor and Mayoress, and just before Mayoress opens the festival we call on the Mayor to say a few words."
>
> Do you know, my husband stood there and said everything that I had written as well as the dates he had memorised.
>
> When it came time for me, I was really stunned. I wasn't used to public speaking but I was forced to think on my feet.
>
> Jack's mother said: "When things go wrong Jack always whistles."
>
> He has a good sense of humour. He is a very good man to go away on tour with. He keeps people happy. If someone has a gripe, he knows how to deal with them.
>
> I recall one man who was growling about everything. Jack turned to him and said, "Look, you've spent a lot of money to come on this trip – why don't you quieten down and enjoy yourself." The man became one of the best people on the trip.
>
> Jack just knows the right thing to say – and it goes back to his sense of humour.'

At the first meeting of the new Council, I told the aldermen that the job they would have to do was not for themselves, but for the benefit of the community generally.

It was the duty of those who accepted leadership to help others less fortunate than themselves.

You are not expected to do extraordinary things but rather you should do the ordinary things extraordinarily well.

Among the invitations I received was one written on a piece of board. It was from a company that invited me to attend a convention to learn more about a new product – described as 'formica laminated plastic'.

My first official duty was to meet the Prime Minister, Sir Robert Menzies, who was in Toowoomba to open the Lionel Lindsay Art Gallery. I had to officially welcome him at the ceremony. Public speaking was not my forte but I managed to get through, despite the fact that I had not slept the night before worrying about it.

Sir Robert apparently realised my nervousness, and after the opening he offered some words of encouragement and then invited me and my wife to join him and his wife for dinner that night.

Toowoomba didn't have the look of a modern city when I moved into the Mayor's office. Many businesses still had awnings held up with roadside posts. The Council had first ordered building posts to be removed from shops in 1940, but building restrictions had held this up.

Work on replacing the awnings started in 1954, and four years later there were still 64 Toowoomba buildings that had to have cantilever awnings erected.

The former Mayor of Rotorua Murray Linton (left) pictured with Jack McCafferty discussing expansion of tourism across the Tasman in the mid 1960s.

Business people responded well to getting the work done and there were few prosecutions against owners who refused to abide by the new regulations.

By 1962, Toowoomba's £1,000,000 conversion from post-type to cantilever awnings was almost complete. Of the 249 awnings that had to be converted only one remained on a suburban shop.

I took up a suggestion that Toowoomba should introduce town maps on roadsides to assist tourists, and that such maps should be illuminated at night.

I opened the £800,000 Myer (Toowoomba) Ltd store in 1962, on an old brewery site at the corner of Margaret and Dent Streets. It was the XXX site, before the company changed to making Fourex beer.

The Myer complex had a floor area of four and three-quarter acres, parking space for 600 cars and stock worth more than £300,000. It was the most modern store of its kind in Queensland and there were 600 people at the opening ceremony.

That same year, tourists visiting Toowoomba and staying at Lennons Hotel, in Ruthven Street, complained to the City Council that the City Hall clock chimes were keeping them awake.

The chimes went every quarter of an hour and they asked if the sound could be muffled between 11 p.m. and 6 a.m.

I took up the request and a mechanic was asked to attend to the clock.

In a bid to retain the city's garden image, I pushed for the employment of full-time gardeners in the city parks and gardens.

In 1958, only nine gardeners were employed by the Toowoomba City Council in an area of approximately 20 square miles. More money had to be allocated by Council if Toowoomba was to keep its name as the 'Garden City of the Downs', and have good displays for the annual Carnival of Flowers.

As Chairman of the Board of the Toowoomba Carnival of Flowers, I sent personal invitations to every mayor in Queensland to attend the 1958 Carnival. The visit by Mayors and their wives gave added publicity to the carnival and enabled the visitors to transmit ideas to their own cities.

That year saw Toowoomba's building boom exceed the figures of any previous 12 months in the city's history. More than a home a day was completed in Toowoomba during the year, and the 374 private homes, built at a cost of £1,011,711, was an all-time record.

On a lighter note, I have been the recipient of a number of hats during my working life.

Election photograph when the Mayor of Toowoomba, Alderman Jack McCafferty, contested the State seat of East Toowoomba on behalf of the Country Party in 1966. Jack is pictured with his wife Lorna and their six children, Ken, Tony, Gail, Kay, Rodney and Neil.

In 1964, during my term as Mayor, I received a black Homburg hat from an anonymous admirer. Following instructions received with the gift, I wore my new hat on my Channel 10 program, *The Mayor Speaks*.

Local government had given me a good start and I made several attempts to enter State and Federal Parliament. Fortunately for my business, I was unsuccessful, but I had a lot of fun trying. I stood as the Australian Labour Party candidate for the State seat of Cunningham in 1956 and as Country Party candidate for Toowoomba East in 1966, and twice for the Federal seat of Darling Downs in 1958 and 1961. Cunningham was a Country Party stronghold and Darling Downs was held by the Liberal-Country Party, but I was determined to give both a shake.

In 1958, the contest for Darling Downs resulted in the Liberals holding the seat with Reg Swartz polling 22,469. Jack McCafferty (ALP) had 13,623, and Margaret Walsh (QLP) 3,680.

Three years later, I was standing again saying, 'We intend to wake the Liberal Party up in this election'.

I took out a full-page advertisement in a daily newspaper addressed to 'Dear Reg' (R.W. Swartz) explaining that 'You may

QUEENSLAND STATE ELECTION — SATURDAY, MAY 28th

VOTING IS COMPULSORY

VOTE **1** **J. F. McCafferty**

YOUR COUNTRY PARTY CANDIDATE FOR TOOWOOMBA EAST

You MUST place a number in EACH SQUARE otherwise your Vote will be Informal

PHONE FOR INFORMATION CONCERNING THE ROLLS, OR TRANSPORT ON POLLING DAY

Committee Rooms: 45 Neil Street — Phone 2 6284

Authorised by E. S. Brown, Toowoomba.   Printed by McDonald & Rosbrook Pty. Ltd., Toowoomba.

Jack McCafferty's 'How to Vote Card'.

have tried your hardest – but let's face it. You haven't got anywhere down in Canberra as far as the Darling Downs is concerned. Tell us, if you can, of one major developmental work done for the Darling Downs since you got into office with Menzies in 1949? Even of a bit of extra business put our way that someone else hasn't got?'

Then there were further full-page advertisements and finally Swartz retained his seat, but with a reduced majority. When there were just a few absentee and postal votes still to be counted, Swartz had 19,981, McCafferty 16,619 and Walsh 2,928 votes.

I have had a long association with the Swartz family and Sir Reginald, who now lives in retirement in the Melbourne suburb of Doncaster, has some views about McCafferty's:

> '*Since my early youth in Toowoomba and later, when our children were growing up there, the name McCafferty had always been synonymous with the name of Toowoomba.*
>
> *As a child I had travelled on a McCafferty bus service and later our children had used a McCafferty bus service when going to school.*
>
> *It would have been difficult then to visualise the expansion and development of the original services to the present dynamic national and international system sponsored by the drive and ability of one man, Jack McCafferty.*
>
> *I had known Jack for many years but became more closely associated with him during my service as Federal Member for Darling Downs between 1949 and 1972.*
>
> *One small service provided by the McCafferty Bus Service during this period remains fresh in my mind.*
>
> *Before I became a Minister and was provided with an official car to travel between Brisbane Airport and Toowoomba I used to travel*

by train on Friday evenings and disembarked at Helidon to continue the journey by McCafferty's bus to Toowoomba.

When Jack McCafferty learnt that I was travelling this way he provided this service free.

This was some measure of real service and friendship which was very typical.

When attending the opening of the new McCafferty Transport Terminal in Neil Street, Toowoomba, I was able to recall this friendly gesture and compare the business expansion which had taken place during this era.'

Toowoomba was progressing and the city now had gangs out sealing streets and extending the sewage system. There were some 6,500 premises connected to sewerage and approximately 6,400 premises were receiving a sanitary service. The night soil man still had an important job in Toowoomba and it would be some time before his role came to an end.

Water was also a problem and I was instrumental in getting the £1,500,000 Perseverance Creek Dam built. With a dam wall height of 170 feet, it was regarded at the time as the highest rockfill dam in Australia and among the 12 highest of its type in the world.

I recall visiting the dam site before it was developed and seeing just a small trickle of water in a stream.

A line-up of Bedfords outside the Toowoomba GPO in 1953.

Jack McCafferty, Mayor of Toowoomba, circa 1958.

The first Comair in 1963.

I asked the engineer just where the dam was going to be, and when he replied 'Where the trickle of water is,' I couldn't believe it.

In 1964, I arranged for 40 people to be taken on a tour of the dam construction site. At the last minute there was a shortage of drivers, and so the Mayor became one of the bus drivers. The group of Toowoomba business people and company representatives took the afternoon off to tour one of the biggest projects ever undertaken by the Council.

In keeping with Toowoomba's motto 'We Prosper as We Grow', 1964 saw many exciting developments. They included a record number of conventions, discovery of more productive oil and gas wells in the Moonie and Roma areas, and approval of Sunday picture shows in Toowoomba, commencing at 7.30 p.m. The new Toowoomba to Warwick main road was completed through Hodgson Vale, and the Anzac Avenue route from Toowoomba to Pittsworth, by-passing Drayton, came into use. A new repertory theatre and the Range Shopping Centre were among other new projects in Toowoomba.

The Toowoomba City Council was desperately short of office space, but when I pushed through plans for a new £330,000 administrative centre in Herries Street it was called by some people 'a white elephant'.

City administrative building, Herries Street, Toowoomba, planned, constructed and opened during Alderman McCafferty's term as mayor – to replace office accommodation in the City Hall building erected 64 years earlier.

I had the entrance beautified with an ornamental fountain and gardens. Today, it remains an attractive building, but I get little satisfaction in that the final building, which Council approved, is far too small for a city with the growth potential of Toowoomba.

A crowd of more than 600 attended the opening on Saturday, December 7, 1963 of the three-storey building constructed of marble, Helidon sandstone and brick and glass. The ceremony was performed by the Governor of Queensland, Sir Henry Abel Smith, who had laid the foundation stone more than three years earlier.

By the time the loans on the new building were repaid in 40 years, interest and redemption would bring the cost of the building to about £500,000. However, if building work had been delayed, by that time construction costs would have doubled.

In that same year, I called on the City Council to design a standard type bus shelter-shed. Serious consideration had to be given to the use of materials that could not easily be damaged by vandals, but would retain a modern image.

Recommendations were for a shed of eight or ten feet in length, which could be used in multiples where required. Steel and iron would be used in their construction, and there would be no glass.

Another much needed project, which I spearheaded, was a new community swimming pool, and the result was the Milne Bay Pool, which was built at a cost of £100,000 and opened by Sir Henry Abel Smith.

Tourism in Toowoomba took another step forward when I opened the new Picnic Point Kiosk in 1958, with dance floor and glass frontage overlooking the Lockyer Valley.

I also oversaw the installation of the first traffic lights in Toowoomba, which were placed at the intersection of Margaret and Ruthven Streets in 1958. The request to erect the new 'motor traffic lights' came from the Queensland Police Commissioner. I also pressed Council to install two-way radio equipment in its vehicles. The cost of equipping six or seven council vehicles and a base station would be £1,000.

With my experience of two-way radio communication in the taxi business, I was certain that Council could save money and valuable time by equipping some of its vehicles with these sets.

Vehicles used by engineers and other specialised workers, if fitted with these sets, would enable the engineers to go from one job to another without wasting time by coming back into the city and then going to the district that they had just left.

I was certain that the time saved would far outweigh the initial expense of the equipment, and unless the City Council acted quickly it would be unable to secure a frequency on which to operate the sets.

Parking meters had been introduced in Toowoomba in an attempt to improve parking for shoppers. In 1962, the charges were sixpence for an hour and one shilling for two hours in most parts of the city; overstaying at a parking meter attracted a fine of £1.

Washers, coat buttons, dummy coins and other objects put into parking meters cost the City Council about £13 in the first nine months of operation.

Among more than 500 such objects removed were a religious medal, several key rings, and a plastic ice-cream spoon. Ninety per cent of the objects were washers. Persons who deposited anything other than 6d or 1/- coins into the meters could face a penalty of £100.

I spoke out against parking-meter pirates in November 1964.

Meter pirates were motorists who pulled into a zone controlled by an unexpired meter and failed to insert a coin into the machine.

I drew the public's attention to the requirements of the State Traffic Act, which stated that when a motorist pulled into a metered zone, he must immediately insert a coin into the meter. I pointed out that I was only drawing motorists' attention to the requirements of the Act. This led to a spate of letters in *The Chronicle* (Toowoomba) including the following:

Letter 1:

'Sir, The Mayor has drawn attention to the so-called "meter pirates".

Whether the motorist puts a coin in the meter or not it is still earning revenue by the hour. Weren't the meters installed primarily to facilitate parking and not to be robbing motorists? There is never any thought given by authorities to refund portion of the money a motorist does not use by leaving before the meter expires.

No wonder the pound is losing its value.

(signed) *Penny-Wise*, Nobby.'

Letter 2

'How dare Alderman McCafferty call these motorists "meter pirates"? If the Council expects to be paid twice for the same thing (meter space), then it is the Council who are the pirates, and not the motorist.....The meters are not put there for the convenience of the shoppers evidently but only as a money-making racket.'

Letter 3

'If I were to park in a meter at 4.45 p.m. and this meter had 15 minutes owing on it, which someone also obviously had paid for, would I have to place sixpence in the meter and pay for the time after 5 p.m. The sign reads from 9 a.m. to 5 p.m.

(signed) *Lady Driver'*

The Editor of *The Chronicle* added just one sentence: 'Under the existing law, yes.'

Yet another writer pointed out that the motorists were paying for the use of the space, not for the time.

A few months later, it was reported that £76,696 has been earned by Toowoomba's parking meters since they were installed a little more than three years earlier.

While Council officers were busy collecting the money, bus operators in Toowoomba were complaining that private cars were parking in areas designated for buses.

Council directed that when the signs read 'BUS STANDS' in a metered zone, 'it was an area strictly for omnibuses'.

No other vehicle could be driven on to a bus stand for any reason. Drivers desiring to pick up or set down passengers and load or unload goods must either occupy a metered space and pay the parking fee or use a loading zone.

The City Council introduced a special uniform for Toowoomba's two motorcycle parking meter patrolmen. The uniform was grey jodhpurs, leggings, leather jacket, black boots, grey shirt and a black tie. They were also issued with a safety helmet, a pair of leather gauntlets and a raincoat. Each patrolman was also provided with four identification badges.

Attempts were being made in 1964 to move the Mothers' Memorial, which was then in Margaret Street close to the Ruthven Street intersection, and what some aldermen considered to be a traffic hazard.

An early move to amend the Council's decision to move the memorial was lost on my casting vote and from then onwards there was daily comment in the Press and I also voiced my opinion on TV. Several women were reported as saying that they would resist by every means the pulling down of the 42-year-old 20ft black granite monument.

A special meeting of Council was called to consider a notice of motion put forward by Alderman Nell Robinson. She wanted

Council to rescind its decision to move the memorial. Her motion was defeated by five votes to three.

At the previous Council meeting, Alderman Robinson had presented a petition signed by about 3,000 people protesting against Council's decision to move the memorial. However, a different council eventually resited the memorial in East Creek Park, near the 4GR radio studios, in a much more fitting place away from a busy intersection.

1964 was also a year in which the official Mayoral vehicle was first fitted with seatbelts, which were to become compulsory.

I was advocating a number of new initiatives for Toowoomba including a lawn cemetery. In a speech in 1964, I said there would be no expensive tombstones in such a cemetery because all that was allowed was a flat slab with the name and particulars of the deceased.

Chapter 9

Mayoral duties and Red Centre Tours

'In those days the band of drivers had unbelievable comradeship. It was nothing to see my wife and other drivers' wives helping to wash and clean the coaches.'

WALLY EMERSON

Toowoomba took a further step forward when it gained its first commercial computer, which was programmed to send out invitations for its own official opening – including one for me as Mayor.

One press report stated as follows:

'The electronic robot wrote the invitations at a speed of 1000 words a minute. Invitations were received yesterday by various organisations and individuals to attend the opening of the Toowoomba Foundry's new Computer Bureau on January 22, 1965 at 4 p.m.'

While mayoral duties were taking up most of my time, the company was going ahead with Red Centre Tours.

Bill Buckle, of Nobby, was on the first Red Centre Tour conducted by McCafferty's in August 1965. He made a 25-minute 8mm movie of the tour and it was later made into an historic video and now forms part of our company's historic files.

It contains much footage of old cars such as the early Holdens and scenes of Alice Springs, then described as 'a thriving town of 5,000 people'.

Coach driver was Tony McCafferty, assisted by Barry Masters.

The passengers stopped overnight at the Victoria Motel, Charleville; North Gregory Hotel, Winton; Isa Motel, Mt Isa; Tennant Creek Hotel and the Oasis Motel, Alice Springs.

At the Oasis, adults using air-conditioned suites were charged £3 a night for bed and breakfast.

Passengers flew to Ayers Rock and the aircraft took them over Palm Valley, Hermansburg Mission and Kings Canyon.

Special souvenir folders coloured blue with gold lettering were produced and passengers placed their tourist information inside.

The tourist information in 1965 contained the following suggestions on clothes to be packed for Red Centre Tours:

> **WOMEN:** Tweed skirt or slacks, blouses, cardigans, pullovers. During winter the climate is warm by day but cold at night, so suitable underclothes should be included to suit these extremes. Strong walking shoes, sandshoes for rock climbing, a heavy overcoat and a rug. Spare slacks, skirts, underclothes and socks. Toilet requisites. Pyjamas, dressing gown, handkerchiefs, a torch, sunglasses, a shady hat and cosmetics.
>
> **MEN:** Ordinary (or sports) coat, sports trousers, sports shirts. A woollen pullover or cardigan for early morning and evening wear. Strong walking shoes and sandshoes for rock climbing. Overcoat and rug, shaving requisites. Spare slacks, shirts, underclothes and socks. Toilet requisites, pyjamas, dressing gown, handkerchiefs, torch, hat and sunglasses.

In January 1965, I introduced a four-point plan to help control Australia's road toll.

I said young licence-holders, between 17 and 21 years, should be restricted to driving low-powered motor cars of up to about eight horse-power. Then after they turned 21, if they had had no serious accidents, they could be given a licence to drive cars of any horsepower.

I also suggested a step-up in the system of snap checks on vehicles on the road, tightening up the roadworthiness of cars sold by used car dealers, and the allocation of more money by the Federal and State Governments to road safety purposes.

Fluoridation of water was becoming a big issue with the Press running hot with letters 'for' and 'against' the proposal. 'Should people take tablets or have fluoride added to the water supply?' was among the questions being debated.

Bakery hygiene also came under scrutiny in Toowoomba and the City Council wanted bakehouses to wrap all bread before it was sold.

The Council sought amendments to the Health Food Hygiene Regulations and Alderman Nell Robinson, who was later to become the city's Mayor, described the bread delivery system as 'hygienically bad'.

More than 1,000 Toowoomba and district people took advantage of special coach tours, introduced in Toowoomba in 1965, to visit cities and towns in Southern Queensland and Northern New South Wales. Many of the patrons were pensioners who received half-fare concessions.

People were now on the move. They wanted to see what was going on in other cities and towns.

This interest was a good thing in the community. It offered people a talking point and a new interest, and allowed them to make comparisons with their home city.

I was astounded at the patronage McCafferty's new services had received.

A round trip to Lismore on a Sunday had drawn bookings for a coach-load of people. The trip returned to Toowoomba via Byron Bay, Brunswick Heads, Murwillumbah and the Gold Coast.

Other trips were conducted to Lismore, Gympie, Maroochydore and Caloundra.

Wendy McCafferty was among the passengers when Wally Emerson drove our company's coach on our first deluxe tour to Melbourne for the Cup. Wally's wife, Jan, and I also travelled to Melbourne to see the national event.

Wendy was at the Cup in 1965 when Jean Shrimpton caused eyebrows to rise when she arrived wearing a mini skirt and introduced that form of skirt to Australian women. On her return to Toowoomba, minis were introduced to McCafferty's travel office and our girls also had beehive hairdos.

Susan Crossley, a former staff member, recalls those days:

> *'We would run a seven-day express to Melbourne for the Cup, and then on to the Oaks and another big race meeting on the Saturday. When our coach left on the return journey on the Sunday one fellow, who was a big punter, had recorded some big wins. He stashed between $1,400 and $2,000 in cash in his wallet and threw his coat up on the rack. When he got off the coach in Toowoomba, he collected his coat but the wallet had slipped out and eventually it turned up at the Brisbane terminal. Staff sent it back to*

Toowoomba and when the punter was contacted he expressed surprise and said, "Oh, I didn't know I'd lost it".'

In 1965, McCafferty's organised a special theatre party coach trip to Brisbane on Saturday, March 20, to see *The Black and White Minstrel Show* at Her Majesty's Theatre.

The stage show had arrived from England in the previous year.

I urged people to attend because it was a type of show the whole family could see without fear of hearing poor type jokes, and because it was the brightest and best presented stage setting we would have the opportunity of seeing in Australia for some time.

Arrangements were made for a three-course dinner at Her Majesty's Hotel next-door to the theatre.

The all-inclusive price was 60/- a person, including coach fare, dinner and reserved seat.

The 'latest type tourist coach' left the depot at 3.30 p.m., arrived in Brisbane at 6 p.m., for dinner and theatre, and departed Brisbane at 11.30 p.m. to arrive back in Toowoomba at 2 a.m.

Efforts were made without success to extend Toowoomba's airport at Wilsonton to allow for the operation of larger commercial aircraft. At that time, very few homes were in the way of allowing longer runways to be constructed across Bridge Street and up to the corner of North and Holberton Streets.

I believe that aircraft of up to 40 seats would have been able to land if an area of ground had been obtained from about the corner of Tor and North Streets to where the Wilsonton State School is now located.

I was the first president of the Toowoomba, Jondaryan and Rosalie Aerodrome Board, which also worked hard in efforts to take over local ownership of the Oakey Aerodrome.

Among my friends over the years Darcy Dukes, who is a pilot and former shire councillor, remembers those difficult times:

> 'I first met Jack McCafferty in the local government days in the mid-'60s. He became Mayor of Toowoomba and I was a member of Rosalie Shire Council.
>
> I suppose we both thought if something was right then we would go all the way with it.
>
> Jack was a staunch supporter of a good aerodrome for Toowoomba, and although I wasn't flying at the time I agreed with his sentiments.
>
> He also supported Oakey to be made the airport for Toowoomba, and we could have had a four-lane highway alongside the railway line towards Oakey but to bypass that town. Oakey is some 18

miles from Toowoomba. It could have been a straight road and passengers could have got to the airport in 20 minutes or less. That is pretty good by overseas standards when you consider how far airports are from big cities.

Today, eight to 10-passenger aircraft are as good as we can get in Toowoomba and for tourism this is just not good enough.

Apparently, Jack thought he had it in the bag, but when it came to the vote one of the supporters went 'twisted'.

It's an unusual thing about local government. You can get a man who will have thoughts and progress in his mind and he will be opposed and even defeated.

OK, Nell Robinson eventually defeated him as Mayor, fair enough, but that was probably one of the worst things that happened to Toowoomba.

Like they said about Clive Berghofer when he was Mayor of Toowoomba and a Member of Parliament – he couldn't have both jobs at the same time. I tell you Clive could have slept in the gutter and still kept up with them.

A successful outcome of the airport debate would never have had any effect on McCafferty's business. Jack was not punting for that aerodrome to build his own business. He knew the impact of tourism for the whole of Australia. Even New Zealand, United States, Europe and the British Isles have gone forward with tourism – and if any place is off the tourist map then it is just a dead town.'

In 1964, as Mayor I had also suggested that the Oakey airport should be investigated as a possible United States air base

I was commenting on surveys being carried out at that time in North Queensland and New Guinea by the U.S. Air Force.

'Oakey might be a possible rear headquarters base,' I said. 'Although not in a frontline area, it could be suitable as a headquarters area. It was well inland and had been an important base during the Second World War, with auxiliary strips at places like Quinalow and Leyburn.

'The presence of 400 or 500 American servicemen at Oakey would give the economy of the area a big lift.'

The Americans didn't come but I had enough on my plate anyway. I served for two years as President of the Carnival of Flowers Board and was later made a life member. I was a member of the Toowoomba District Abattoir Board, the Toowoomba Club and the Toowoomba Golf Club, as well as being a long-serving trustee of the Toowoomba Athletic Oval.

I backed an appeal by the Australian Broadcasting Commission (later Australian Broadcasting Corporation) in Toowoomba to increase the number of local concert subscribers so that the city would not lose its annual concert series. In 1963 I also appealed to people to support the Darling Downs University Establishment Association. Notices were sent out to 15,000 people on the Darling Downs in the hope of boosting membership from 2,350 to 10,000.

The chairman of the association, Dr A.R. McGregor, spearheaded the setting up of enthusiastic membership drive committees all over the Darling Downs and South-West Queensland. Unfortunately, Dr McGregor was later killed in a road accident in France.

I was president of the association that helped establish the foundations for what today is the University of Southern Queensland.

A leading Queensland newspaper dubbed me with the title of 'Mr Toowoomba' for what it described as my 'outstanding efforts to improve the city'.

When the Red Cross Blood Bank launched its appeal in Toowoomba, I 'hit the road' myself. I went out selling Red Cross badges of various sizes and personally canvassed business houses in the city.

At another time, I ran into trouble with women across the nation when I suggested that stiletto heels should be banned from city footpaths.

Bitumen footpaths were being damaged and it was costing ratepayers thousands of dollars in repair bills. The stiletto heels were leaving a trail of holes that even Blind Freddie could track, particularly in hot weather.

One of my new coaches also had its upholstery severely damaged by young women wearing stiletto heels.

Another unusual matter to be brought to the Mayor's notice was a complaint about excessive noise from Marching Girls practising in the vacant allotment near the library, which was then in Little Street. The Council asked the Marching Girls to use 'softer' whistles and looked into a suggestion to cover the wooden library floor with good-quality rubber tiles.

In March 1963, I gained national coverage after complaining that brains were not well represented in Toowoomba's annual Show Princess contest.

I was chairman of a panel judging 17 local beauties, and after the judging I said that fewer than half the girls knew the order of knighthood (the Thistle) the Queen had bestowed upon the Prime Minister, Sir Robert Menzies. Nor did they know the name of our local Federal Member of Parliament.

Before the winner was announced I said that all the young people of Toowoomba seemed to want to do was sit in coffee lounges, drink espresso coffee and live it up. When I asked them what they thought could be done to improve Toowoomba for the younger people, they gave answers ranging from more coffee lounges and other places of recreation to the thought that we should have a 10-pin bowling alley. No suggestion of anything cultural came from them.

My comments made newspaper headlines such as 'Beautiful – but so very dumb' across the country and a number of hilarious cartoons. One male chauvinistic reporter wrote: 'Perhaps it is time the organisers of beauty contests went back to first principles. A beautiful girl stops the traffic by her looks, not her conversation . . . Men in Toowoomba, or elsewhere, are ready to forgive a beauty contestant her ignorance of politics.'

'Downs council puts crackpot gag on Mayor' was the heading in one newspaper a month later. The Toowoomba City Council had voted to fine people and newspapers who made unauthorised news about Council doings.

I had held Press conferences regularly for five years and was astounded by the Council's decision to gag me.

I carried on holding Press conferences despite moves to enforce a by-law providing a £20 ($40) fine for the unauthorised release of Council information to the Press.

I believe the moves were politically motivated because I was the ALP member on the Council, and were probably started by an official of the Liberal Party in a bid to unseat me.

When Princess Alexandra visited Toowoomba during the State Centenary celebrations in 1959, I was chosen to ask her for the first dance at a special ball. The problem was that although I liked attending country dances, I had never learned to dance properly, and now I had to take time off work for dancing lessons. I don't think I impressed the Princess with my style and later I said tongue-in-cheek that any chance of gaining a knighthood had quickly faded from view.

The second time Princess Alexandra visited Toowoomba and met me I said: "You probably remember me, I stood on your toes when we last danced together."

In 1962, I was on a different dance floor when I was encouraged by our schoolgirl daughter Gail to dance to the beat of a new dance craze called 'the twist'. I remember the applause as I stepped onto the dance floor at Picnic Point. It was later reported in the local press:

Meeting Princess Alexandra.

'He began a two and a half minute Mayoral "twist" after which, between gasps, he announced he was exhausted.
    "Let's twist again," said Gail, but the Mayor said, "No, but perhaps another time".'

Lorna recalls Gail's education and family involvement with McCafferty's:

'Gail went to the University of Southern Queensland when it was known as the Darling Downs Institute of Advanced Education. She did primary and pre-school with honours and majored in early childhood. She now teaches in Brisbane and has two children, Lucinda and Damien, who both work for McCafferty's in Brisbane. Gail was formerly married to Jim Warren, of the Department of Trade and Industry, Canberra.'

On the occasions when Princess Alexandra visited Toowoomba there was tremendous community support for members of the royal family. On the first occasion, there was great excitement as the original Australian tour, planned for Princess Elizabeth and Prince Philip, had been cancelled due to the death of the King. My daughter Kay was under a hair dryer at the time, and she remembers the Princess's visit all too well:

> 'That day I went to have my hair done and was sitting under one of those massive hair dryers. Those old dryers were hot, horrific things with wires everywhere and someone called out, "She's coming, she's coming now".
>
> I rushed out with a towel around my head, and my father, who had already met the Princess said, "Oh, my daughter's over there".
>
> When the Princess was leaving later that day she turned to me and said "I saw you this afternoon with a towel around your head."
>
> That was not something you'd expect a princess to say, but she was so beautiful. She was such a lovely person and an absolute delight.
>
> Dad enjoyed meeting her because she was such a fun person.'

In 1965, Lorna and I were among the official guests at special functions at Ipswich and Grandchester to mark the centenary of Queensland Railways. The centenary dinner tickets were the shape of a steam locomotive.

A year later, I attended another official engagement – the dedication ceremony at the Cooby Creek Tracking Station. The Applications Technology Satellite Ground Station was constructed for the Commonwealth Department of Supply, acting on behalf of

Three Bedford Comair coaches lined up outside the Toowoomba City Council Administration Building in 1964.

A Commer shown in use in July 1963 taking a group of footballers from St Mary's Christian Brothers College, Toowoomba, to Pittsworth.

the National Aeronautics and Space Administration of the United States.

The station was opened by the Minister for Civil Aviation and Member for Darling Downs, Mr Reginald Swartz, who then lived in Toowoomba.

One of the unusual matters I had to deal with as Mayor, when smoking and chewing tobacco was still in vogue, was the problem of people spitting on city footpaths.

I described this filthy habit as a health menace and appealed for thoughtfulness and consideration to stop what was becoming a too-common practice.

A City Council by-law provided for a penalty of up to £20 ($40) for spitting on footpaths, and I instructed council staff to keep a close watch out for offenders.

I called meetings to form many local branches of organisations such as the National Association for the Prevention of Tuberculosis in Australia, the Spastic Welfare League and the Bush Children's Health Scheme. I was president of numerous organisations including the Toowoomba branch of the Queensland Road Safety Council and the Toowoomba Municipal Band.

On one occasion, I received a letter from a ratepayer stating that she had broken her spectacles when she fell over a heap of dirt left on a footpath in James Street. I arranged for the woman to be reimbursed for repairs to her spectacles.

In 1961, when Toowoomba's population stood at 50,134, I had been re-elected Mayor unopposed. Three years later I was back for a third term as Mayor with 15,754 votes. My opponent N.E. (Josh) Reynolds had 8,592, and there were 1,014 informal votes. I had my Mayoral allowance increased by £150 a year to £1,700, made up of a mayoral allowance of £1,400 and an aldermanic allowance of £300.

I remained as Mayor until 1967, when I was defeated by the daughter of a Toowoomba shopkeeper, Miss Nell Robinson.

During my nine years as Mayor, Lorna and I cared for our six children – Kay, Tony, Rodney, Gail, Kenneth and Neil – as well as attending to family business matters. Wendy Masters, who later became Wendy McCafferty on her marriage to Tony, recalls how I was viewed by the young staff at City Hall:

> *'I was a young woman, fresh out of school, working as a junior at the Toowoomba City Council in 1961, when Jack McCafferty was Mayor.*
>
> *Jack used to park his car alongside the old City Hall and enter by a side door. I worked with the switchboard girl, and he always acknowledged everybody with a "Good morning" or "Hello".*
>
> *I was very young when I stumbled while carrying a cup of tea into the Mayor's office and dropped the spoon. Without thinking, I picked it up from the carpet and placed it back in the saucer and handed it to the Mayor. I thought nothing of it but I was reminded of the incident some time later when Jack's son, Tony, who had also been in the room at the time, told me about it.*
>
> *When the 80 staff moved from the 60-year-old Toowoomba City Hall to the new Administration Centre, Tony began to take more notice of me and when we became engaged I still found it very difficult to address Mr and Mrs McCafferty.*
>
> *At work it was "Your Worship". I never did get round to calling them Mum and Dad and unfortunately our marriage didn't work out as we planned.*
>
> *I now teach marketing at TAFE on the Gold Coast and I draw on my experiences with McCafferty's to enhance the textbooks. I cannot speak too highly of my time with the company.*
>
> *When I first started going through all these theories I thought 'Gee, you know McCafferty's never did any of this and yet they still survive.' Then the more I went into marketing I realised that Jack is the big researcher, he is on the ball, listening and talking, finding out things and checking them out.*

Take the big trip he did in January 1994. He went to Cairns, Darwin and Alice Springs, came home for a weekend and then went down south. He is remarkable. I would have been worn out.

On top of that a week later, I came across a McCafferty's newsletter with pages written up about where Jack had been and what was happening. He had written it in an inspirational style and got it printed. Although I no longer work for McCafferty's I felt "Wow, aren't we going places".

Even today he maintains an exhausting schedule. I've known him drive down to the Gold Coast for a weekend and drive back at 4 a.m. on the Monday morning in time to see the first coach leave the Toowoomba terminal.'

QUEENSLAND RAILWAYS

TIME TABLE OF CO-ORDINATED RAIL-ROAD SERVICE BETWEEN

BRISBANE AND TOOWOOMBA

via HELIDON

Friday, 29th January, to Tuesday, 2nd February, 1965

IN CONNECTION WITH

AUSTRALIA DAY HOLIDAY, 1965

s. d. 16 6 SINGLE	s. d. 29 6 SAT-SUN RETURN	s. d. 30 6 RETURN

BRISBANE TO TOOWOOMBA					TOOWOOMBA TO BRISBANE			
Date	Central	Roma St.	Helidon	Too-woomba	Date	Too-woomba	Helidon	Roma St.	Central
	Depart	Depart	Depart	Arrive		Depart	Depart	Arrive	Arrive
January, 1965— Friday, 29th	a.m. .. .. p.m. 1 29	a.m. 8 15 9 0 p.m. 1 33 4 30 5 50	a.m. 10 49 11 11 p.m. 4 8 6 48 8 29	a.m. 11 19 11 41 p.m. 4 38 7 18 8 59	January, 1965— Friday, 29th	a.m. 7 40 8 20 10 40 p.m. 3 20 5 30	a.m. 8 15 8 57 11 15 p.m. 3 59 6 5	a.m. 10 10 11 45 p.m. 1 10 6 30 8 5	a.m. 10 13 p.m. 1 13
Saturday, 30th	a.m. 10 51 p.m. 12 8	a.m. 8 15 10 55 p.m. 12 14 6 25	a.m. 10 49 1 19 p.m. 2 34 8 54	a.m. 11 19 1 49 p.m. 3 4 9 24	Saturday, 30th	a.m. 7 40 8 20 12 40 3 20 4 45	a.m. 8 15 8 57 1 22 3 59 5 20	a.m. 10 10 11 45 p.m. 2 35 6 30 7 30	a.m. 10 15 p.m. 3 38 7 35
Sunday, 31st	a.m. 8 35	a.m. 8 42 p.m. 4 20 5 50	a.m. 11 15 p.m. 6 39 8 21	a.m. 11 45 p.m. 7 9 8 51	Sunday, 31st	a.m. 8 15 p.m. 6 12	a.m. 8 55 p.m. 6 50	a.m. 11 23 p.m. 9 13	a.m. 11 25 p.m. 9 17
February Monday, 1st	a.m. 4 48 p.m. 12 31 ..	a.m. 4 51 8 15 p.m. 12 35 4 30 6 30	a.m. 7 51 10 49 p.m. 3 22 6 48 9 1	a.m. 8 21 11 19 p.m. 3 52 7 18 9 31	February Monday, 1st	a.m. 7 40 8 20 p.m. 3 20 5 45	a.m. 8 15 8 57 p.m. 3 59 6 20	a.m. 10 10 11 45 p.m. 6 30 8 53	a.m. 10 13 p.m. 8 57
Tuesday, 2nd		a.m. 8 15 9 0 p.m. 4 30	a.m. 10 49 11 11 p.m. 6 48	a.m. 11 19 11 41 p.m. 7 18	Tuesday, 2nd	a.m. 7 40 8 20 10 40 p.m. 3 20	a.m. 8 15 8 57 11 15 p.m. 3 59	a.m. 10 10 11 45 p.m. 1 10 6 30	a.m. 10 13 p.m. 1 13

Passengers holding Co-ordinated Rail-Road Tickets and travelling between Brisbane and Toowoomba should travel on the above trains only.

Particulars of Fares, times of Trains from and to Intermediate Stations, and other information may be obtained on application to Station-masters, the City Booking Office or Tourist Bureau, Adelaide Street, Brisbane, or at the office of McCafferty's Bus Service, 28-30 Neil Street, Toowoomba.

Mr. J. F. McCafferty, trading as McCafferty's Bus Service, is responsible for the road portion of the journey between Helidon and Toowoomba.

Brisbane, January, 1965 (5)   Issued by Order of the Commissioner for Railways

I organised and promoted overseas tours in a big way. Tours were also organised to various parts of Australia, including trips to Central Australia in a DC3 and others to the Great Barrier Reef. One of the largest groups taken overseas was a party of 141, who flew to New Zealand in 1966. They included the mayors and shire chairmen from areas around Toowoomba.

When the group arrived in New Zealand, we were given special treatment by the mayors of the cities we visited – Wellington, Auckland, Rotorua, Dunedin and Christchurch. At Rotorua, I challenged the Mayor of Rotorua, Murray Linton, to organise a group of New Zealanders to visit Toowoomba. This he did with a group of 70 and established a bond of friendship between the two countries with many visits in both directions.

Toowoomba Travel Office in the National Mutual Life building in Margaret Street. At the counter is Wendy McCafferty.

The first travel office operated by McCafferty's at the National Mutual Life building in Margaret Street, Toowoomba, in 1966.

It was in 1966 that I became the proud owner of land in New Zealand – even if the plot is far too small to stand on.

In a New Zealand publicity gimmick, I became one of four million owners of a half-acre property in the village of Katahi, Rotorua. I was given the title deeds for a square inch allotment in the village. The gift was part of the site set apart by the Lands Association in New Zealand for goodwill gifts to personalities throughout the world.

I maintain a great belief in the future of tourism in Australia and particularly in my home State of Queensland.

I told a journalist in an interview in 1966 that 'Queensland is the premier state of Australia with unlimited development and business possibilities.

'The only thing that can stop this development and consequent drop in unemployment would be the people themselves – should they not want to make the effort. Some people give up too easily and do not try long enough or hard enough for success.'

McCafferty's Travel Office opened its doors in Margaret Street, Toowoomba, in 1966. There was a need for a higher profile for the travel industry and I chose a location in a busy street near Tattersalls Hotel.

The company moved into the National Mutual building and our second son, Rodney, was appointed manager.

Rodney had his early education at Downlands College, Toowoomba, where he was prominent in sporting activities.

Before taking up his position with the company's new offices at 190 Margaret Street, he had worked in various McCafferty's travel offices for 11 years and had travelled extensively around the world on many agents' educational tours.

Lorna is proud of Rodney's achievements as she outlines here:

> 'He was senior athletics winner of his year at Downlands, played junior A grade football for Queensland, and for Rangers in Toowoomba, as well as showing good form on the cricket pitch. He has won many sporting trophies over the years.
>
> He was in charge of the shirt department at Myer, Brisbane, and he was well trained in business management. He was there from when he left school at 18 until his mid-twenties when Jack said "You're in the business".
>
> Rod has been in travel ever since.'

Chapter 10

Losing the Mayoralty

(1967-1969)

'You're life is mapped out for you from the time you are born, my sister told me that. There is nothing you can do about it.'

LORNA McCAFFERTY

One of my biggest disappointments occurred when the people of Toowoomba put me out of the Mayoralty in 1967. But in one way it did me a good turn. I took Lorna on a long, well-earned break travelling around Australia.

I felt that there was still much to be done in Toowoomba. I would have liked to have seen a central police station, instead of having police offices scattered over the town, and I would have made sure that the Range highway was improved.

There were probably two reasons why I lost my seat. One was because I was trying to promote the Toowoomba Airport and the other was because I had left the Labour Party in 1965 and had joined the Country Party. Previously, I had supported the Labour Party, as had my father.

I considered that I had been elected by the people and I didn't take kindly to being directed by a committee of the Trades and Labour Council on how to vote on contentious issues.

I'm afraid that this didn't suit me at all. After I resigned from the party, they still put the knife in and I lost my seat. Under present conditions, the ALP would never allow such a situation to happen – but conditions were certainly different in 1967.

I was getting an allowance of £100 a month as Mayor, which is a bit different from the Mayoral allowance today.

There was also a lot of jealousy when I was Mayor. This was because I was operating a successful travel agency and came up with a lot of new ideas for boosting tourism. I think most small towns think the same way; they don't particularly like success.

There was a considerable backlash after I left the Labour Party. Anonymous letters appeared in newspapers and we received nuisance calls at the house. I lost some friends and acquaintances.

I remember I used to say I would do what I thought to be right and if the people didn't like it they could vote me out. And in doing so they did me a favour.

I had been conditioning myself to resigning from the Australian Labour Party for 12 months before I actually pulled the plug.

The Chronicle said news of my resignation dropped like a bombshell in Queensland political circles:

> 'The Mayor, known Australia-wide for his outspoken criticism of practically everything from the Federal Government down to stiletto heels, said he had adapted his way of thinking from the Labour point of view to that of the Country Party. He said he now viewed himself as an Independent.'

Lorna had quite a bit to say on how our family life had been affected during the Mayoralty:

> 'When Jack was in the Mayoralty, our son Neil was two years old and he was 12 when Jack left that position. Ken and Neil saw very little of us because of public commitments,
>
> When Jack was out of the mayoralty, Neil put his arms around me and said: "Tell me, you mean you are going to be home all the time. You are never going out any more, you are just going to be home."
>
> You know I could have wept. I felt what our comings and goings had meant to the children.
>
> Our children were often called in to assist while we were in the mayoralty. The boys put on white shirts and bow ties for photographers and the girls wore pretty dresses when presenting bouquets. During a road safety campaign, our children went out on trikes and bicycles to demonstrate how to handle traffic signs.
>
> Neil went to the Darling Downs Institute of Advanced Education and did a Diploma in Arts. He was among the first 25 to be chosen when the DDIAE opened its Arts course. They had some exceptional teachers in those days.
>
> Today, he lives in a forest in the Kempsey district, and he and Kerry (née Flanagan) have two children, Mardai and Aya. Their children's names originated in Indonesia where Neil and Kerry studied art.'

I never use notes when making speeches and I maintained an excellent rapport with the media when I was Mayor.

In my speech at the declaration of the poll, which handed over the reins to Nell Robinson, I said, 'After a complete break from public life, I intend to devote all my time to my expanding bus and travel business, which at times has had to be neglected because of public duties, as I am confident Toowoomba has a very bright future as a tourist city. ... I would like to relinquish office, hoping that during my 12 years service on the Council I have contributed in some small way to the present chapter of Toowoomba's history.

'Past history has proved that to make any progress at all in Local Government and to be sincere and to do some good for the community – without bowing to pressure groups – it is not possible to please everybody.'

An inscribed silver tray has a special place among the furnishings in our home. It was presented to Lorna and I by the Citizens of Toowoomba in 1967. The night of the presentation was a wonderful affair that we will never forget.

As I think back over the years there were times when I really enjoyed being Mayor and having the ability to do positive things for the people of Toowoomba. Ron Goodenough recalls one such incident here:

> 'I believe that one incident encapsulates Jack's approach to his job as Mayor.
>
> I was busy in the workshop when an old fellow came in and said he wanted to see Jack McCafferty. "Well, join the queue like the rest of us," I told him. "There's always a queue to see him."
>
> He said, "Jack's a terrific bloke. He's the only decent mayor this city's ever had.
>
> Where I live we are in a bit of a gully. When we get heavy rain the water pours through the back fence and underneath my house. If I happen to be out or asleep it even flows into my car. I've appealed to all the previous mayors of this city but nobody has done a thing except Jack.
>
> A couple of months ago we had a big storm during the night and I was ropeable. I had to drive my car out to higher ground and when I returned home I rang Jack McCafferty at a quarter to one in the morning. I told him what I thought of him and his Council.
>
> I put the phone down, made a cup of tea and had just climbed back into bed when there was a knock at the door.
>
> I asked myself what fool would be knocking on my door at this time in the morning? I opened the door and there stood Jack McCafferty.
>
> He said 'You are in trouble, fellow. I came down to see it for myself.'

Jack then went out and climbed over the fence to see where the water was coming from.

That morning at half-past-seven there was a noise outside in the street and I thought what the devil's going on? Council workmen were out there and by ten o'clock the problem was fixed and I have never had any trouble since."

When Jack lost the election I arrived at work on the Monday morning to find a lot of long faces.

"Well Jack that's the best b....y thing that ever happened to the company," I said.

"What do you mean?" he asked.

"Well, you've been tossed for Mayor and you're off the Council and when we want to see you about something to do with the company we won't have to join the queue of 50 or 60."

And that's what happened, the company just exploded from then on. The staff believed that Jack had been neglecting his own business to look after the city.'

My friend Sir Reginald Swartz also explained how he viewed my terms of office as Mayor of the city:

'As Mayor of Toowoomba for some years Jack McCafferty made a lasting favourable impression and revealed the business astuteness

Opening the Helidon Railway Station in August 1968. Gordon Chalk MLA is on the left with Bill Knox the Transport Minister, who performed the opening ceremony, Ted McCormack, Chairman of Gatton Shire Council, and Jack McCafferty.

and drive in that administration which was later displayed in his own business.

Perhaps the term "pioneer" could be applied to Jack McCafferty, because his vision for the future for his bus transport business assisted in the opening up of areas in outback Queensland, which depend so much on a reliable and regular transport system.

This "pioneering" spirit has been rewarded by the continuing strong support which his company receives from many outback areas, particularly in Queensland.

During my many years in public life Jack McCafferty and I had always remained friends. On the occasion we contested a Federal election I learnt at first hand something of the drive and energy which was later used in the development of McCafferty's Express Coaches.

The award of an OAM in the Order of Australia in 1992 was a fitting recognition of the continuing part that Jack McCafferty has played in this Toowoomba, Queensland and Australian development and it was also a tribute to Lorna McCafferty and family, and the staff of McCafferty's who have played a significant role in the development of the company.'

When my term as Mayor finished officially in 1967, I decided to pack up and drive to Darwin, Alice Springs, Adelaide and back home with my wife and two friends, Ken Briggs, who had just retired from the ANZ Bank, and his wife Jean.

While we were away, Tony, without telling me, purchased a 45-seater Hino touring coach, fully imported from Japan.

I nearly had a fit as we didn't know how much use we had for a unit as big as this. However, Tony soon had it booked for charter and tour trips and once again McCafferty's stepped into another era – long-distance coach services with air-conditioned coaches.

Tony remembers those days well:

'We were still bus drivers in those early days. We had been using Bedfords on tours to Alice Springs, the Snowy Mountains and the Barossa Valley.

I realised that a more upmarket type of coach was required and I happened to be at the Brisbane Exhibition in 1967. Freighter Industries were displaying an air-suspended rear-engined Hino coach. It had the airbag suspension instead of conventional springs and it was the first time it had been seen in Australia.

I was suitably impressed and was taken for a test drive and then given it on loan for a week. McCafferty's purchased it for $15,000, $2,000 below the list price.   It had 41 reclining seats and extra leg room, but no toilet or air-conditioning – it was cooled by jet air. It was a beautiful touring coach and ideal for what we wanted.'

One of McCafferty's first Hino coaches, built by Freighters, Adelaide, 1971.

McCafferty's first new Hino, bought from Freighters in Adelaide.

But the Hinos did come in for some opposition from the mechanical staff.

Mechanic Ron Goodenough at first wanted us to knock back the order. He and another staff mechanic crawled under the first bus and said they thought that there would be a tremendous amount of maintenance required because of the new suspension.

However, they were overruled by management and the first Hino was one of nine similar coaches purchased in the years from 1967 to 1972. They were used for tours to places such as Melbourne for 'the Cup', Perth, Darwin and Alice Springs. The Hino coaches filled the bill for our company until the early '70s, when a much more powerful General Motors diesel in a Denning coach came on the market.

As I mentioned earlier, getting a bus licence was nowhere near the hassle that you encounter today. Jack Warnecke, who was a driver from 1967 to 1979, recalls what happened when he made his application:

> *'I carted wood during the Second World War and when I joined McCafferty's as a driver in 1967, I went to the Toowoomba Police Station to get a bus licence.*
>
> *The policeman said, "You've driven trucks before?". When I answered "yes" he just gave me my licence.*
>
> *Today, I'm 75 and proud of my association with McCafferty's.'*

The General Manager of Freighters Industry (SA) Pty Ltd, Adelaide, Mr A. L. Wheatley, shaking hands with Jack McCafferty on the delivery of the third new Hino coach. In the background is former chief mechanic Ray George.

Special McCafferty's 50th anniversary drinking glasses are on his sink, while in his wardrobe, at his Toowoomba home in Sourris Street, is a very historic uniform. It's the one he received in the 1970s, grey with a brown tie. Tony McCafferty also wore a similar uniform.

Jack Warnecke remembers his first pay packet in 1967:

> *'I was paid $8 an hour casual rates when I started and because I was a casual driver there was neither holiday pay nor sick pay.*
>
> *The smallest vehicle I drove was an Austin five-seater panel van which was used on the Toowoomba to St George run, which McCafferty's had taken over from Western Transport.'*

McCafferty's was servicing many farming communities on the Darling Downs. From Toowoomba two daily services were running on the 90km route to Millmerran via Pittsworth, and there was a twice-weekly service on the 322km run to St George.

We had won the tender for the licensed service to Pittsworth and Millmerran, which followed the withdrawal of the Railways rail motor service. A year later, in 1971, I purchased the Toowoomba, Moonie and St George run from Western Transport with a Commer Mini bus and a Mitsubishi coach. Unfortunately, it didn't fit in with our other operations and was later sold to Ian Graham.

Our company won the tender for the licensed service between Toowoomba and Coolangatta in May 1970. At the same time a new inland route from Brisbane to Rockhampton was pioneered.

Roads were not good in those days as Jack Warnecke recalls:

> *'On one occasion at Moonie, I got bogged in sand and had to get assistance from a grader from the Main Roads Department.*
>
> *I also drove SB Bedfords, with four forward gears and one reverse gear, driving Sunday mornings on the Toowoomba Grammar School church run and on special trips.*
>
> *I was also one of the drivers on the co-ordinated run, which began at 7.30 a.m. from Toowoomba to catch the train at Helidon. The bus then returned at 8 a.m. on the school bus run serving Helidon, and then there were also school runs to Murphys Creek and Blanchview. Another school bus service operated between Nobby and Toowoomba.*
>
> *Bedford buses were used on the Toowoomba-Gold Coast run and I often stayed overnight at Tweed Heads. It was in the days before poker machines, and passengers were a mixture of young and old.*
>
> *I drove the Millmerran coach when the rail motor ceased. It was a very quiet run, supported by the students who travelled to the high school at Pittsworth and Toowoomba.*

One of my most memorable trips was in July 1970, when I helped transport a group of four dancers and a young manager from the Queensland Ballet Company around western Queensland. I drove an 11-seater Mitsubishi from Winton to Longreach, Muttaburra, Barcaldine, Tambo, Charleville, Tara and Dalby for performances at local schools.

It was a great trip. I lost my voice when I got 'flu near the end of the journey, but the young people treated me like a brother.

Back in Toowoomba I was driving Albion and AEC double-deckers. Gears were still on the floor on most of these buses but there was one double-decker with a pre-selector gear shift. It was often used on the army run between Toowoomba and the Motor Vehicle Transport Company at Cabarlah.

Around town, drivers of double-deckers had to pick their streets to avoid hitting the overhanging branches on big trees.

McCafferty was a top man, one of the fairest men. He treated me right.

I know my pay never worked out to me anyway and I always seemed to get too much. I questioned Mr Mac once about it and he told me I was being paid for the work I had done. I never had a row with him or a hard word.

I had a personal motto: "Whatever you do, do it right and don't muck about, because it's just as easy to do a good job as a bad job".'

Jack Warnecke left what he termed his 'fine working mates' in 1979, when the company began using V6 Denning coaches.

He had been more used to driving Bedford diesel and petrol coaches and the Scania, an ex-Redline Coach, which always seemed to be missing a speedo and rev counter.

One driver of the Scania claimed that he had been booked by the police down south for doing 70 mph in a 50 mph zone. He was wild about it and I couldn't believe that the bus had actually done that speed. Then next time it left the terminal I got into my Chevrolet car and followed – and it really did achieve that speed. I was astounded.

On one occasion during an airline strike, the Scania was used to take a rugby union team back to Sydney from Toowoomba. It was during this particular strike that staff at the Townsville terminal reported having problems with people seeking coach seats.

They were the people completely unused to coach travel and had been pampered by the airlines. When they rang the McCafferty's Coach Terminal they were prone to asking how many meals were included in the ticket, and where they would be accommodated overnight?

Chapter 11

A woman behind
the wheel

'Coral Probst became the first woman to gain a licence to drive omnibuses or heavy vehicles, other than a semi-trailer.

She undertook a tough oral examination and then came a really stiff driving test. She came through with flying colours.'

NEWSPAPER REPORT IN 1967

Coral Probst got her photograph in the newspapers in 1967 when she became the first Toowoomba woman to hold a commercial bus driver's licence. She had held an ordinary driving licence for 16 years.

To gain the licence to drive a bus she answered questions on heavy transport, attended a traffic lecture school at the Toowoomba Police Station, and went on a test bus drive in a Comair. Newspaper reports in October 1967 and January 1968 recorded Coral's achievement with glowing praise:

'For the first time in Toowoomba's history a woman driver took charge of a full-sized bus and drove a group of school children from Toowoomba to Helidon.

The driver was Mrs Coral Probst, who is in charge of McCafferty's Service Centre office.

Jack McCafferty said that Mrs Probst would take charge of special tourist trips and do general bus driving.

"Charter bus work is entering a new era," Mr McCafferty said, "and there is a very definite place for women drivers".'

In January, 1968, media attention turned to Coral Probst again at the wheel of a 40-passenger bus.

The story in *The Sunday Mail* said in part:

'Toowoomba's steep range highway holds no terrors for the city's most recently qualified bus driver.

Yet this particular bus driver is an attractive young woman – Mrs Coral Probst.

Her usual job is secretary to McCafferty's where she has worked for many years.

It was at Jack McCafferty's suggestion that she took instruction in bus driving. Now she has several trips up and down the range to her credit, driving the co-ordinated bus run which shuttles rail passengers to and from Helidon Railway Station...... Mrs Probst also drives smaller 21-seater buses on school and kindergarten runs around Toowoomba.'

Coral stayed with McCafferty's 21 years and today her husband is still driving for the company.

In the days when there was no power steering and McCafferty's were buying second-hand buses down south, it was not unusual for Alf and Coral Probst to finish work on a Friday night, jump on a coach to Brisbane, fly to Melbourne, bring back a coach to Toowoomba and start work on the Monday.

On one occasion they left Melbourne in an OB Bedford but ran into problems approaching Albury. Alf continues the story:

'It was at a time when service stations in Victoria had to close at 6 p.m. at weekends. The service station owner didn't want to know us. I parked the bus and checked the engine and found that there was a loose stud on the generator. Fortunately, the stud was still there and I tightened it up and we continued north. But then, getting closer to Tamworth, the bus got slower and slower. We got a good night's sleep at a motel, and I bought a new set of plugs the next morning, but they made no difference.

We crawled up the hills, the muffler had fallen off, we had only four cylinders working and I needed both hands on the lever to change gear.

The bowl under the carburettor had come off and petrol had flooded everywhere and we crawled into Toowoomba at 1 a.m. on Monday, and were back to work at 8 a.m.

The mechanic told us later that two of the overhead rocker posts had broken and the gearbox was full of ground metal!

On another occasion we experienced what I believe is a coach driver's worst nightmare – having no brakes going down the Toowoomba Range. It was a day that I will never forget.

Coral was among the passengers on the OB Bedford coach which was doing the co-ordinated run from Toowoomba to Helidon and she too noticed something was wrong.

I couldn't believe it. I'd just driven the bus off the maintenance ramp, it was fully loaded with passengers and we were descending the Range in second gear when the brakes failed.

What could I do? I pulled on the handbrake, but there was little reaction and the coach began to pick up speed. Don't wait for something to happen I told myself – start planning. I contemplated running the coach into the bank, but there was too much traffic about, and then I took a chance and went to change down to bottom gear........I knew it might not do it, but then it held.

I felt so relieved, and when we stopped at Helidon a fellow came from the back of the coach and said, "You had no brakes coming down the range, eh?" I don't know how he knew. But Coral told him that she knew something was going wrong because my face had gone white.

I have never been involved in an accident or had a traffic fine. I was driving buses before I joined McCafferty's. I got my bus driver's licence in 1959, and sold my South-East Toowoomba Bus Service (Geddes Street and Hume Street) in 1986 to work for Jack.

One of the earliest buses I remember McCafferty's having was one which had all doors alongside the seats on one side. It was used on the Sydney-Blue Mountains trip and to take picnickers to The Washpool, which was used for swimming at Helidon Spa. That was before the highway was widened and a traffic lane was built over one of the spa water springs.

We still have the folder of a McCafferty's Grand Round Australia 30-day coach tour of 10,000 miles, which departed from Toowoomba on September 30, 1968. The tour took passengers north to Cairns, then to Normanton, Mt Isa, Katherine and Darwin, then on to Kununurra and the Ord River, Wyndham, Halls Creek to Broome, Pt Hedland, Carnarvon, Geraldton, Perth, Albany, Norseman, then across the Nullarbor Plains to Iron Knob and on to Adelaide, Melbourne, Sydney and finally on the coastal run up to Brisbane and back to Toowoomba.

Coral typed out very detailed instructions to all tour passengers and they were signed by Jack McCafferty.'

One letter we mailed out concerning last-minute details for a Central Australia Coach Tour in August 1968 urged travellers not to forget to bring a good pair of walking shoes. 'You will find them most useful around Alice Springs – also a fly veil could be helpful as generally when there is a lot of green grass about the flies are bad, also whilst out walking in the bush. A brochure containing all details of the tour will be presented to each passenger at Toowoomba. In this brochure the printed words of many popular songs will be included so it is to be hoped everybody will be in good voice to join in the singing. .....Indications are that this tour

Special paintwork on a Bedford coach for a visit to Toowoomba by the Queen in 1954.

Above: Rod Hood of Denning (left) with Jack McCafferty and John Osborne pictured with coaches at the Toowoomba terminal in 1990.

Below: The new 'stretchliner' 56-passenger coach – the longest in Queensland – introduced by McCafferty's in 1994.

group will be the happiest one ever to leave Toowoomba and I do hope you join in the spirit of the party and have a jolly good time.'

Among the 30 songs typed out on the two-page sheet were *It had to be you, I wonder who's kissing her now, Two Little Girls in Blue, Pack up Your Troubles, If you knew Susie, You Made Me Love You,* and *I've got a Lovely Bunch of Coconuts.*

One popular form of entertainment on board was to get all the passengers on the left-hand side of the coach singing "Three Blind Mice", and after they had started, get those on the right-hand side singing the same nursery rhyme.

That was in the days when fuel was not readily available, and we used to carry spare drums of fuel in the cargo hold, and the fuel had to be siphoned out when the main tank ran low.

They were great pioneering days as former driver Clive Fletcher recalls:

> 'When I went to Perth for the first time in 1968, Ray George and I were on one Hino coach, and Tony and another driver were on the second Hino.
>
> The tyre people in Toowoomba said the tyres would never make it half-way across, but we went to Perth and back and never changed a wheel.
>
> That same year I also did my first trip to the Centre with Alf and Coral Probst, and again we never changed a wheel, but we didn't have the same luck during my first 30-day trip around Australia. That was in October 1968 and we were really moving to maintain the schedule. At Fitzroy Crossing, we had a problem with a tyre which blew and we started for Derby without a spare.
>
> Once in Derby I asked a snack-bar man if there was anyone around selling tyres. He said, "Your luck must be in because the tyre man has just flown in from Perth."
>
> He had a suitable tyre and tube, but then there was a problem of paying for it as the money was being carried on another coach running behind us.
>
> "Well, you've come so far I'll charge it to Toowoomba," the tyre man said. Heading for Wyndham I saw a speck in the mirror. It was the other McCafferty's coach, and I felt so relieved I let them catch up, but I never had another flat tyre on that trip.'

In Toowoomba promotion was the name of the game and we undertook promotions in the Toowoomba City Hall. We would hire the hall and fill it up with no trouble at all. People like Ted Egan, who was nobody then, joined forces with Barry Tognilini, the Liberace-style pianist who used to play on the Indian Pacific. We gave away prizes, sample bags and trips on the coaches.

The McCafferty family in 1969: Seated are Ken, Lorna, Jack and Tony. Standing are Neil, Kay, Rodney and Gail.

Many of the early coach tours started in Brisbane, and when they reached Toowoomba I would go out and introduce myself to the passengers and wish them well on their trip.

John Clough, the company's Financial Controller, is Tony's cousin. Without John's hand on the till McCafferty's may not have got where we are today.

John, who had previous transport experience in Mackay, brought a maturity to our company's accountancy.

I once heard a terminal staff member say:

> 'The company owes a lot of success to people like John Clough. He
> is one accountant who you can talk to. John and Tony started the
> new brigade and it was John who first put in computers.'

In 1968, we had the ultimate travel agency in rented premises in Margaret Street, Toowoomba. It had a motto: *"The meeting place of tourists in the Garden City'*, which appeared on all letterheads of McCafferty's Travel Information Centre.

Tom Mahon, who had worked with TAA and was McCafferty's first marketing officer, wanted an all white format for the new travel office. However, a Toowoomba company, Lanes Interiors, changed it to a Boeing jet design – even the carpet was from an airliner.

The company's first remodelled travel office in Margaret Street, Toowoomba, in premises that were previously the Flying Dutchman Restaurant. (1969).

All the people who came from Brisbane were amazed by the decor. Staff decorated the recessed windows. On one occasion, during a promotion for Hawaii, sand was placed inside one window on plastic covering the carpet and then additional sand was placed on the footpath outside the window to give an illusion that the beach went straight through the window. It was all right when staff left for the day, but then a westerly wind blew the sand across the street overnight.

Early days in travel are remembered by former travel officer Jan Emerson:

> 'I was among the staff who worked in McCafferty's first travel office at the National Mutual Insurance building in Margaret Street, which was "a tiny hole in the wall".
>
> It was great when we moved across the road and transferred our work to the TAA Tarzan computer link in the larger Boeing office in Margaret Street. We had 10 or 12 travel consultants in a great atmosphere.
>
> In those days, individual travel consultants welcomed their regular customers in the airline-style office with its blue and purple carpet. The women fitted in with their corporate uniform comprising a blue skirt and jacket and multi-coloured scarf.

We took tours to China and New Zealand. It was in the days when the Chinese wore very sombre colours such as black, brown and khaki.

The travel industry was very buoyant in Toowoomba.

It was very personal, staff knew all their customers, and there were a lot of big business accounts including the Toowoomba Foundry, Cargill Seeds, Pacific Seeds and the Queensland Graingrowers' Association.

Many of the customers would send the staff postcards when they were away and on return they would come back into the office to talk about their trip. It was a real family thing and very personal.

The Margaret Street office had an atmosphere which has disappeared from many travel agencies today.'

McCafferty's Melbourne Cup Coach Tour

TOUR "A" INCLUDES

Return Coach Fare.

Melbourne Cup and Oaks Day Admission Tickets.

Return Rail Tickets to Races each day.

Bed and Breakfasts :
  4 nights Melbourne Travelodge Motel.
  1 night Canberra Travelodge Motel.

FARES : $88.00 (PENSIONERS $78.00)

TOUR "B" INCLUDES

Return Coach Fare.

Melbourne Cup and Oaks Day Admission Tickets.

Return Rail Tickets to Races each day.

Bed and Breakfasts, Overnight Motels :
  4 nights Melbourne, Parkville Motel.
  1 night Canberra, Travelodge Motel.
  1 night Dubbo, Motel.
  1 night Singleton, Motel.

FARES : $100.00 (PENSIONERS $90.00)

DEPOSIT OF $20.00 REQUIRED TO CONFIRM EACH BOOKING — BALANCE TO BE PAID BY SATURDAY, 12th OCTOBER, 1968.

McCAFFERTY'S TRAVEL SERVICE

190 Margaret Street, Toowoomba

Phone 2 6793 (A/H. 2 4921)

McCAFFERTY'S SPECIAL COACH TOUR

We're off to the MELBOURNE CUP

McCAFFERTY'S TRAVEL SERVICE
190 MARGARET STREET TOOWOOMBA
PHONE 2 6793

DOWNS PRINTING CO. PTY. LTD., TOOWOOMBA

My idea of promotion was to use Miss Australia and Carnival of Flowers quest competitors who were outgoing. People used to gravitate towards McCafferty's Travel because of the quality of the service and the staff.

Posters were placed along the walls and there were no brochures out at the front. We didn't know in those days the scientific theory behind all this.

It had to look tidy at the front. Years later another leading travel company announced that it had found the way of boosting its activity by removing all the brochures from the front.

Again I never really attempted to build a chain of offices. We had agents all the way up to Rockhampton selling tickets and taking travel enquiries.

Among the junior staff in September 1975 was Susan Reinke. She recalls the time when she worked in the travel office in Margaret Street that was built like a Boeing jet:

> *'I was the first person to be employed by John Clough, who had started with the company in June that year.*
>
> *Mr Mac had an office in the front of Travel, and I made tea for the six staff members. Mr Mac always had his tea with milk and one sugar. There was always a biscuit on every saucer.*
>
> *I wasn't even the youngest person in the office but I never quibbled about the work, it was a question of doing it efficiently and seeing how fast it could be done.*
>
> *We used to watch each morning when Mr Mac walked in and we knew instantly whether we were in for a good day or if something had gone wrong.*

The window of the remodelled travel office in Toowoomba.

If he was happy everyone would feel relieved. However, if something had gone wrong there would be an 'atmosphere' throughout the office and I would sit there waiting for him to call someone to his office and hope it wouldn't be me.

Mr Mac has tremendous charisma and doesn't believe in beating around the bush.

I did everything from agents' returns to clerical work and handling the switchboard.

When I first started with the old manual switchboard there were about six plug-in cords and I just loved answering the phone. My enthusiasm sometimes got the better of me and John Clough called me in and told me that I wouldn't be allowed to continue working on the switchboard if I spent too long talking to people. I wanted to be polite and I liked people, that was my problem.

John would sit in his office close to the switchboard and he would be thinking, but the girls always thought he was watching them on the switchboard and they found it intimidating. I was shortsighted so it didn't bother me.

The Sydney bus would come in at 4.30 a.m., and people would ring up two days before and say, "Next Thursday can you tell me what time next Thursday's Sydney bus will arrive in Toowoomba and will it be late?"

The Gold Coast service would leave at 3 p.m. and we would get other equally frustrating calls such as, "Excuse me, could you tell me what time the three o'clock bus to the Gold Coast is leaving?".

All the staff knew each other across the network and it was just like a big family. On one occasion I went round to the terminal in Neil Street to collect my pay. There was no bitumen and we just parked on the dirt. One of the cleaning staff came out and put a balloon on my exhaust as a joke. When I returned to my car and started the engine there was this big bang. Staff used to do things like that.

When McCafferty's started in travel there was little opposition, but within a few years other travel agencies started and even the banks introduced travel sections.'

Many of the good points of the airline companies were taken on board by the coach companies in Australia. We began trials with ticket printers, similar to those in airlines, in 1993. The printers were needed because extra space was required on the computer system.

Staff sometimes suggested opening a travel office at Miles or Wandoan, but it wasn't our scene.

Why did we take steps in the right directions instead of the wrong ones? Our Financial Controller John Clough has his own viewpoint:

'I remember saying concentrate on the things you do best. Get rid of tours and some of the charters and concentrate on the express. It paid off because the express services have forged ahead at the expense of other services.'

Chapter 12

Safari tours and some funny names

(1970-1974)

'There were 45 passengers and two drivers on one trip. A young passenger kept wandering around with a sack on his arm and it always seemed to be moving. He turned out to be a snake collector who had to be asked to remove his sack from the coach and put it outside the passenger area.'

WALLY EMERSON

The coach side of the business really took off in 1970 with eight buses and a staff of 15. Fifteen years later, there were 70 coaches and about 260 staff scattered around the State and in Sydney. I told a *Courier-Mail* reporter:

'I don't think I realised what the end result would be when I bought the first bus back in 1940.

'I am a person who plods along and grabs opportunities when they become available. There are still opportunities around. Someone could do today what I have done but they would have to work long and hard.'

The State Transport Department called tenders in 1970 for a regular daily service from Toowoomba to the Gold Coast and we were the successful tenderer with one service each way daily.

I was so impressed with the growth of the Gold Coast area that I opened two booking offices at Beach House Plaza, Coolangatta, and in the Cosmopolitan Building (opposite 'The Islander') at Surfers Paradise.

Some of the experiences of our early drivers make interesting reading, especially when they were travelling in the Australian outback. Here's an account from Wally Emerson:

'One of the hardest trips I ever did was a safari tour in the 1970s when we became stuck at Kingoonya in South Australia.

We passed another McCafferty's coach driven by Ray George, not long out of Port Augusta. Heavy rain, and I mean inches of rain, was falling and Ray was doing the same safari tour but coming around the top way in the opposite direction. When I asked him what the road was like through the Centre, he said it was just like the Pacific Highway, except that it was all dirt.

The rain came down in buckets and the co-driver Eric Nuss and I were marooned in Kingoonya, which at that time was on the actual highway.

Kingoonya had just a few buildings, including a railway station, hotel, store, a couple of shanty houses, a jail and the policeman's residence.

We were held up there for a week surrounded by water. I slept in the jail, it was the most comfortable bed in Kingoonya, the rest slept in the hall.

Every day we went out with the local police sergeant to check flood levels. There were seven or eight other coach parties also marooned in the town and we played cricket with the local Aborigines, using a pitch in the main street.

We drank the pub dry and ate the store out of provisions. By the end of the week we decided that enough was enough and I got the map out with a group of Marist brothers who were stranded with their Volkswagen Kombi van.

They said that instead of heading north they could go to one of their colleges in Perth, and so we decided to accompany them across the lake country and the Nullarbor to get to Perth.

We towed the Volkswagen through water and it took us 24 hours to cover 40 miles. We dug and shoved and kept going and came out on the Eyre Peninsula. It was a Centre tour that went wrong and we ended up in Perth instead of Darwin.'

I never cease to be amazed at the nicknames staff give to other staff members. Most drivers who work for McCafferty's seem to pick up nicknames along the way. The names are handed out in good humour and many stem from a single incident when something allegedly went wrong.

The next time you board a coach the driver could be Rambo (rarely wrong: always right) or Flex (always combing his hair), Two Bricks (thick as two bricks), The Garden Gnome (talks incessantly about gardening), Paddle-foot (could have been a police officer with his feet), Chiminey (it's the way he says 'chimney'), Tea Leaves (his surname is Bushell), Cunning Bob, Rainforest (thick and dense), Side-lights (not bright enough to be a headlight), or Captain Midnight (black as the ace of spades but a terrific driver). Then there's Keg (you will recognise his shape), Double-keg (twice Keg's size), The Pope (a head of pure white hair), The Reverend (doesn't drink or swear), Ailment (always talking about his medical problems), Flipper (doesn't mind flood waters), Viking (has striking red hair), Shortcuts (always trying to get there quicker than other drivers), Peewit (small fellow will always adjust the driving seat when he boards the coach), Einstein (good on theory), and Breakfast, Dinner and Tea (a driver with stains on his tie).

There's also a Kiwi with Maori connections whose coach is usually a few minutes late. When challenged by senior staff to give a reason his standard reply is: 'Listen, I drive slow and safe – not like you white fellas'.

Then there's Boss Hogg (one of the Alice Springs staff who likes hot-air ballooning and is named after the cartoon character), and there's also Milo (he used to feed his cattle with a variety of sorghum called milo, and you can usually spot him around the Rockhampton terminal).

Another driver we used to call 'Bex", because every day before he started work he had to have a Bex (headache powder), and several more during the day. There was another driver who was called 'Utility', because his first name was Laurie – but his mates wouldn't call him 'Lorry' because of his small stature. One very reliable driver I do remember was Vince Francis.

When I started the Brisbane to Rockhampton service in 1972, I gave a job to an ex-truckie – a big chap with plenty of muscle. One day we were waiting for him to arrive in Toowoomba at 5 p.m., and when we looked out of the terminal window his bus was coming in with a police car chasing him. I believe he went through a speed trap and hadn't stopped. He eventually talked himself out of it.

An accountant with curly hair has gained the nickname Colonel Gaddafi, after the Libyan leader, and a woman who has been in charge of Reservations is often referred to as Maggie, after Maggie Thatcher the 'Iron Lady'.

There was one occasion when I walked past 'Maggie's' desk and said jokingly 'Hear you're retiring Maggie'. I didn't elaborate and she found out later that I had read in the newspaper that Margaret Thatcher was retiring as Prime Minister of England.

But the nicknames among the drivers and staff are mild compared to some that have evolved in the McCafferty's Toowoomba Workshop over the years. They range from Toe-nails

131

The scene at McCafferty's Toowoomba terminal in the early 1970s.

to Johnny Zero, Herr Krueger, Pedro, Agro, Mullet, Smelly and Rocket.

The drivers also have their own names for various routes in the system. They call the Dawson Valley run, which began on Christmas Eve 1972, 'The Valley', Townsville to Rockhampton 'Rock Vegas', Mt Isa 'Siberia', and Mt Isa to Brisbane 'Down the Guts'.

Coach drivers also have their own particular brand of humour. There's a standard answer whenever a passenger asks a question such as, 'How long's the Gold Coast coach, mate?' 'Oh, she'd be about 40 foot,' is the reply.

Every driver has an unusual story, which is usually concerning a moment of embarrassment. This one's from a Rockhampton driver:

> *'I was on a Central Queensland service run and the last passenger had been dropped off so I headed back to the base on my own. Feeling well pleased with the trip I pulled down the microphone, put on a tape of Slim Dusty, and accompanied the country singer at the top of my voice.*
>
> *I was enjoyed myself, jigging around in the seat and slapping and clapping my hands.*

> *I pulled into the depot and was putting everything away when I heard a noise. A bloke had been having a lie down on the back seat. He came down the aisle to get off the coach, turned to me and said: "Well, I've met some b——y idiots in my day, but you take the cake".'*

The rumour went around Toowoomba that when Myer built its store in the city I, as Mayor, had got a whole new house of furniture.

But when staff came to the house they could see no new furniture. Every time Lorna brought up the suggestion to improve the furnishings my reply was : 'Oh, the grandkids will only kick it apart, let's make do with what we have.'

During a violent hailstorm in Toowoomba in 1976, Lorna was standing in the kitchen in a raincoat holding up an umbrella trying to prepare meals as water flowed through the roof and ceiling. The ceilings caved in and that was when we got our new lounge suite. Lorna sets the record right to straighten out the rumour:

> *'No, no, we didn't get our furniture as a gift, but we did receive a canteen of cutlery inscribed on the box at the opening of Myer.*
>
> *As Mayoress I always went along with Jack. He has been a very lucky man to have me. I never ever went against him, because he was that kind of man who wouldn't take it and you'd be out.*
>
> *He had definite ideas of what he wanted and if you didn't go along you'd be left behind. We have wonderful understanding.*
>
> *I always saw there was good food for the children when we went out.'*

We opened our Brisbane travel office in Mayfair Arcade, Adelaide Street, in January 1974.

I told staff that there was little point in placing a coach in service with 'SYDNEY' or 'BRISBANE' on the destination sign and then expecting passengers to flock on board without some form of publicity.

We realised that some solid advertising saturation was necessary to educate prospective passengers about the Daylight service and to counter competition from other services and other forms of transport. So we briefed our advertising agents to prepare an attractive campaign in the press and on radio. In three months we spent over $60,000 on the campaign, but it was worthwhile and our share of the business was well above expectations.

When the first Central Queensland service started on June 11, 1974, there were only a few two-way services each week.

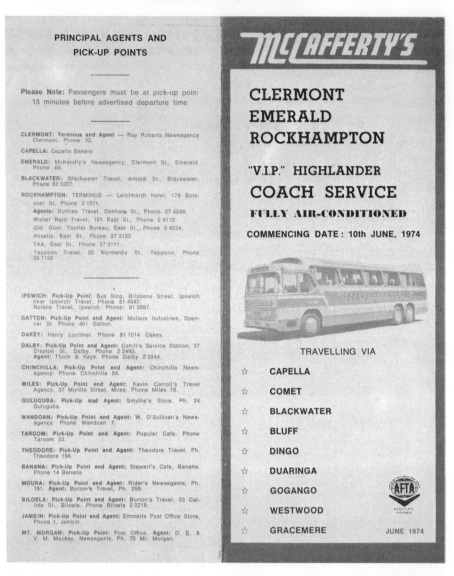

PRINCIPAL AGENTS AND PICK-UP POINTS

Please Note: Passengers must be at pick-up point 15 minutes before advertised departure time

CLERMONT: Terminus and Agent — Ray Roberts Newsagency. Clermont, Phone 32.

CAPELLA: Capella Bakery.

EMERALD: McKendry's Newsagency, Clermont St., Emerald. Phone 66.

BLACKWATER: Blackwater Travel, Arnold St., Blackwater. Phone 82 5207.

ROCKHAMPTON: TERMINUS — Leichhardt Hotel, 178 Bolsover St. Phone 2 1371.
Agents: Duthies Travel, Denham St., Phone 27 4588.
Walter Reid Travel, 101 East St., Phone 2 4112.
Qld. Govt. Tourist Bureau, East St., Phone 2 4234.
Ansetts, East St., Phone 27 3133.
TAA, East St., Phone 27 3111.
Yeppoon Travel, 20 Normanby St., Yeppoon, Phone 39 1152.

IPSWICH: Pick-Up Point: Bus Stop, Brisbane Street, Ipswich near Ipswich Travel. Phone 81 4842.
Nolans Travel, Ipswich. Phone: 81 3987.

GATTON: Pick-Up Point and Agent: Mullers Industries, Spencer St. Phone 401 Gatton.

OAKEY: Henry Lorrimer, Phone 91 1014 Oakey.

DALBY: Pick-Up Point and Agent: Cahill's Service Station, 37 Drayton St., Dalby. Phone 2 2492.
Agent: Thorn & Keys. Phone Dalby 2 3344.

CHINCHILLA: Pick-Up Point and Agent: Chinchilla Newsagency. Phone Chinchilla 54.

MILES: Pick-Up Point and Agent: Kevin Carroll's Travel Agency, 37 Murilla Street, Miles. Phone Miles 78.

GULUGUBA: Pick-Up and Agent: Smythe's Store. Ph. 24 Guluguba.

WANDOAN: Pick-Up Point and Agent: W. O'Sullivan's Newsagency. Phone Wandoan 7.

TAROOM: Pick-Up Point and Agent: Popular Cafe. Phone Taroom 33.

THEODORE: Pick-Up Point and Agent: Theodore Travel. Ph. Theodore 194.

BANANA: Pick-Up Point and Agent: Stewart's Cafe, Banana. Phone 14 Banana.

MOURA: Pick-Up Point and Agent: Rider's Newsagents, Ph. 191. **Agent:** Burton's Travel, Ph. 299.

BILOELA: Pick-Up Point and Agent: Burton's Travel, 33 Callide St., Biloela. Phone Biloela 2 2218.

JAMBIN: Pick-Up Point and Agent: Emmerts Post Office Store, Phone 1, Jambin.

MT. MORGAN: Pick-Up Point: Post Office. **Agent:** D. E. & V. M. Mackay, Newsagents. Ph. 70 Mt. Morgan.

McCAFFERTY'S

CLERMONT EMERALD ROCKHAMPTON

"V.I.P." HIGHLANDER COACH SERVICE

FULLY AIR-CONDITIONED

COMMENCING DATE: 10th JUNE, 1974

TRAVELLING VIA

☆ **CAPELLA**
☆ **COMET**
☆ **BLACKWATER**
☆ **BLUFF**
☆ **DINGO**
☆ **DUARINGA**
☆ **GOGANGO**
☆ **WESTWOOD**
☆ **GRACEMERE**

AFTA ASSOCIATE MEMBER

JUNE 1974

One of our agents who helped us get established in Rockhampton was Les Duthie. In 1972 he operated a hotel and travel agency in Rockhampton and he was our main agent in that city.

The coach service originally operated from the footpath in front of Duthie's Travel Agency, Rockhampton, where sometimes up to six coaches lined up in the street.

Unfortunately for Les, our services increased so much that no longer could we expect the public to wait on the footpath with all their baggage, and at times we would have five or six coaches loading. Rockhampton City Council asked us to stop blocking the

The scene at the old terminal in Rockhampton in the late 1970s.

streets with all this congestion, and we then purchased the freehold of used car showrooms, belonging to Palm Motors, in Denison Street, Rockhampton.

For a while this suited our operations, but with the expansion of our services we were forced to look for even bigger premises. A site on the Northern Highway, just over the bridge, was selected. It was a large restaurant called 'Big Al's'. We did modifications to it and made it into a serviceable terminal that we are still using today.

All our mechanical repairs in Rockhampton were done initially by Sel Murphy's Garage, and because of the condition of some of the roads we had to traverse there was always plenty of work for him. Today, with the improved road surfaces and more dependable coaches, the maintenance is all done in our Toowoomba workshop and only emergency repairs are carried out in Rockhampton.

Floods in Central Queensland sometimes cause us major headaches. *The Chronicle* (Toowoomba) recorded the following story on January 30, 1974:

> '*Mr Ted Collins, who was once manager of Kianga Station (owned by Mr Rex King) for nearly eight years, and who left for Salisbury, S.A., to become manager on an irrigation project, owned by the*

First Rockhampton terminal in Denison Street in about 1975.

Rhodesian Government, is at present on two months furlough to Australia with his wife.

This trip, after seven years away, is to fulfil a promise to visit his aged parents, now in their 80s, who reside in Toowoomba.

Mr and Mrs Collins left Salisbury on December 27 by Jumbo Jet, but on returning will travel by boat. While in Toowoomba they decided to make a special trip to Theodore to visit old friends and to see the progress of the district.

They travelled by McCafferty's Coach and hit the middle of the flood period with falls of 150mm. In other places which the coach travelled through falls were heavier.

Mr Collins told of almost impassable roads and creeks but the coach got through. They could not speak highly enough of the courtesy and attention received from the drivers.

Only once during the flood did the coach fail to get through, and that was from the Rockhampton end.

Twice on the trip from Taroom luggage was placed on top of the vehicle, and the luggage compartments opened to allow the water to flow through and stabilise the bus. Four feet of water was passed through this way.

When the river at Theodore was impassable, the passengers were transferred from the coach to the shire council boat, then to a coach from Rockhampton. Thus all passengers travelled from Brisbane to Rockhampton, and vice versa.

> *On one trip when the water was over Palm Tree Creek, 12 miles from Taroom, they by-passed this by deviating via Cracow and Gorge Road to Wandoan. Several times they were pulled out of a bog near Mr Lewis Green's property.*
>
> *With no trains during this period, the advantage of this splendid service was realised during the flood. McCafferty's Coach Service is something the Valley can be proud of. Like the old Pony Express – "Come Hell or high water" – McCafferty's always get you through.'*

The Rockhampton Terminal is in the hands of Ray Shaw, a former ambulance officer of 23 years, who started working for our company in 1985.

Also on the staff at Rockhampton is long-time employee and Operations Supervisor Tom Craig, who was a truck driver before he joined McCafferty's in January 1974.

Tom drove Denning coaches from Rockhampton to Wandoan and back and enjoyed every minute. He took up a position behind the counter in March 1992.

Back in 1981, the company was operating drive-through facilities for coaches in Denison Street, Rockhampton. A large volume of passenger and freight traffic was handled for the Brisbane coastal and inland routes as well as the Rockhampton to Emerald and Mackay services.

Ray Shaw, of Rockhampton, receives the award for Best Transport Operator at the Central Queensland Tourism Awards presentation in April 1994.

Ray Shaw, Manager at Rockhampton, with the trophy.

McCafferty's Rockhampton operation won the 'Best Tour and Transport Operator Award' in the Central Queensland and Southern Reef Region Tourism awards for 1994.

Tom and Ray agree that the company has developed some really great coaches – but you can't please everyone and they still hear from the not so tall drivers who say there's a need to be able to lower the seats even more.

When the floods come in the Rockhampton region they cause many problems, and 24-hour delays for coach traffic are not unusual.

On one occasion, drivers at Rockhampton never turned a wheel for 11 days and the railway and airport were also closed. If the floodwaters had risen just a few centimetres more, they would have been inside the terminal office.

Our old manual switchboards were often overloaded at times of crisis. Susan Crossley remembers what happened:

> *'In the early days, when there were floods in Rockhampton, the switchboard in Toowoomba would be jammed by relatives and*

Rockhampton terminal and Ray Shaw, Tom Craig and Assistant Manager Gavin Lucke, in 1994.

> *friends seeking information about coach movements. It was hard going working the old manual switchboard and three of us – Debbie Schultz, Sharon McGuire and myself – would work in shifts. Sometimes the operator would last an hour before calling for someone else to take over.'*

Sleeping on the road was par for the course during floods as Mick Manteit recalls:

> *'I took a group of boys from Downlands College in Toowoomba to Sydney, and before I picked them up on the Friday, floodwaters were over the bridge at Helidon and the Condamine River was in flood at Warwick.*
>
> *Jack was optimistic and he needed the money so I continued down the road, but when I got to Warwick there was no way I could get the bus into town. Traffic was halted by massive floodwaters.*
>
> *I rang Jack and he told me not to bring the passengers back but to see what I could do.*
>
> *I walked across the railway bridge into town and got accommodation for the boys in two hotels. We should have been at Glen Innes that night.*
>
> *Saturday came and we were still stuck there and all the boys were in the picture theatre when word came through on the grape vine that trucks were starting to continue south via Tannymorel, where the level of the Condamine was falling.*

I went back to the picture theatre and told the boys to pack up and walk back across the railway bridge.

When other drivers saw our bus start up they came over and asked if they could follow.

We stopped at Killarney for the boys to buy pies and when we reached Tenterfield that night the boys curled up in the lounge room at the Telegraph Hotel.

The next day, when we were heading for Armidale, we came across more crossings and creeks under water. I sent one of the students out each time to see the depth of the water. If it came up to his knees then I could drive through. If it was a bridge, I just hoped that the decking hadn't given way.'

People often can't understand why coach drivers can't drive through flood water. The problem is that once a coach enters the water, it can lose contact with the ground and be pushed along by the river. But flood waters aren't the only problems according to Ray Shaw:

'Tom Craig and I agree that the worst passengers to handle are those who are drunk. You can't refuse to sell a ticket but you can refuse to put them on a coach. If you find a passenger drunk on board then you put him out on the roadside to sober up.

Then there are the ones who come into the terminal at Rockhampton to go to Duaringa; they arrive sober in the morning, and then go on the beer all day and come back drunk. "How am I going today, boss?", one of the regulars often asks me. I take one look at him and tell him to come back tomorrow. There was one fellow I wouldn't allow on the coach for three days until he had sobered up.'

In the early days, coaches used to stop for motorists broken down, but now there are too many hoons on the road and coach drivers often don't know if it is a genuine breakdown. It is not worthwhile to stop, but exceptions are made if we come across a coach that has broken down.

Radios on board coaches have made a big difference and our drivers radio in to each terminal and often to roadhouses to advise of their arrival time. However, as Australia grows as a multicultural country communication needs special skills as Ray Shaw records here:

'Staff in Central and North Queensland are especially patient with Asian travellers who find the English language difficult.

There are also many Vietnamese travelling north to Airlie Beach and Cairns. They can understand us, but sometimes we can't understand them.'

It seems that coach drivers when they retire never get tired of talking over their old days. Wally Emerson relates here that although he left McCafferty's some years ago he can't get away from his old firm:

> *'My wife Jan and I have never forgotten our association with McCafferty's. It's amazing, for the past 10 years we've been away from McCafferty's, running a music business in another part of Toowoomba and yet travellers still drop in regularly to talk about their trips and we have become a sort of club for former drivers.*
>
> *I believe the strength of McCafferty's is directly related to Jack McCafferty's personal interest in the business. Even now he still sells tickets. Quite recently I asked him if he knew all the drivers by their first names, and there are about 300 of them. He looked at me for a moment and answered "Just about".*
>
> *I left McCafferty's at one stage and worked with Greyhound for three years but returned as Operations Manager and later became Marketing Manager, before leaving to establish my own family music business.'*

Marketing remains today as one of the most dynamic sectors of our company. I notice many things as I walk around the offices. There are three trays on one of the main desks in Marketing bearing the labels 'URGENT', 'Non-Urgent', and 'Fat Chance'. It's the bottom tray that is overflowing!

As the 1970s rolled on, so too did the country areas. With the search for coal those areas in Central Queensland serviced by McCafferty's began to thrive, with new towns springing up to meet the challenge of the new frontiers.

Like the stage coaches in old westerns, our coaches were breaking new ground and were a part of the growth of the nation, to service new areas along the coast and inland.

The company won the tender, from five submissions, for the service between Brisbane, Toowoomba and Rockhampton via the inland route (Miles, Wandoan, Theodore and Mount Morgan) and made the first run on December 23, 1972.

This was not achieved without opposition from a handful of other coach operators who expressed their views to the State Transport Department.

The 525-mile (900km) route was envisaged as a twice-weekly service, to be followed on June 10, 1974 by another long-distance service covering 850km twice daily between Rockhampton, Emerald and Clermont, and then in 1978 with a daily service to Mackay via Moranbah. Ted Bignall was the first driver on the

Mackay-Moranbah run, while Brian Henderson had opened up the Clermont to Rockhampton route four years earlier.

The Clermont service was extended to Mackay in 1978.

Among the first casual coach drivers on the Clermont to Rockhampton run was Vince Lester, who operated a bakery at Clermont, and later became a Minister in the Bjelke-Petersen Government.

At times in 1974, when we were operating Rockhampton to Emerald and Clermont, we were short of drivers and Vince used to help us out.

When he was the State Member for Belyando, Vince Lester supported our application to extend our coach service from Clermont to Mackay, taking in Dysart and Moranbah. He wrote to the Acting Transport Minister, Mr Fred Campbell, in support of the application and added the following three paragraphs:

> 'Mr McCafferty has pioneered the inland run from Brisbane through Toowoomba, Miles, Theodore, Moura, Rockhampton and out through Blackwater, Emerald, Clermont and Capella, and at times, with floods and other inconveniences, has had to put up with low passenger numbers, but has always maintained the best possible service.
>
> I would personally be disappointed if another operator were to get the run from Clermont to Mackay. This extension would complement McCafferty's already good service to the people.
>
> I would appreciate knowing when the successful applicant will be announced as a number of Moranbah people have been enquiring in this regard.'

One of my most disappointing times in my career was when I convinced the State Transport Department through Gordon Chalk MLA, after a lot of lobbying with other politicians, to open up a licensed service from Rockhampton to Emerald and Longreach.

McCafferty's were the only operator between Rockhampton and Emerald and I was looking to extend from Emerald to Longreach.

Tenders were called and when Greyhound was awarded the licence, I couldn't believe that this was true.

We had done a lot of lobbying to get the service from Emerald to Longreach, and when Greyhound gained the licence they promptly doubled the fares and reduced the frequency of travel between Longreach and Rockhampton from four services a week to three.

'The service has never paid,' Greyhound general manager Peter Collins, was reported in the media as saying later. 'It has been subsidised by revenue from other services.'

The service was getting a passenger loading of only 25%.

Barcaldine Shire Chairman Jim Bennett said Greyhound might be doing people of the west a greater service if it handed over its Longreach to Rockhampton route to McCafferty's.

Councillor Bennett said the franchise didn't allow Greyhound to pick up passengers between Emerald and Rockhampton.

In some respects Greyhound paid dearly for this as they didn't last too long on the service. Eventually McCafferty's got the licence and Greyhound faded away.

Vince Lester, who's had a long association with McCafferty's, records how it all began and how some political decisions can be both 'idiotic and stupid':

'I first met Jack McCafferty as a lad when he was Mayor of Toowoomba and I had just won both the 100 yard and one mile races in an athletics program in Toowoomba in 1960.

I was 16 years old, and at the presentation of awards I listened to Mr McCafferty telling us that we all had to get out in the world and work. We had to treat the rest of the world with respect and never be frightened to compete.

As an apprentice baker in Tara, and with no money whatsoever, I didn't have a bright future.

I left the sports meeting and decided to take Mr McCafferty's advice. I went out to the flour millers and told them that I wanted to run my own small business.

Fourteen years later I met Jack McCafferty when I was a baker in Clermont and also a member of the Belyando Shire Council and chairman of the Central Highlands Tourist Association.

This time I approached Jack about the re-development of the bus run from Rockhampton to Emerald and Clermont to Springsure through Emerald to link up with his major services.

When he ultimately got the licence for Clermont to Rockhampton, I got a commercial bus driver's licence and on odd occasions I drove for McCafferty's, mainly between Clermont and Emerald.

On one occasion a group of nuns were waiting for the bus to arrive, and as I drove in they recognised me as a member of the Queensland Parliament. They all made the sign of the cross and said they hoped that the coach would make the journey without incident. I never had an accident with a coach.

I was saddened when Jack McCafferty missed out on the Longreach contract. It was an idiotic and stupid decision made by the Transport Minister. The decision was based on deregulation and "open tenders". The Minister saw his action as being a "test of survival of the fittest of two contenders".

There were not enough passengers for both coach companies and it would have been far better to have awarded the contract to McCafferty's and to have made the company more profitable. Greyhound did not operate for long on that Longreach run.

Jack McCafferty never feared competition. His strength was in pioneering coach runs even if passenger numbers didn't initially justify those runs.

He stuck by the people in the outback areas and this has made McCafferty's the most successful coach operator in Australia.

I have observed Jack McCafferty looking always towards the future and sometimes taking 10 steps at a time. In some ways his

An early photograph of McCafferty's Sydney Office in Kings Cross.

vision is similar to that of the former long-serving Queensland Premier Sir Joh Bjelke-Petersen.

A lot of my own success was inspired by Jack McCafferty. He has gone out and conquered his own world. I went out and made it into Parliament. I have much to thank Jack McCafferty for as well as the O'Brien flour milling family in Toowoomba. They have helped and inspired me.'

Vince Lester was on the Belyando Shire Council in 1967 and entered Queensland Parliament in 1974. He was a minister from 1983-89, and today holds the seat of Keppel.

We started our Sydney service following frustrations with Queensland bureaucracy, and particularly over our problems with the Longreach service. When we saw an opening for a good express service between Brisbane and Sydney we initiated an overnight run via the New England Highway and Toowoomba in late 1979. This particular route also had been formerly serviced by Cobb & Co.

This route was already serviced by other operators running overnight schedules and we figured that another operator like McCafferty's would generate a lot of new business, and this proved correct. After six months' operation, loadings were averaging 75 per cent each way, and we followed this up almost

145

six months later with a daylight service on the Pacific Highway coastal route.

Under Section 92 of the Constitution we could operate interstate, because there was free trade between the States.

One of the first drivers out of Sydney on the run from Kings Cross was Gary Barnes in July 1979.

He was the eighth driver to start with McCafferty's. Other early ones included Mick Manteit, Clive Fletcher, Ray Tobin, Don Tincombe, Bill Hooper, Wally Emerson, Steve Cooper and Jack Warnecke. Billy Fett was the cleaner and Coral Probst was in the office.

McCafferty's carried 43,000 passengers in the first two years of operations on the Brisbane-Sydney New England Highway route.

Gary is among the drivers who have seen the colour scheme of the coaches change from red, white and blue for the Hinos; to blue with red strip on roof; then white with magenta, pink and blue; and then to grey and now to the current gold.

Cobb & Co had gone into receivership, and in 1979 McCafferty's purchased the licence to operate their second long-distance service, this time from Brisbane to Rockhampton along the coast. This gave us a circular route from Brisbane to Rockhampton via the inland route and the coastal route.

Jack McCafferty surveying the Brisbane-Mt Isa route in 1979.

Business was booming and on Friday, November 13, 1981, an additional daily service was introduced from Brisbane to Rockhampton and return, via the coastal route.

Our company had also acquired Cobb's 'Tuckerbox' safari tour program and two Mercedes and two Domino coaches.

When I decided to begin the service from Brisbane to Toowoomba and Sydney via the New England Highway Greyhound was the only operator, and with McCafferty's in opposition it was only a matter of time before we became the front runners on the route. Likewise, on the Brisbane to Cairns run, Greyhound and Pioneer were the only operators. We were going as far north as Mackay and that was as far as I was allowed to run by the State Transport Department. I believe they protected Greyhound and Pioneer licences even though there was an increasing demand for extra seats on this run.

I tried all avenues to get the Transport Department to open this run up to other operators, and in about 1980 public tenders were called for extra licences on this route and we were successful. Other operators were VIP, Deluxe, Sunliner, Intertour and Bus Australia.

By 1994, we were operating up to seven services daily each way Brisbane to Rockhampton and five services daily each way Cairns to Brisbane. The opposition had become a conglomerate of Greyhound-Pioneer, Bus Australia and Intertour, running four services a day each way between the cities.

After we established the services from Rockhampton to Emerald it was necessary for us to look for our own premises in Emerald, as we had a contract for six coaches to the BHP coal mine and the town council was complaining about our coaches being parked and washed on the street.

A suitable block of land was purchased with a large house on it. This house was sold for removal and we built a terminal sufficient to suit our requirements with plenty of space to park our coaches off the street. Later on improvements were made by concreting all the parking area and building a cover over the coach loading area.

Ray Medlin, who started with us as a coach driver, and his wife Laurie, run this terminal in a very efficient manner, and it is a credit to both of them. It is a showpiece in our network of terminals.

Before opening up our new terminal in Emerald our managing agent was newsagent Bill McKendry. He still takes an interest in McCafferty's operations and can be seen at the terminal at times checking on things and collecting his papers.

Harold Braun, of Capella Store, was another agent who helped us get established in the area. Likewise in Clermont, Ray Roberts,

Ray and Laurie Medlin at Emerald.

who was then operating the newsagency, was our main agent. Unfortunately today I am sorry to say that through ill-health he has been forced to give up the agency and retire. Ray and his wife Betty were stalwart supporters of McCafferty's.

Agents like Les Duthie, Bill McKendry, Harold Braun and Ray Roberts did a lot to help us get established in their areas. They were aware of the benefits we would bring to their towns and they all worked hard to make it a success for which I am very grateful.

Passengers travelling on McCafferty's fleet of ultra-luxury Jumbo Express Coaches in the 1970s enjoyed many comfort and safety features. These included refrigerated air conditioning, tinted, anti-glare panoramic windows, deeply upholstered reclining seats and footrests, massive under-floor luggage compartments, powerful, quiet GM Detroit diesel engines, 'Air-Ride' suspension system, reclining seat backs, toilets and washrooms, taped, soothing music, drinking water, and the important safety features of power steering and three separate braking systems.

There were some fun and games when we took delivery of our first Denning coach in December 1972 and set off in style to open up the Rockhampton route.

I later recalled the inaugural run from Brisbane to Rockhampton with a chuckle – but that was many years after a most embarrassing incident:

We departed Brisbane at 7 a.m. with our coach captain Wally Emerson and 17 excited passengers who were to be greeted at a civic reception in Rockhampton by the Mayor, Alderman Rex Pilbeam, at 7.30.p.m. that day.

Everything went smoothly until about 3 p.m., when the coach just decided to stop outside Taroom on the way to Theodore.

The outside temperature was 110 degrees F. with dry and dusty conditions. Coach Captain Wally Emerson eventually discovered the fault. The fuel feed line on the 500-litre long-distance aluminium fuel tank had broken just below the top of the tank and was sucking in air. Wally continues:

> 'I remember Jack McCafferty calling out to us: "Can't you fellows fix this b....y thing."
> We drained the fuel, went right back through the lines, bled all the lines and then borrowed a hose off a header on a property up the road to effect repairs.'

No one came past during the time of the breakdown, so we were unable to alert Alderman Pilbeam of the delay and three hours later we were merrily on our way to Rockhampton.

When we eventually arrived, we heard that the Mayor had thrown the flowers he had to present to McCafferty's into the air in disgust and had gone home.

It's all a very funny incident now, but at the time it was darn right embarrassing. The Rockhampton run was very important as Wally Emerson outlines here:

> 'The Rockhampton run was significant because of the great rural characters drivers encountered on the run, especially at flood times.
> One woman would wait at the front gate for the driver to throw the **Morning Bulletin** to her as the coach went past.'

McCafferty's first long-distance coach service from Brisbane to Rockhampton traversed a route from Brisbane via Ipswich, Gatton, Toowoomba, Oakey, Dalby, Chinchilla, Wandoan, Taroom, Theodore, Banana, Biloela, Dululu and Mt Morgan to Rockhampton. A full meal stop of 45 minutes was made at Stan Allen's Cafe in Taroom.

We introduced the first blue and white Jumbo coach to Queensland for the Rockhampton service and it set the standard for what was described then as the largest and most comfortable coaches for group charter travel within Australia.

Agents were advised in advance that the coach would be the new 42-passenger first fully air-conditioned G.M. Jumbo in the fleet with trailing axle – 316hp, radio, taped music, cold drinking water, full reclining seats, toilet and wash bowl. At the time, the Jumbo, which cost $72,000, was one of the largest coaches in Queensland, 40ft long, with more than ample leg room.

Each passenger was allowed one large suitcase and one overnight bag to be carried free, and there was an excess baggage charge of $1 for each additional bag irrespective of weight and distance.

Parcels were being carried to towns not serviced by rail and the charges were 60 cents minimum up to 7lb, then four cents for each additional pound.

On Fridays, passengers from the Rockhampton service were able to connect with McCafferty's Gold Coast service, 5.30 p.m. from Toowoomba direct to all points along the Gold Coast as far as Coolangatta.

Within two years, the Brisbane-Rockhampton inland run was a twice-daily service Monday to Saturday, and one service a day each way on Sunday. Today, it is a twice daily each way.

From its inauguration, departures were timed for passengers' convenience and the services provided a vital public facility, mainly in areas where trains had been discontinued or where they had never operated.

On the Rockhampton coastal service McCafferty's coaches complemented, rather than competed with, the parallel rail service.

From humble beginnings with one employee in 1972, ten years later McCafferty's coach terminal staff in Rockhampton had grown to 16.

The service came about when the Taroom Progress Association, under the guidance of Mr Stan Allen, pressured the Government for a coach service in the area.

With the combined efforts of the association and McCafferty's, the State Government called for tenders.

The Queensland Bus Proprietors' Association recorded that it wouldn't be a viable proposition, but my enthusiastic staff proved this theory incorrect.

By 1982, the Rockhampton service had grown to two return services daily and isolated towns such as Taroom, Theodore and Moura had become regular stop-off points.

The only complaints McCafferty's received was that before the service was introduced people who ordered goods used to have to wait weeks until they were delivered, and they wouldn't receive the bill until much later.

With the new service, they received their goods almost immediately, and as the 'locals' said, unfortunately they now also got their bills immediately because of the prompt mail service.

McCafferty's freight service proved a winner. Windscreens could now be delivered quickly to stricken motorists in Wandoan, and gearboxes to Rockhampton.

While the fare-paying passengers were carried in comfort 'up top', cargo was carried in baggage compartments 'down under'.

In many cases, the cost of sending essential materials by coach was way below that of general carriers. But even better than that was the reputation for reliability. McCafferty's really did deliver the goods at the same time as they delivered the passengers.

For primary producers in Queensland's bush, machinery failure can halve a harvest, and in these places time is money. A sudden change in weather and any delay in spare parts delivery can literally cost a primary producer a large slice of the year's income.

Farmers dread the thought of a machinery breakdown. It's incredible the amount of time and money a farmer can lose at harvest time if his harvester breaks down and he has to wait a week to get replacement parts.

So that's where McCafferty's come in. In many cases we are only a phone call away. Often it was possible to arrange overnight delivery.

What's the most common cargo today?

Well, there's still a fair few windscreens for people stuck out in the middle of nowhere with nothing but shattered glass between them and the elements.

Documents are also transported in courier satchels and there are also deliveries of medicines.

Magazines are another regular commodity for the coaches.

But, perhaps we are best remembered in the country as the people who got that spare part out there on time when it was needed.

And, because the company does service so many areas and our primary function is passenger transportation, I believe we can offer some of the best freight rates available.

In the early days, our coaches often got bogged on roads that weren't sealed, and the drivers got a lot of assistance from locals to get their vehicles rolling again. Providing a speedy freight service to the farmers became one way of saying 'thanks'.

Ray George recalls one memorable trip when there was too much mud to get the coach door open:

'It was Boxing Day 1973 when we left Sydney with a load of school teachers organised by Malcolm McIntyre for a two-week trip to Darwin, Alice Springs, Ayers Rock and down to Port Augusta and back to Sydney.

It was a fairly uneventful trip to Dubbo and then via Bourke, Cunnamulla and Charleville to Winton. We camped at Winton Swimming Pool and the next morning had to decide whether to go via Kynuna or Boulia to Mt Isa. I decided to go Kynuna way as I was familiar with this road. After getting bogged six times and only going 70 miles in seven hours and the road ahead looked an endless bog, we turned back to Winton and made it with no further delays.

Next day we took the Boulia road and got within a mile of the Hamilton Hotel before coming to a stop with the road completely blocked with seven road trains held up with the mud.

As it was New Year's Eve, I walked down to a creek and brought back some logs for a camp fire. We unloaded the cooking gear and food and were preparing to set up camp. By this time the road trains had formed a line behind each other and had barred the vehicles all together and with the train moving back and forth and the ones on firm ground pushing or pulling the rest of them they managed to get through the mud and on to the higher ground and the pub.

One of the prime movers came back to pick up one of his dogs (trailer) and offered to tow me through which I accepted. As he wasn't going to wait for the others from our coach they had to run along side with all the kitchen gear and food. We camped in the hall that night.

We pushed off next day and after lumbering in and out of mud holes got within 16 miles of Boulia. Here we were so deeply bogged that we couldn't open the door so I had to climb out of the driver's window and dig a hole next to the door, so the passengers could get out. We slept the night in the bus and it was oppressively hot and steamy and if you stepped outside you were up to your ankles in mud. No one had complained as yet.

Next morning I noticed a wind generator tower over behind some trees a couple of miles away and on going over found a homestead called Maclands. Talking to Mac the owner I explained our situation and he very kindly offered to let us use the shearer's quarters if necessary. I rang Boulia Shire Council and they sent out a road grader to try and get us out. The road was that bad that the grader got bogged on the way. On his arrival we hooked a heavy steel rope to the two towing hooks on the front of the bus.

I asked the grader driver to wait until I got air up to lift the airbags and also to use the power of the bus to help. However, as it was the New Year's holiday and he had left his dinner to come out I don't think he was too happy. He took off before I was ready and instead of shifting the bus the rope pulled off the front bumper assembly and we were just bogged.

152

I told him he might as well go home and I rang the shire again and they sent out a bigger grader with a jovial driver called "Yap Yap". He was true to his name and very helpful. We dug a trench under the bus and fed the steel rope back to the differential and got plenty of air up. With the extra power of the bigger grader we managed to get out of the bog and on to firmer ground. "Yap Yap" said it would be impossible to tow us back to Boulia till the road dried out a bit so we wished him a Happy New Year and sent him on his way.

All the passengers and our two cooks, Jerry and his wife, walked over to the homestead and I stayed with the bus. After a couple of days I worked out a track along which I felt I could get the bus through to the homestead. Fortunately Mac had been a mechanic in the army and he had a lot of gear in the shed such as welders and drills so I spent the rest of the week repairing the damaged front of the bus.

With Mac's Land Rover we were able to get into Boulia for food supplies and by the end of the week "Yap Yap" came out again with the grader and towed us into Boulia, only breaking the steel rope once.

As the Bourke River was still rising we decided not to camp at the caravan park but to go across the bridge into town. There, through the courtesy of the shire council, we camped in the shire hall, which was very comfortable with toilets, kitchen and mattresses which were used during race meetings. The pub was next-door and the open-air picture theatre opposite. The current show was "The Chastity Belt" and we sat under the canvas chairs to keep out of the rain.

After a few days we got through to Mt Isa when the rivers went down.

Our next problem was at Camooweal where the Georgina River was flooded and flowing about a foot over the low-level bridge. As there were no guide posts to show where the bridge actually was, I managed to drop a front wheel over the edge of the bridge. As the door was out over the fast-running current, passengers had to crawl out of the driver's window to make it to shore.

After four hours, with the help of the local policeman and a chap from Main Roads and a wallaby jack and a block and tackle, we were over that hurdle.

As the Stuart Highway was flooded up towards Newcastle Waters, we had to abandon the Darwin section of the trip. Heading south via Tennant Creek and Alice Springs to Ayers Rock we encountered no major problems. Then, on towards Coober Pedy with sometimes a bow wave a foot up the windscreen and at one sharp dip the water came right over the roof and down through the roof hatches waking quite a few up.

Finally at about 4 a.m. we came to Wintana Station where the creek was running a banker and quite impossible to ford. The station owner kindly let us use a shed on the property where the men slept and the women slept in the bus.

I and my 10-year-old son Michael slept in an old caravan which had hit a gum tree and half of it kept the rain out. They had 12 inches of rain during the three days we were there, normally a year's supply.

Some of the other coaches further down the highway were getting food drops from aircraft, but we managed OK with rationing the food.

Jerry and his wife did a marvellous job with what supplies we had. Once again we were on the track, and were towed out with bulldozers in a few places where the road was washed out and there were temporary detours which were pretty soft.

I walked down along the highway where the water was deep before driving through so I got to know it pretty well. We arrived back in Sydney three days late, but everyone on board declared that they had thoroughly enjoyed the trip and it would be one that they would always remember. I was looking forward to heading north to Brisbane, but when I got there it too had been deluged by heavy rain and parts of the city and Ipswich were inundated.'

A second Denning Jumbo air-conditioned coach came on the scene in 1973, and the company purchased a workshop in Dent Street, Toowoomba, from Mick Mooney.

The initial Denning Jumbo was the first one to be registered in Queensland. Denning, which is a public company today, began as a family business and was later taken over by Leyland, Jaguar and Rover Australia.

Over the years we became the largest Denning operator in Australia.

One of the reasons why we standardised on Dennings, apart from passenger comfort and reliability, was their very adequate bin (underfloor) space.

Our company's long-distance coach services carry a large volume of freight, and underfloor bins with convenient access on both sides ensure that, with very minor exceptions, all the freight and parcels available as well as passengers' effects can be carried.

Freight complements the passenger business on routes, including the express runs interstate, and provides a vital service for developing areas, including the Queensland coalfields.

Having faith in Denning coaches was something I shared with Ron Goodenough as he states here:

'McCafferty's never looked back after switching to Denning coaches.

> *No bus is good to work on but Dennings were better than the others. Everything was still placed out of the way and every possible method was used to keep them as quiet as possible.*
>
> *We would get 200,000 miles on the old Hinos without a major service. Now Dennings do two million kilometres.*
>
> *The early Hinos were extremely expensive for short running and the brake system was very hard on the linings.*
>
> *The first time we got a Hino to the workshop we couldn't get it inside unless we deflated the airbags. It's a wonder Jack ever retained his hair.*
>
> *At times, I was called away from the workshop to carry out coach maintenance in distant parts. On one occasion I went to Glen Innes where a SB Bedford had burnt out a big end, and another time I travelled to Longreach to replace a blown-out piston in the No. 12 Hino.*
>
> *Everything had to be serviced properly. Reliability was what it was all about. Even drivers who left McCafferty's told me years later that McCafferty's coaches were serviced better than those of some other operators.*
>
> *Jack never interfered inside the workshop. In 22 years I saw him in the workshop only half a dozen times. Jack's idea was to employ someone to do a job and if you were doing the job correctly he would leave you alone.'*

Ron Goodenough had started with our company in 1953 on £30 a week and with three weeks' annual holiday. When he retired in August 1975, he was in charge of the maintenance of the coaches.

The Dennings were definitely the best he ever worked on with the designers giving more thought as to how mechanics would have to service them.

It was the Denning coaches that had helped to improve our company's image.

We favoured Denning coaches because they proved ideal coaches for Australian conditions. Their styling is pleasing, and has a lot of passenger attraction; their seating, air-conditioning and toilets are first class and provide the best on-road facilities for our passengers.

They are a 'go-everywhere' unit and do not have to be confined to highways and freeways. We can send them off on tours confident that our passengers will have no complaints when they return.

The Den-Air suspension is great and provides excellent riding characteristics under all conditions. In fact, Dennings became part of our philosophy for customer relations.

Chapter 13

Filling up the seats

(1975-1976)

'Often we'd leave Toowoomba with only mail and no passengers on board. The mail would be packed on every seat and you'd drive straight to Rockhampton and unload and come straight back again.'

MURRAY 'ACTION' JACKSON

We had commenced the Brisbane-Sydney service via the New England Highway, with the first trip on December 14, 1979. Brisbane travel had received IATA accreditation, and the Brisbane/Sydney express ran above expectations with over 10,000 passengers in the first six months.

Our fares were below our competitors at $39 (Brisbane to Sydney) and $36 (Toowoomba to Sydney).

More coaches were still being bought and they included nine Pioneer coaches, which cost the company $27,500 each, and our fleet had increased to 45 coaches. The acquisition of the Cobb & Co. terminal at 167 Stanley Street, Brisbane, in 1980 saw the opening up of yet another McCafferty's coach service. This time it was the old Cobb & Co. service from Brisbane to Rockhampton via the Bruce Highway.

In 1982, McCafferty's provided two return services daily from Brisbane to Sydney via the Pacific and New England Highways.

We started to Sydney using the Pacific Highway, and then in 1984 we eventually won a licence up to Cairns.

It was an exciting time. We were taking thousands of holidaymakers on trips all round Australia, serving isolated areas of inland Queensland, carrying mail, goods and freight to thousands of people throughout Australia, and providing express services between cities and towns from Mackay to Sydney.

We celebrated our 35th year in business at the function room at the old Toowoomba Show Ground on Friday, March 14, 1975.

Full-length gowns in a riot of colour stole the fashion scene. Toowoomba's daily newspaper, *The Chronicle*, reported the event and described many of the gowns. Mrs McCafferty was in a black jersey gown featuring floral swirls in grey, lime and blue, while Lady Chalk favoured a lipstick-red gown of French crepe with an unusual trim of small crochet circles in deep navy on the bodice with larger circles highlighting the slim-fitting skirt.

Our company's prominence in business and the community was on everybody's lips. There was mention of some of my favourite sayings such as 'Don't be afraid of hard work', and 'Look for the opportunities and openings because they won't come looking for you'.

Sir Gordon Chalk, who was State Treasurer, told the gathering that complexes such as a bus terminal envisaged for Toowoomba could be financed by the State Government Insurance Office or similar financial institutions.

Earlier, I had suggested that such a bus terminal should be subsidised by the Federal Government. I said the estimated $500,000 cost of the project was beyond private enterprise and I argued that a bus terminal should be regarded with the same priority as railway stations and airports.

Official guests at the function included, as well as Sir Gordon and Lady Chalk, the managing director of Cobb and Co., Mr Bill Bolton jnr; Mr Col Sykes representing TAA; managing director of Bush Pilot Airways Mr Syd Williams; and Mrs Fay Naylor of Coober Pedy.

In 1976, we purchased four more Denning Jumbo coaches and bought five acres of land in Taylor Street, Toowoomba, for a new workshop that was to cost $120,000. Our company sold off its former workshop in Dent Street.

With a leading coach company such as McCafferty's, safe arrival begins long before departure and it starts in the company's main workshop. That's where more than $1 million of spare parts for our company's expanding fleet are stored and ready for use.

Those parts range from window seals and windscreen wipers to half-a-dozen G.M. Detroit diesel engines.

The company's policy of having a caring role with its passengers and coach captains has paid off and the company has an enviable record of safety on the roads.

Maintenance means painstaking scrutiny of each bus both before and during runs. It means a company policy of keeping coaches for a maximum of seven years for long-distance express services.

That seven-year rule always makes sense since it means we always get maximum resale for the vehicle. That, in turn, means we buy only the best when it comes to replacement coaches. After all my name is up front . . . and I just won't associate myself with anything but the best.

During McCafferty's round Australia journeys – clocking up something like 20,000 kilometres – the coaches are serviced en route by company mechanics.

Let's face it, we just can't take chances on some of these outback roads. To cover the distance our vehicles have to be in top condition. Safety doesn't stop at the workshop, either. The company's coach captains are highly trained professional drivers.

McCafferty's fleet had become standardised on Denning coaches well before Denning's 100th coach rolled off the production line in 1981. The 12.2m coach was fitted with carpet and toilets, and it had Thermo-King air-conditioning. The 100th coach followed extensive testing of the suspension under rigorous conditions in Central Australia.

Our fleet in 1981 consisted of 22 three-axle 12.2m units powered with the Detroit 8V71 engine, and 11 two and three-axle units had 6V71 Detroits.

In addition, there was one three-axled 8V71 powered Domino, which had been added to the fleet at a cost of $163,000, two Toyota Coaster 20-seater diesels, and five out of nine MCI 4106s purchased from Ansett-Pioneer as stop-gap vehicles in 1980 to meet urgent needs when the coalfields and Nanango services began.

McCafferty's in 1978 opened its new Rockhampton terminal at the Palms Centre at 168 Denison Street, and in August that same year we began acting as managing agents in Toowoomba for East West Airways with a three-year contract.

Our coaches continued using the Rockhampton terminal until 1986, when the premises became too small and very congested with up to six coaches endeavouring to use the facilities at the same time. The most we could handle was three coaches at one time and so we moved into our present North Rockhampton Terminal, which we purchased and renovated at a cost of around $350,000.

The terminal was developed on a former American-style eatery known as Big Al's, on the corner of Brown and Linnett Streets, North Rockhampton.

At that time, General Manager Tony McCafferty told the media that the Rockhampton City Council had asked his company to contribute $8,500 for external roadworks. He continued with the words:

> *'We are the only company in the city which offers a terminal for passengers to seat themselves. People travelling on other company coaches are required to wait on the footpath.*
>
> *Are those companies whose passengers are waiting on the footpaths required to contribute to the upkeep of the footpaths?*
>
> *I don't think it's fair that we should have to contribute to roadworks when the service is wanting in Rockhampton and we're prepared to spend money on building our own terminal.'*

Our main competitors in the city – according to *The Morning Bulletin* – were Greyhound, Pioneer, VIP and Deluxe coaches.

In August 1986, the $750,000 air-conditioned Rockhampton coach terminal was open from 5.30 a.m. to 9 p.m. daily. Facilities included a spacious reception area with TV, wash rooms, undercover loading and unloading facilities, off-street parking, taxi loading zone and STD telephone.

There were six return services operating daily from Rockhampton to Brisbane and a new non-smoking service was departing for Brisbane at 11 a.m. daily. To encourage non-smokers to board this coach there was a special introductory fare of $35.

In 1981, a twice-daily service was operating each way between Rockhampton and Clermont, with one through connection Brisbane from Mackay and Clermont. Feeder services were provided from the new mining town of Middlemount, and departures had been added to the main trunk route at Capella with an extension also from Springsure to Emerald using a Toyota.

By November, about 1,000 passengers a week were travelling on Central Queensland bus services with McCafferty's Coaches. To the passengers who passed through the tiny township of Banana, the drivers were explaining the origin of the name as the coach passed by the lifesize statue of a bullock in the main street.

The absence of a proliferation of banana trees made many passengers ask the same question. They were told that a dun-coloured working bullock called Banana was used in the early days to lead wild cattle into a crush at Leith-Hay's Rannes Station, south-west of Rockhampton. This was in the days when all the use that could be made of cattle was the sale of hides and tallow.

Many of the cattle brought in from large western runs were so wild they were difficult to handle. Banana proved an excellent

A popular postcard available in the Central Queensland town of Banana.

decoy to lead the cattle into the rush. In 1880 the bullock died in a nearby gully, which was known to stationhands thereafter as Banana's Gully.

Today, Banana has a number of postcards on sale to tourists. Of course the statue of Banana as a working bullock is the prime favourite. Another 'best seller' features a McCafferty's coach dwarfing the tiny Banana Post Office.

The Emerald to Springsure feeder service, which began a twice-weekly operation in 1982, is still operating, and a similar coach service from Emerald to the Gemfields was discontinued because of poor patronage, but is now serviced thrice weekly by the Rockhampton-Longreach service.

Attempts to run a service from Emerald to Moura, via Springsure and Rolleston, in 1975 were abandoned after a few months because of the poor road conditions.

The purr of coach engines, computers and domestic cats is music to the ears of our company's Financial Controller, Brisbane-born John Clough. He is responsible for financial control, the company's superannuation plan and personnel recruitment program, and liaising with government departments on matters of legislation.

On his desk close to a wall map of Australia in relief showing roads, towns, mountains and rivers is a copy of *A Standard Guide to Cat Breeds*.

John Clough and his partner Lia both love cats. She is a group two judge of short-haired cats such as Siamese and Orientals; John is a group three judge, which includes Burmese, Abyssinians and Rex.

When he started at McCafferty's in Margaret Street, Toowoomba, some 18^{1}/$_{2}$ years ago, the company had account books that were all completed manually. The writing on the pages was monitored by a public accountancy firm, R.N. Elliott and Co, of Toowoomba.

John takes up the story:

> *'We invested in one of the very first Sharp-style computers which ran with the aid of a new typewriter. It was an innovation. The typewriter was connected through an interface to a large calculator. You could program this large calculator and information could be transposed on to cards like a ledger. In fact, it was very similar to mechanised accounting.*
>
> *The new equipment produced a trade debtors', creditors and agents' ledger which was a sophisticated form of debtors' ledger. The payroll was all done manually and eventually this was placed on computer.*
>
> *The move to get everything mechanised began in 1976-77, when McCafferty's had 100 staff on the payroll, including six working in accounts. Today, the company has more than 500 staff and 24 work in accounts.'*

Our company purchased its first computer in 1978, and by the end of that year we had a bank of three Canon AX-1 computers. There was a switch to Canon CX-I computers early in 1982, and then plans were made to upgrade again to a hard disc drive system.

There was little doubt that the computers were cutting down the work load, and by 1982 we had slashed the time taken to produce the payroll for 160 employees from two days to two hours.

We had been using the same office accounting equipment for several years and when it came time to upgrade we went to a Canon mini-computer system in 1979.

It was the first of a series of Canon computers before our company moved its accounting section from the rear of its travel office in Margaret Street to the Neil Street terminal in 1981. It was then that the system was upgraded to the next range and since then there have been further improvements. McCafferty's have stayed with Canon equipment, working closely with Matrix Office Systems in Toowoomba.

John Wilce heads McCafferty's Operations today, with a larger staff than when the previous Manager of Operations, Murray 'Action' Jackson, joined the company in September 1976. Then there was only one person – today there are four.

Murray had been driving for NZ Road Service, of Dunedin, for nine years, operating on the Queenstown-Franz Josef tourist run. He married Noela O'Leary in Australia and began driving Bedford buses for our company when we had no more than a dozen vehicles. He recalls the first time he went out with a V6 Denning coach:

'I drove out to St George in No. 31 and and when I returned the next morning, Jack came over and walked around the coach to see if there were any marks on it.

I went on Round Australia tours three years in a row – 1977, 1978 and 1979. There were three coaches on each tour and they were on the road for 50 days, each carrying 40 to 41 passengers.

The tours, from Brisbane to Brisbane, were extremely well organised and they called into Melbourne at the time of the Melbourne Cup. Playing bingo, telling clean jokes, listening to music on the tape recorder and singalongs were all part of entertainment on board the coach.

The worst road I ever encountered as a driver was the first Round Australia tour I did in 1977. The road between Broome and Port Hedland was just red dust and there was just one stopping place, the Sandfire Roadhouse.

On another occasion, I was driving a brand-new coach, No. 40, on one of the railway access roads into Mt Tom Price, in 43-degree heat, when a tyre blew.

The perspiration was pouring off me and I couldn't expect much assistance from the mainly elderly passengers who were aged up to 92. It was while I was underneath jacking the wheel up that I heard a hissing noise and saw to my consternation a tyre on the opposite side of the coach going down.

At Mt Tom Price, I got a patch placed on one of the tyres at a cost of $20, and the next day going into Carnarvon the coach blew another tyre. I stopped a police car on the highway and they radioed back to Carnarvon and organised two tyres for the coach.

Among the freight which caused problems in the late 1970s was a huge amount of mail as the result of McCafferty's gaining a contract to carry letters and parcels between Brisbane and Rockhampton.

We had to load as much mail as we could underneath and inside the coach. Then we'd get to Toowoomba and be told that we had to change coaches. All the mail would have to be off-loaded and we'd leave Toowoomba absolutely buggered.

I also did a lot of Cairns tours, especially when Cobb & Co "tripped". I would do five or six Cairns tours back-to-back, coming home on Saturday night and leaving again on Sunday morning.

On one occasion, a coach on a Central Australia tour was delayed by flooding at Kynuna. I flew to Mt Isa so that there would be two drivers on board to catch up on the schedule once the floods subsided.

Driver Steve Cooper brought the coach through and we left Mt Isa at 8 a.m. and drove express to Katherine, arriving there at 3 a.m. the next morning. When we reached Darwin, the coach was back on schedule and I flew back home.

My worst trip was on a long weekend. I arrived at Rockhampton and was asked how I felt. When I answered "all right", they asked me to take a coach back to Brisbane, carrying a maintenance crew which had been working at the coalfields.

They had sent another driver to pick them up in Mackay and so I had a two-hour break to get a shower and have a cup of tea.

When the maintenance crew arrived in Rockhampton they were drunk. They had booze everywhere and they had broken the curtains. I sat in the driver's seat and switched on the microphone.

I told them my name and that I wasn't a hard bastard to get on with but this coach wouldn't be moving until every bit of grog went inside the luggage compartment underneath the coach.

I pulled the keys out and hopped off the coach and opened the luggage compartment.

They called me all the names they could, and pushed the emergency roof hatches out, and they did heaps more damage to the coach, but there were a couple of decent fellows among them and slowly but surely the grog came off the coach and went underneath.

It was a very long night, I know that much. Then, it started to rain and the water came in through the open roof hatches.

When they yelled that they were getting wet I told them that they had opened the hatches and there was no way we could close them. They kept yelling at me and it was the most frightening trip of my life, down the Bruce Highway and back into Brisbane. When we reached the terminal at 7 a.m. I was glad to see the back of them.'

Murray Jackson continued driving until the end of 1979. He then spent one year as Assistant Operations Manager before becoming Operations Manager, a position he occupied until he retired for health reasons in January 1994.

As Operations Manager he was on duty 24 hours a day. He did the rosters, allocated coaches for different services and organised drivers' holidays. This is how he saw his job:

'I started work every morning at a quarter to six and did that for 13 years. In the early days I wouldn't finish until six at night, and then any problems such as breakdowns or accidents would result in phone calls to my house throughout the night.

My wife never minded the phone ringing and it was rare that we would go to bed without receiving a call between 10 at night and four in the morning.

I'd get some silly calls at times. One driver rang from Tenterfield after midnight to say he was running half an hour late.

I knew that he could make up that time, and when I got to work that morning he had reached Toowoomba on time.

At 6 a.m. each morning I received calls from various network managers regarding coach movements. Decisions were then made as to whether any coach had to be returned to the workshop for maintenance. This system enabled McCafferty's to keep unnecessary breakdowns to an acceptable level and avoid any inconvenience through delayed services.

I had good backup from John Fett, who took over from me on days off. Then, there was also excellent backup from Vin Clarke.'

The Operations Room is the nerve centre of McCafferty's. Radio provides the link between the terminals and coaches. Staff in Toowoomba operate on two different radio frequencies and they are able to talk with drivers on the road as far west as Miles, and staff in Brisbane and on the Gold Coast .

We've recently been in a major drought, but it is flood time that provides major headaches with people ringing up at night asking 'Where's the coach?' Five years ago there was flooding in the Taroom area and out west between Longreach and Winton and the phones rang hot.

I maintain a close liaison with Operations as Murray Jackson recalls here:

'Jack McCafferty always maintains a keen interest in what is happening in the Operations Room. He would come into my office every morning at 7 a.m., leave at 7.45 a.m. and return at 9.15 and leave again 30 minutes later to handle the mail. He'd be back in after lunch at about 2.30 and you could set your watch by him.

He is a great man and a very firm boss. You know where you stand with him.

The Operations Room is always a hive of activity, and the pressure is on whenever a coach is delayed or an accident occurs. Fortunately, the company has a good driving record, but emergency procedures are always in place.

It was disappointing but not unusual to get a call at half-past four in the morning to say that a driver, who was due to start work at five o'clock, was sick and wouldn't be in.

If a driver had a problem with a coach out of Sydney we would tell him to hang on while we organised another coach. We then rang another operator to see if we could hire a coach and then we decided if their driver or one of ours would be used. If a coach was running very late then we had to tell the Reservations room so that the information could be passed on to all the agents and the roadhouses which provided meals.'

Chapter 14

Should we buy an aircraft?

(1977-1980)

'McCafferty's has grown into one of the largest and most successful family coach and transport companies in the Commonwealth.'
JACK DUGGAN, TRANSPORT MINISTER

The company considered moving into aviation in an attempt to conquer what the movie makers call 'the tyranny of distance'. Agents, coaches and passengers had to be provided with service across the continent, and normal air schedules were sometimes not acceptable. There was also a problem that regular airlines didn't service many cities and towns in the McCafferty network.

McCafferty's first aircraft, a Piper Aztec, bought in 1977 and pictured at Uluru.

We held a Board meeting and considered purchasing our own aircraft. This was a gamble. Speakers suggested that it could be used to ferry coach drivers to country towns, as well as to answer calls for spare parts, and when not in use it could be made available for outside charter work.

The project was approved after much pressure from Tony McCafferty, who had joined the Darling Downs Aero Club in 1963 and obtained a student licence. He had qualified for his full flying licence in 1967 and was appointed club president in mid-term and was elected president twice.

Our first aircraft was a twin-engined, six-seater Piper Aztec brought in Melbourne in 1977 from Ensel Electronics, the forerunner to Dick Smith.

Tony used it to fly across the Simpson Desert and later McCafferty's executives travelled from Toowoomba to Perth, leaving at 4 a.m. and arriving at 4 p.m.

As well as being used for company business, the aircraft was available for charter work by the Darling Downs Aero Club.

Four more Denning Jumbo coaches were purchased in 1977, and five more in the following year.

It was a year that saw a move in Brisbane from Coachlines to the Cobb & Co terminal in Stanley Street, South Brisbane.

A memo distributed to staff and agents sought a smooth change to the new location with the least inconvenience to passengers. We had been using Coachlines facilities for nearly five years, but the build-up in passenger numbers and the quantity of freight necessitated a depot of our own. A toilet, rest room and telephone facilities were now available for passengers' comfort and we also had the advantage of linking our services to Cobb & Co services to and from the Gold Coast and between Brisbane, Sydney and Melbourne.

The Clermont-Moranbah, Nebo and Mackay service was extended to a twice-weekly service in December 1977, and in 1978 the Central Queensland service was extended to Mackay through Moranbah.

By 1981, we had four sales representatives on the road, calling into our agents, travel offices and any place where we could get a leg in the door.

In addition to the services, we also operated a daily service from Toowoomba to Oakey (31km), providing the airport-city connecting link for East-West Airlines flights to and from Sydney. The Toowoomba airport, on the outskirts of the city, was not large enough to handle East-West Airlines' Fokker F27 aircraft.

Our company also provided a twice-weekly service from Toowoomba to the Surat oilfield (400km), changing over drilling crews.

We had Avis hire car girls at McCafferty's at a time when our company promoted many film nights. Promotions often ran to $1,000 each but gained the company excellent publicity.

When the premiere of *The Irishman* was arranged in Toowoomba, one of the girls decided to fly out clover from Ireland, but she didn't realise they had to go through a long delay in Quarantine. Everybody was to get a sprig of shamrock – the national emblem of Ireland usually worn on St Patrick's Day – but when they did get out of Quarantine the consignment had been sprayed and our special three-leaf clovers had wilted.

An occasion, which some employees would rather forget, is recalled here by Wendy McCafferty:

> *'One of the film nights when staff turned out in force was for the screening of **Winning**, with Paul Newman, and Joanne Woodward playing the part of an Avis girl.*
>
> *We turned up at the cinema on opening night, wearing our neatly pressed Avis uniforms of red skirt and white blouse. But our smiles turned to looks of concern after watching the film and seeing Paul Newman shooting through with the Avis girl for the weekend.*
>
> *We thought it was a bit embarrassing and people would think they could rent an Avis car and the girl too. After that first night our subsequent appearances in the cinema foyer were definitely not in uniform.'*

We were still busy operating the co-ordinated service from Toowoomba-Helidon-Brisbane, and Toowoomba-Gold Coast, and conducting Red Heart tours to Darwin and Alice Springs, and the Perth Wild Flower tours. The duration of Australia-wide tours had increased from 30 days in 1968 to 33 days in 1969.

On one wild flower trip McCafferty's actually lost a passenger, as Tony McCafferty explains:

> *'We were travelling to see the wild flowers in Western Australia and there was a young lad on board with his grandfather.*
>
> *I counted the passengers on leaving Nyngan, and the grandfather was missing. "Where's your grandfather?" I asked the young fellow. "He's in the toilet," was his reply and he pointed to the back of the bus.*
>
> *Ten miles out of town I looked in the mirror and noticed that the grandfather's seat was still vacant. When I went and asked the young fellow to check on his grandfather, he looked at me strangely*

Another Round Australia trip in 1977.

and said, "Oh, he's not on the bus, he was in the toilet at the last town". I turned the bus round and eventually we picked up grandfather.'

John Clough travels to our different terminals about once a year. This takes in centres such as Cairns, Townsville, Emerald, Rockhampton, Brisbane, Toowoomba, Surfers Paradise, Sydney, Melbourne, Adelaide, Alice Springs and Darwin.

They are all McCafferty's terminals manned by the company's own staff. Other centres are serviced by our agents.

How things have changed is outlined here by John:

'Our company is involved in more accounting today than ever before, but it is much more sophisticated than it was 10 years ago. Financial data is coming off at a much more frequent rate.

We now produce a full profit and loss balance sheet on our company every month. For example, figures for the busy month of December are available by the end of January.

Should we buy an aircraft?

> *In the old days it was very difficult to get out an accurate financial report, and we would produce indicator figures and rely on the June 30th balance sheet to set targets for the next 12 months.'*

In 1979, we replaced the Toowoomba Terminal with a new $200,000 two-storey coach terminal on the same site in Neil Street.

We did consider putting up a multi-storey building with a motel and office block with shops and terminal at the lower levels. However, a shortage of finance was against this proposal, although some staff still think that it should have gone ahead.

Our passengers now had full lounge and rest-room facilities within the main terminal building. Coach drivers were provided with shower and kitchen facilities and a bed-sitting room to enable them to relax between driving assignments.

The terminal and office building now included a coach terminal, travel agency and administration centre. The terminal, which is in use today, has access from two streets and coach movements are strictly controlled in and out. There are six saw-tooth loading bays where passengers can board or alight under cover in addition to a covered taxi stand. The ground floor features a functional waiting room with easy-to-read information on departures and a section for freight.

Opening the extensions to the Toowoomba terminal and head office building in Neil Street, Toowoomba, in 1979. Seated in the front row was the Catholic Bishop of Toowoomba, the Most Reverend Bishop Kelly.

The terminal provided a much updated facility for travellers. By 1979, the days had gone when buses could get away with loading and unloading from city footpaths, where passengers and their friends had to wait in darkened areas without seats or facilities.

The amazing transformation of the Neil Street site was mainly due to the builder and job supervisor, Mr Allan Elliott, who is our son-in-law. At that stage, the terminal had more than 40 coach movements a day using the terminal, and the travel agency remained at the terminal until 1994, when it moved across the road alongside our Marketing Division in Russell Street.

Among the workmen who remember helping construct the terminal is carpenter Ron Crossley:

> 'We worked hard to complete that terminal. Allan was a great builder but a workaholic and would work till he dropped. We removed the fuel tanks from the petrol station and that is where the women's toilets are today. The freight counter went in where the hoist and lubrication area used to be.
>
> Allan's son Brett worked with us and another person who was in the team who helped build the terminal was Neil McCafferty. He was a nice, quiet guy with a lovely personality.
>
> When it came to building furniture for the terminal, Mr Mac wanted apple green and black and so I made up the desks. I worked for McCafferty's on and off for about 20 years.'

The opening of our new terminal in April 1979 was an auspicious occasion as the then Minister for Transport and Deputy Mayor Toowoomba, Jack Duggan, explained:

> 'I officially opened McCafferty's Depot in Toowoomba almost 25 years ago. Few of us who were present on that occasion would have visualised that in the intervening years this firm would, from such humble beginnings, grow into one of the largest and most successful family travel coach and transport companies in the Commonwealth
>
> I feel this success story can be attributed to Jack McCafferty's own personal drive, imagination and willingness to introduce innovative ideas and keep abreast of current needs and developments. His family and a loyal staff have been no mean contributors in achieving these goals.
>
> The concept of a centralised depot with its attendant facilities for inter-city and interstate passengers is an excellent one.'

Bus services using McCafferty's new terminal included Skennars, Border Coaches, Cobb & Co. and Sternbergs (Orchid

The Beechcraft Baron twin-engined six-seater. (1980)

Tours). On the corner of Neil and Bell Streets, near the terminal, was Jasper's Snack Bar, operated by my wife's brother-in-law. Work on further extending the Neil Street terminal was finished in January 1981.

We had sold the Piper aircraft in 1980 and invested $250,000 in a much faster Beechcraft Baron B58 twin-engined six-seater.

Tony took delivery in Melbourne and flew it to Toowoomba in four hours.

The company's charter business was also expanding and we welcomed charter pilot Kev Sullivan on staff.

In July 1980, we had 120,000 supplements produced for our 40th anniversary and these were distributed in Toowoomba, Rockhampton and the Brisbane suburbs. We had also joined the Queensland Bus Proprietors' Association.

Birdsville was once again on our minds and in September 1980 we sent five coaches from Brisbane and Toowoomba and two from Rockhampton to the races.

Two years later I flew to the Birdsville Races and, to gain Australian and international media attention on Queensland, hoisted the State flag at the dusty outpost.

This was not without some misgivings that the personal flag of the Queensland Premier, Sir Joh Bjelke-Petersen, might be stolen. The Premier's aides feared that one of the 5,000 anticipated

Birdsville Hotel during the race weekend in 1981. Most of the drinking was done outside and the Diamantina Shire Council had the mammoth task of clearing away a mountain of empty cans left over at the end of the big weekend.

Birdsville revellers would assault the pole and knock off the prestigious flag.

In league with a local Member of Parliament and Cabinet Minister, Mr Bill Glasson, I set up camp away from the main action and sank a 7m steel pole in concrete. Bill Glasson's job was to borrow the Premier's personal flag from the Executive Building in Brisbane with or without his knowledge.

The Premier's staff knew of the plan but at the last minute got cold feet in case the flag 'disappeared'. They sent an urgent message to Birdsville advising me to 'grease the pole'.

I obliged and the pole was caked with heavy lubricating oil to prevent an assault on the flag.

I told reporters that I had been to every country in the world except Russia, but Queensland was still the best place. The picnic races at Birdsville attract international attention and our State flag should fly in that neck of the woods.

The flag incident gained us excellent media publicity.

We suffered a setback, however, in November 1980, when a fire at the South Brisbane terminal caused about $100,000 damage to McCafferty's section. Ten drivers' cars were burnt and the Department of Works declared the building unsafe, and we moved to the South Brisbane Suburban Station. The scene at South Brisbane is recalled by Ron Crossley:

Fire caused serious damage to the old South Brisbane terminal and the former Cobb & Co office. The premises were shared with the Hallet carrying company.

After the South Brisbane terminal was damaged by fire, McCafferty's took over terminal premises at the South Brisbane Station in Stanley Street. Fay Sutton and Michele Rolls are assisting passengers who are about to board the midday service to Rockhampton.

Toowoomba-based staff in 1980.

'The South Brisbane terminal was a real mess when we arrived. The Cobb & Co freight section had been destroyed as well as the drivers' cars. Allan Elliott measured up our new 'home' at the South Brisbane Railway Station and we worked round the clock – all Friday night, all day Saturday, all day Sunday. We crashed on the floor when we needed sleep and by Sunday afternoon we had the job under control.

We had taken out two old heavy lift wells, and rebuilt the place using colorbond on the ceiling.

On the Sunday afternoon we were having seafood and beer in the old freight room at South Brisbane Railway Station when suddenly Mr Mac arrived and said, "Oh, oh, who's paying for all this?"

I said, "I'm sure as hell ain't." He had a drink with us and then left us to it.'

Everything seemed to be happening at once and there were so many decisions to be made.

Fax machines had not been invented, and to keep in touch with the various branches, six telex machines were installed at Toowoomba (travel office and terminal), Brisbane (travel office and terminal), Sydney and Rockhampton. In addition, a centralised reservation system was operating at South Brisbane and this enabled our staff to handle many thousands of express bookings during busy periods.

The 1970s saw record expansion of coach services throughout Queensland following the relaxation by the Transport Department of all restrictions on licensed services in the State.

Chapter 15

More planes and the right uniform

(1981)

'If he had something coming up and you went to Jack with an idea he never treated advertising as an expense but as a very necessary part of developing his business.

His philosophy has certainly proved him right, because he got to the stage where he developed it to a point where the company almost ran itself.'

JIM FAGG

Our Beechcraft Baron aircraft took part in an inspection trip from Toowoomba to Rockhampton and Emerald in 1981. In about 4$\frac{1}{2}$ hours flying time our party covered 850 air miles. If we had gone by road we would have covered more than 2000km and taken at least two days. In its first 12 months, the Baron flew more than 500 hours.

A year later the Beechcraft Baron, with its call sign VK-KEW, was replaced by a zippy eight-seater, twin-engine Cessna 402C Business Liner. It cost $350,000 and had the call sign VH-KEZ (Kilo-Echo-Zulu).

We needed it to service our coaches. We now had 55 buses, which operated long, scheduled routes in Queensland and New South Wales, and which travelled around Australia on tourist trips.

We also had to ferry drivers about by plane when changes were needed on long-distance bus trips, and when there were breakdowns, which could happen anywhere. We couldn't have a busload of people waiting around for spares, so we flew in the parts.

While we operated out of Toowoomba we had important centres of operation across the country. Our executives needed to be able to move freely among those centres, and the plane allowed us to do so.

The fully-equipped Cessna, with all-weather colour radar, radar altimeter and air-conditioning also had a bar and toilet facilities. There were dual controls for long-distance flights and an in-flight hostess.

It was an aircraft that was used mostly for company business to position drivers, visit agents and customers, and for charter work when required. Pilot Kev Sullivan used a Telecom radio pager to keep in contact with the office.

The Cessna was only 12 months old when the company bought it in Texas, USA, from Hardy Burton the Third, of Jefferson.

After some years of operation, it too was replaced by a Duke Beechcraft purchased from Tom Ingram, who had oil wells in New Mexico.

This six-seater, which had only done 700 hours, was one of the fastest twin-engined aircraft powered by 380hp engines around at the time. It had a pressurised cabin and was McCafferty's flagship for five years. The Duke Beechcraft served our network well before finally being sold to a chemist in Spokane, Washington, USA.

The Beechcraft Duke at Toowoomba.

Staff selection was now becoming increasingly important and we couldn't afford to keep 'dead wood'.

Our executives began to take more time to select their staff and today they are always on the look-out for people who are orientated towards a family-style of business.

It's a more personal type of relationship. A lot of people come from big businesses where they wouldn't see the boss. The situation is vastly different at McCafferty's, where management has a very active role.

We select people who have a certain flair, who want to work and who demonstrate keenness and have an ability to show loyalty and support after being offered a definite career path.

Our company asks for all things to be submitted in a resume. If an applicant is selected to attend an interview then he or she is asked to write something out by hand to check for literacy. Good handwriting is essential in the coach and travel industry. As one executive put it, 'poor handwriting can often translate into bad habits'.

When our company began using Denning Den-Air air-conditioned toilet-equipped coaches on the Sydney-Brisbane services we went to a lot of trouble to select the right type of drivers for our operations. We train our drivers well, fit them out with attractive serviceable uniforms, give them a coach they are proud to handle and back them up with McCafferty's good name.

It's a recipe for success that has paid off, but we don't hand the driver a schedule and an ignition key and put him on the road. He gets a long break at the end of his shift in a very comfortable hotel or motel and a lot of other benefits.

All our drivers and staff members wear uniforms. Drivers are issued with pale-blue shirts epauletted to take a nameband. These bands carry gold bars denoting length of service, and drivers also wear a dark-blue tie and are issued with an attractive namebar. Our drivers wear dark-blue shorts and long knitted socks in summer and can change to trousers in winter if they prefer.

The uniform is serviceable and practical and it creates a good impression among customers.

When you think about it, it's all part of an overall advertising/public relations/promotional campaign, but we don't leave anything to chance. Coach operators have a service to sell, just as a shopkeeper has goods to sell, and I am a firm believer in advertising as the best way to promote a company's activities.

Our company often expounds its policy on advertising in journals such as *Truck & Bus*. In one of the issues in 1981, I stressed how advertising had benefited my business:

'If there's any special secret to our success, it has to be advertising.'

I have always been a firm believer in the value of advertising. In my opinion, no advertising is lost.

Advertising is intangible and it is often difficult to estimate whether it has brought any worthwhile results in dollars and cents. But that is not the point: although you may obtain only a small response, you have still presented your name to the public and you have made them more aware of who you are and what you are doing.

Over the years we have placed most of our advertising in the press, followed by radio and television.

The printed word is lasting, it endures and it is there for people to read over and over again, until they are firmly convinced of your presence and services.

I admit to being an avid newspaper reader. Before coming to work each morning I read the Brisbane and Toowoomba daily papers. They keep me informed on local, national and world events. I like to discuss news and trends with my employees and the people I meet during the day.

In 1981, our company was using a top Queensland advertising agency and it was spending about $250,000 a year on advertising, publicity and promotional activities.

A jingle composed for the company's Daylight service cost $2,000. It was a quality product and proved its worth.

But, our advertising doesn't stop at newspapers, radio and TV: it reaches much further to take in tour and travel brochures, posters for display at key points, and other promotions. Advertising is used to expose more potential users to the full extent of the McCafferty's operations – services, tours, charters and travel. Even such gimmicks as named pens, rulers, coasters and balloons are included.

But, there's no point in advertising if you haven't the goods and services to back up your claims.

It's been hard work but I've enjoyed every minute of it and I have never been afraid to spend money on advertising. I'm convinced that it has paid off well for the McCafferty's empire.

I am never one to miss a publicity opportunity. Dozens of photographs have been taken of me over the years, driving coaches, meeting people alongside coaches, at the opening of new services and terminals, and escorting tours across Australia and overseas.

This is how the former radio announcer and advertising executive Jim Fagg recalls tours in Central Australia:

'I remember Jack McCafferty promoting his first Red Centre Tour, which took off with 32 passengers on May 20, 1961.

In those days holidaymakers could also venture to the vineyards of the Barossa Valley and day trippers could head for more local destinations closer to Toowoomba such as Heifer Creek, Cooby Creek and Stanthorpe.

This was before TV and before the introduction of express coach services.

Jack also promoted the co-ordinated run with the bus from Toowoomba to Helidon to connect with steam trains to Brisbane, before the diesels took over.

In those early days Jack was competing against Pioneer tours, which were Australia wide, and other tours by similar companies. He was the small operator in a very big arena.

We got on extremely well. Jack knew what he wanted, he knew what he was about and he knew his own product. He was adept at saying, "No, no, that wouldn't suit" or "Yes, that would suit". He had a feeling for getting his message across to his market.

On many occasions, Jack came into the radio studio, particularly when there was a new coach or a new service.

He was as strong on radio as in the print media. If there was a travel feature, then McCafferty's would dominate it.

After two years in radio, I took on advertising agency work and my liaison with McCafferty's extended for more than 30 years.

I worked on the promotion of the first express coach to Rockhampton and successfully incorporated radio, press and TV.

In radio, print media and TV, Jack called the shots. Jack's advertising was a continuous thing. You would have a product and advertise for so many weeks and then he would be on to something else.

Entering the Redex trials had put McCafferty's on the map. As well as being a keen sporting contest it opened Jack's eyes to opportunities for coach travel across the continent. He was flying the McCafferty's flag.

Jack McCafferty's tenacity in some ways resembles a man with a different political background – Winston Churchill.

I see Jack's strength as being the ability to see an opportunity and to know what he wants. He will go through hell and earth to get there and he doesn't give up. He is a man who would find it hard to accept a corporate structure and he remains as a father figure for several hundred employees.

Jack has a way of dealing with difficult situations, and he won't continue with confrontations. There is no half-way.

When Jack went on to the City Council his business suffered, but when he returned to it he made it his life's work. He is a man who just doesn't have a "too hard" basket. He has put Toowoomba on the tourism map.

McCafferty's is today regarded as one of the best known and widely respected privately-owned coach companies in Australia. It has grown from one coach into a nationwide long distance, express, tour and charter undertaking with widespread ramifications in associated activities.'

I remember Jim Fagg and his wife Joy going on a McCafferty's trip to Sydney and Katoomba for their honeymoon in 1948. Then in April 1975, Jim and Joy escorted a party to New Zealand for a 15-day McCafferty's tour of that country. Each passenger paid $616.

Most trips are highly successful, but there are a few that some drivers would rather forget. Tony McCafferty's wife called him from the shower on one occasion to answer a phone call from Kununurra in Western Australia. Tony continues:

'The driver of one of our latest Denning coaches said: "I've got a problem with the coach, the dashboard lights have all gone crazy and there's been a fire at the back of the bus."

He had gone into the motel to get the room keys for the passengers and when he returned to the coach all the lights on the dashboard were flashing and alarm signals were sounding.

He ran to the back of the coach to check the engine and saw flames coming out so he grabbed a hose from the motel laundry and put out the fire. The wiring was burnt, the lights and gauges were crazy and the alarms were still sounding. What should he do?

I told him to get hold of an auto electrician in town and get him to call me back.

Some time later the auto electrician called and said, "She's shorted out a lot of wires and needs a new harness around the engine; it's done major damage to the wiring harness in the front of the bus."

"Can you fix it?" I asked.

"Yes, I can fix it but I haven't got all the cables, but I could get them from Darwin."

"How long will it take to get the coach rewired?"

"Oh, about two weeks."

"That's no good, these people have to leave tomorrow, they are on a round Australia tour."

I then rang Denning in Brisbane, and their auto electrician said he had a harness which was just about to be placed on a new chassis.

"Grab it," I shouted. "I'll get McCafferty's chief mechanic and we'll fly to Kununurra straight away."

We flew to Kununurra and worked through the night to rewire the coach.

When the tourists came out of the motel after breakfast in the morning, they hopped on the coach and set off. They didn't know we had worked all through the night to redo the wiring. The distance we had flown was equal to that from Australia to Fiji; it really was a mammoth task.'

Perhaps this is the best example of the importance of the company having access to its own aircraft.

Technology continues to advance in so many ways and for many of us it is hard to think of the time when we didn't have computers. Among the staff who can recall those days is Maree Quinn, who began her career with our reservations staff straight from school in January 1979:

'Staff who join the company today say they cannot believe that we used to do everything manually without the aid of computers.

When I was interviewed for the job I was asked to write on a piece of paper so that my handwriting could be checked. But even today, legible handwriting is very important when notes have to be typed into a computer.

It was exciting coming in straight from school and working in the Margaret Street office with older people and learning in a new environment. I started doing agents' returns, making morning teas, sorting mail, doing deliveries, banking, switchboard and telexing.

There were six of us working in accounts and the number of agents then was fairly small.

All the training was 'on-the-job', and with any growing company training is still a problem. The travel industry requires specialised knowledge and staff have to learn the whole network. You have to know the names of towns throughout Australia, and then learn three-letter coding for different towns, such as TWB for Toowoomba.

In the 1980s, once Reservations had details of all the tickets in from the agents, each ticket had to be checked manually for mileage for road tax.

There were many well-known names among our company's early agents. McCafferty's used to have such agents as Woods Travel Agency in Mackay run by a former Senator, Ian Wood. Even years after retirement from Canberra, Ian Wood was still called "The

Lew Carroll receives a telephone call for Eight-Double-Eight Taxis at the Neil Street terminal in November 1955.

Senator" and used to ride to his travel agency each day on a very old bicycle and never drove a car. But I remember his travel agency as being a very competent establishment, and today the former Senator's bicycle is on display in the Mackay Historical Society's museum.

In the early days there could be 44 or 45 seats on a coach and a number of seats had to be allocated to different terminals. All details were recorded in a diary and everything was done without computers.

Our agents are now much more advanced and travel is more sophisticated. Timetables are easily followed and agents know exactly what they want.

I remember the excitement among staff when the new terminal was being built in Neil Street and they were looking forward to getting more office space. One staff member suggested that the company should purchase the whole block fronting Neil and Bell Streets, right up to a commercial radio station on the corner, but this was not taken up.'

The move to the new terminal saw older staff battling to learn how to handle new office equipment.

The old plug-in manual switchboard caused some problems. On occasions, Maree pulled out the wrong plug and disconnected senior staff. She said it was disconcerting to hear my voice boom out through an open office door, 'What happened to my call?'.

The first telex machine at the Neil Street terminal was installed in February 1981. These machines were seen as being very cost effective.

Five years later I encouraged staff to send telexes rather than make phone calls. I wrote in the staff newsletter, 'With the high cost of electricity today, it is imperative that attention be given to electricity wastages, such as lights left on unnecessarily, fans and air-conditioners running when nobody is about. The same applies to the use of phones, especially trunk line calls. Use the telex wherever possible instead of the phone. With electricity and phones these accounts are astronomical and increased charges will make it worse. So please note this request.'

Things were moving along very quickly in 1981, and Reservations needed staff with a bright personality and who were not scared of people on the other end of the phone trying to make a booking. They had to demonstrate an ability to handle people under different circumstances and to remain cool and relaxed. With some people, staff could reply with humour, but with others they had to be very careful.

In the early days, staff were not trained as they are today. If callers got too abusive the call was passed on to management.

Staff were always encouraged to widen their knowledge through travel as Maree Quinn records:

> '*I got my first plane ride when a group from McCafferty's flew to Alice Springs to meet three coaches which were on round Australia tours. Included in the group was Dennis Densley from the Toowoomba workshop, whose job was to service the coaches.*
>
> *While the coaches were being serviced, we visited a camel farm and I jumped up on a camel with coach driver Keith McNicol in the rear seat. It was the first time I had been on a camel.*
>
> *I didn't know then that camels could run so fast. I think everyone got a good laugh from that incident*'.

Maree left McCafferty's to have a daughter in 1991, and returned in the following year. She told me that she was amazed to see just how much the company had advanced and how many new staff had come on board. She explains how things have changed:

> '*Travel industry staff need lots of training. There are so many new services to take in and no longer is it a job where a person can walk in off the street and start work sitting behind a desk.*
>
> *People ring up and ask to be dropped off at a certain cattle station in the Northern Territory, and they laugh if you don't know*

184

Reservations (Toowoomba) in 1987. Maree Quinn is on the left with Sharon Mills, Carolyn Kohler (née Ziebell), Lucinda Warren, Samantha Kellard, Chris Martin and Paula Donoghue.

exactly where the station is. Australia is such a big country with so many names to learn.

I feel sad that the days have gone when McCafferty's staff all knew each other. I would love to have a training centre established in Toowoomba, where all the staff in head office would have a chance to meet new staff members from other centres.

We talk to them on the phone, but we have no idea what they look like. We used to know everyone at head office – now we don't.

When I became Reservations Assistant Manager I received a job description which stated that Reservations was the largest single department with McCafferty's. Number one on the duty list was updating the computer database and handling computer maintenance and problems. I also had to handle customer, agent and staff complaints and problems, carry out fare construction for Reservations, Marketing and Administration, fare construction for overseas tour wholesalers and travel agents, and construction and bookings of package holidays.'

Craig Wilson started with McCafferty's in September 1980 at the same time as Coral Padget, when Ray George was the manager. By 1987, Reservations had become a separate entity. It started with six staff and two microcomputers, seven computerised booking locations and a 12-line Commander phone system. By 1992, the system had grown to five microcomputers with 26 booking locations and 11 full-time staff and three casual employees. There was also a 24-line phone system and sixteen 008 lines. In December 1991, an average of over 850 bookings a day were made from the 1,700 calls that were received.

Today, 28 people work in Reservations and in February, 1993, Reservations staff in Toowoomba took 22,000 phone calls including 11,600 bookings. This is how Craig Wilson views his work:

> *'I love a job which would send most people around the bend. Each day, Reservations receive between 3,500 and 4,000 calls and one of the biggest problems is that everyone seems to want a window seat.*
>
> *If they can ever invent a coach with window seats in the centre then our prayers would be answered.'*

Just before Christmas 1992, an additional computer reservation system was installed in the Toowoomba office at a cost of $800,000. This brought the total outlay on McCafferty's computer reservations system over five years to $3 million.

In the early days, staff were called on to handle a whole range of tasks and it was the best part of working on the counter. Later,

Some of 1993 Reservation Staff: Craig Wilson on the left with Margot Wilson, Colleen Carroll, Sue Donnelly, Heidi Tait, Helen MacDonald, Chris Martin, Carol Mallinson and Anthony Kuster.

Coral Padget was taking the phone calls and channelling them to the right sections.

Although 'the customer is always right' is the maxim for business there are still difficulties created by some passengers.

Mostly these passengers regard themselves as 'better than others' and rarely is everything right for them. Even if they went by plane, they would be the type who would still complain about meals and other services. They want everything done for them and to hell with the rest of the passengers.

Computers don't come easy to some staff as Janelle Leaman recalls:

'Maths wasn't one of my strong points. It was 1980 and I just walked in to McCafferty's off the street and got an interview. I joined the company as a receptionist but found myself working the Canon AX1 computer at 203 Margaret Street, Toowoomba.

Jan Emerson was in charge of travel with John Clough working hard as the accountant. Val Flohr was in charge of staff working on the payroll and handling the accounts.

There were two computers in a tiny room at the back of the Travel Centre, but in those days I thought it was a good environment and modern for the time.

The main work involved keeping track of tickets and doing the accounts for McCafferty's agents. Every ticket sold by a driver, agent or the terminal went through the computer along with commissions and the road tax had to be worked out on the number of passengers on each journey.

Accuracy was one of the biggest things. If a slip of the fingers meant that you typed in 100 passengers instead of 10 passengers going to Rockhampton then it could be really embarrassing when you had to pay road tax.

A computer print-out was sent to each agent and this stated how much money was owed to McCafferty's.

When the Administration and Accounts Section moved from Margaret Street to Neil Street, there was a different atmosphere. It was no longer a small company growing up, it had matured. I helped set up the new office and I went up the ladder from computer operator to office manager and assistant accountant.

I watched the company develop from two computers to a huge bank of computers operating at incredible speeds and diversification.

Every fortnight each agent sends in a return for passengers and freight to McCafferty's head office.

McCafferty's now have nearly 1,600 accredited agents.

A good agent is seen as one who is especially nice to customers, who writes the tickets out neatly and gets returns in on time.

Staff still have trouble at times deciphering writing and it seems to get worse rather than better.

I organised the company's first uniform for female staff. Office staff wore a navy skirt, white blouse and pink, white and navy scarf bearing McCafferty's name.

In the early days, power strikes were a real problem and staff often had to bring out candles and work with paper and pens until the power came back on.

The company moved at a more leisurely pace. I used to enjoy attending corporate luncheons, which were held in the old Board Room in Neil Street.

It was an important part of building up the company's image and local business people and McCafferty's financial people would be invited along. Toowoomba restaurateur Mr George Levonis served prawns, crabs and other seafood, chicken and bread rolls and two smartly attired women waited at the tables.'

John Clough, as well as being the company's Financial Controller, is also secretary to the McCafferty's Board, which meets regularly. The Board is headed by me as chairman; and the members are Tony McCafferty, general manager; Rodney James McCafferty, travel consultant; Kenneth Aubrey McCafferty, reservations clerk; and John Clough, secretary, who records the minutes.

McCafferty's is still very much a family company. My wife Lorna and I have one-third each, and our six offspring have the other third.

Over a period of years, what can go wrong with some businesses that have shareholders is that money is used for purposes other than for that business. We channel money back into our business. We also own a lot of freehold land and our own premises.

When a company strikes a rough patch, it must have reserves and some companies have nothing to fall back on.

McCafferty's prides itself on its staff. Management look at the family background of the person being considered for an important position in the company. Stability is essential and our company needs people who will fit in and grow with the business and put their heart and soul into it.

Lorna explains about one of our sons:

'Kenneth does everything for me. Kenneth left teaching and has been jack of all trades. He's been out on the road, seeing agents, working in Toowoomba and at Surfers Paradise, and now he's an expert in coach timetables and coach routes.'

188

In the Board Room. Rod McCafferty (left) is pictured with Ken McCafferty, Jack McCafferty, Tony McCafferty and John Clough.

The first family meeting in the new Board Room in the Neil Street building was held on January 19, 1981, and the family partnership was incorporated into a proprietary company, McCafferty's Management Pty Ltd in 1981.

The first luncheon for VIP account customers and firms was held in the Board Room on February 13, 1981, and on the same day the company took delivery again of Coach No. 52. This was a coach that had been refurbished by Denning after being burnt out in the fire at McCafferty's premises in Stanley Street, South Brisbane, in 1980.

Today, every department within the company presents a report to Board meetings:

Marketing – John Osborne handles all aspects of advertising, promotions and sales; **Operations** – John Wilce is in charge of the scheduling and control of all the coaches and control of terminal staff; **Reservations** – Craig Wilson handles all bookings from public and agents; **Workshop and Maintenance** – Dennis Densley is responsible for the work and maintenance on all the coach fleet; and **Finance** – John Clough is the Company Secretary. John Clough and John Krause prepare all the financial information and an analysis of these figures is presented to the Board for discussion. John Clough is also one of the trustees of the company's superannuation scheme.

The hey day of the co-ordinated service was coming to an end in 1981.

A few long-distance passenger trains were still climbing the Toowoomba Range, but intercity trains had been cut at Helidon, connecting with the coach service to Toowoomba, leaving the rail tracks clear for more profitable freight trains.

We were still selling railway-type card tickets to Brisbane and various rail destinations and a ticket dater was at the terminal counter to validate the card tickets sold to passengers using the co-ordinated service.

However, more and more cars were coming on to the road, and people were driving themselves to and from Toowoomba and Brisbane.

We were forced to stop the Toowoomba-Helidon co-ordinated run. The last driver on the final run on November 7, 1981, was Nev Horan. The service, which had been operating for 35 years, had carried 2.5 million passengers, had covered a distance of two million miles and made 100,000 trips.

On the day after the closure, we began a new Metrolink electric train and coach service between Toowoomba, Ipswich and Brisbane. It cost $7 single, to travel from Toowoomba to Ipswich and took one and a quarter hours.

Coaches from Toowoomba to Ipswich now connected with the electric train to Brisbane and the metropolitan area. This service proved a winner and was regarded as the most popular way of travelling from Toowoomba to Brisbane.

Other services such as Sydney were also forging ahead and there was one day that staff at Kings Cross in Sydney will not forget in a hurry. Back in 1981, Clem Cheers was preparing for an early morning departure at 6.30 a.m. A woman passenger arrived late and raced into the terminal to purchase a ticket. She left her possessions, in a green plastic garbage bag, on the footpath near the coach.

It was while she was at the counter that a passing garbage truck stopped briefly and picked up the garbage bag. The coach had to leave without the woman, who was last seen chasing the garbage truck up Darlinghurst Road.

On a note of trivia, I've always been intrigued how the Cross developed its name. I was told that Kings Cross was actually called Queens Cross from 1897 to 1905. I feel any further comment is unnecessary.

We opened our Sydney office there on December 15, 1980, with Ms Val Keyse as Manageress. From day one there were numerous problems with parking of coaches, changing phone and telex numbers and not the least was a mix-up with the previous agent getting all our bookings over the phone as the McCafferty's Express Service was still listed under his name.

Initially, there was a high turnover of staff at Kings Cross, which has a strong population of itinerant workers. In 12 months there were 16 new staff in an office that normally had six. It took time to sort out the situation and to come up with a fine complement of staff.

Airport controllers staged rolling strikes, which started in January 1981 and lasted five weeks. They gave our Brisbane-Sydney coach services a great kick along at a time when Richard Whitlock became the new Sydney manager.

The Kings Cross office continued to grow and there was a marked improvement in bookings out of Sydney once the new phone books came out with McCafferty's number under our own name instead of the previous agent.

There were eight coach operators on the Brisbane-Sydney service, but we were getting more than our share of customers. Our services were more reliable and drivers were encouraged to offer a little extra service, to speak nicely to the customers and to help them with their baggage.

In 1981, there had been a most successful open day at Tarong Power Station, and Queensland Electricity Generating Board hired 14 McCafferty's coaches to take 4,000 people on inspection tours.

Line-up of coaches at the Tarong Power Station site.

Some of the drivers who were employed in the early days of the Tarong contract when the company had 20 coaches on the route.

Our staff had now grown to 160 and the company began the CAPCOAL school run from German Creek to Middlemount and Dysart in May 22, 1981, using a new Denflex coach built in Sydney.

An eight-week contract was obtained with Queensland Government Railways to take a coach-load of men from Emerald to Gregory out and back six days a week to build the new loop line to Gregory.

McCafferty's had tendered successfully to transport the workers to the Tarong Power Station from Yarraman and Nanango. We entered into a seven-year contract with the Queensland Electricity Generating Board for the Tarong site.

This involved 17 drivers and coaches providing services from nearby towns to the power station site. By March 1982, McCafferty's had 19 coaches operating at Tarong.

It was just as well our company had bought 15 acres of land around the workshop complex at Nanango, and the first manager, Ron Rolfh, had moved into a house on the site.

Initially, I had purchased 10 acres for a coach stabling and maintenance depot and a three-bedroom manager's residence. Seven Denning coaches, fitted with two-way radios, were stationed at Nanango to handle the Tarong operation.

The contract was successfully carried out, but, when the seven years ended and it came up for renewal, we missed out and it went to another operator.

Problems had also developed at Nanango because of a shortage of water to wash 15 coaches. We brought in a water diviner but the project was not a success. The water diviner believed water was available at 75ft, but the drill was still going down when it reached 100ft and struck granite. There was no water but we got a bill for $1,800.

Chapter 16

A new office at Emerald

(1982-1985)

'When you consider that the early timetables were the same as in 1994, it is incredible. In the same time coaches have improved by 150%.

I remember the first Emerald service. Things were a little slow to start with. Bill McKendry, who had the newsagency, used to patrol the streets looking for people to ride the bus, at least to Clermont, so we could say the service was being used. Mr McKendry played a major part in pioneering the service.'

RAY "RAMBO" MEDLIN (EMERALD)

1982 was a year in which our company achieved a new record for charter work. Thirty-one coaches were booked out in the month of March and the Toowoomba workshop was working on a seven-day roster that had been introduced in the previous year.

Since 1980, our company had also had a contract with the Gregory Mine, with seven coaches operating on a journey between the mine and Emerald, Capella and Dysart.

When we began the Nanango service, McCafferty's had the second-largest fleet of Denning coaches in Australia, our 33 trailing behind Australian Pacific's 45.

Other units in the fleet included three fixed-axle, full-height trailers used for mail and freight on the Rockhampton-Emerald service and occasionally on the Rockhampton-Brisbane inland route at peak times.

In those days, the highway between Rockhampton and Emerald was not the best, with narrow strips of broken bitumen, gullies instead of bridges, and what bridges there were, were narrow.

Ray and Laurie Medlin run the Emerald terminal on strict rules, which according to Ray began on day one and will continue until they finish their careers.

Woe betide a driver who arrives at the Emerald terminal with an incorrect passenger count; Laurie balances the books every day – and they are never one cent above or below what they should be.

Coaches are washed at Emerald and some minor maintenance is carried out.

But there is a lot of humour at the terminal, where smartly dressed staff and local knowledge pay off.

Ray, who was born at Mt Morgan, started driving for our company in 1974, left in 1976 and then returned to the company and has been manager since 1981. Ray started with the company at the same time as Tom Craig, the supervisor in Rockhampton.

Ray cut his teeth on the early Bedfords and moved to Dennings in the days when roads connecting Emerald, Rockhampton and Clermont were gravel.

McKendry's Newsagency was the Emerald agent for McCafferty's as pick-up and set-down point for passengers and freight for eight years. It was on December 7, 1982, that we opened our own office in rented premises in the Wong Yong Building at 99 Clermont Street.

Many complaints were received from the local council and chamber of commerce concerning visibility at corners where the coaches were parked. The company picked up its goods and chattels and moved to the industrial estate west of the town, where coaches were parked on the road, and a garden shed was erected in the yard of Oates Engineering and Automotive. There were up to seven coaches there at times.

We exhibited plans for our new coach terminal in September 1981, depicting a site we had purchased at 115 Clermont Street, Emerald. At the same time, the *Central Queensland News* reported:

> *'A house on the site will be moved to* **'Poinsetta'**, *Rubyvale, for Mr and Mrs W. Horne, to replace the homestead burned on the property.'*

The new building, made of concrete blocks, was 18.3m long and 6.5m wide, and at the rear was a large area for parking coaches, six cars, a washing area and room to manoeuvre coaches.

The plans included a waiting room, ticket-sales counter, freight room and toilet block.

I told the media that traffic would flow in from Dunning Lane and out into Clermont Street.

By 1981, the company was spending $500,000 annually on advertising its services, which now included two new twice-weekly services in the Central Highlands; the Emerald to Springsure feeder service and the Emerald, Anakie, Sapphire and Rubyvale service.

The same year saw the commencement of the Tieri school run and the new overnight Rockhampton to Brisbane via the coast service three times daily. Another service started was the Rockhampton, Moranbah via Dingo and Middlemount, and the overnight service from Brisbane to Sydney via the Pacific Highway, was running three services daily.

We were conducting personally escorted tours to China in 1981, including visits to the Great Wall, Peking, Shanghai, Nanking, Canton, Soochow and the Ming Tombs.

Express coaches, carrying passengers and freight, were operating from **Toowoomba** to **Sydney** using both the New England and Pacific Highways; **Cairns** via Rockhampton, Mackay, Airlie Beach, Townsville and Innisfail; **Rockhampton** via Chinchilla, Miles, Taroom, Theodore, Moura, Biloela and Mt Morgan, and **Rockhampton** via Gympie, Maryborough, Hervey Bay, Bundaberg and Gladstone; **Mackay** via Rockhampton, Blackwater, Emerald, Capella, Clermont and Moranbah; **Moranbah** via Rockhampton, Dingo, Dysart and Seraji; **Gold Coast** via Ipswich, Mt Gravatt (Garden City), Sunnybank, Beenleigh, Dreamworld, Southport, Burleigh Heads and Coolangatta; **Brisbane Metrolink** via Ipswich and electric train to city (fare from Toowoomba to Brisbane $8.10); **Millmerran** via Westbrook, Pittsworth and Southbrook; and **Melbourne** via Tenterfield, Armidale, Dubbo, Narrandera and Shepparton.

I drove my Ford LTD more than 4,000 kilometres in 10 days visiting agents in 1982. The journey took me from Toowoomba to Mackay, then to Townsville and back through Rockhampton, Biloela, Bundaberg and Maryborough and through Tarong to Toowoomba. During a two-night stopover at Emerald, I checked the company's new block of land next to the bakery.

I made the following diary notes: 'Impressed by the way Ray Medlin carries out his job . . . The books he keeps are very precise and detailed with a record of all coach movements, mileage, number of passengers carried, weather details etc. In fact, a daily report of every activity. This is excellent and something I have always looked for. Now, we have it at last! Thanks Ray and his "offsider" Laurie who devotes a lot of time to the bookwork.

At the Emerald terminal – Don Johnson (Rockhampton driver), Ray and Laurie Medlin, and Ian Madden (Emerald driver).

A word of praise too for Vin Clarke and his staff at that time at the Rockhampton terminal, for the cleanliness of the terminal and the general "air of dedication" by the staff.'

Our company introduced its first superannuation scheme in 1982, initially for heads of departments. At the same time we endeavoured to introduce a scheme limiting the age of permanent drivers to 60 years.

Among the factors were the ever-increasing traffic problems which necessitated 'sharp' reflexes, together with sophisticated requirements of the new $180,000 coaches.

Our company came in for some praise from the Queensland Transport Minister, Gordon Chalk.

Mr Chalk said the action of McCafferty's, in supplementing their existing fleet of road vehicles with two ultra-modern coaches, was in keeping with a policy always followed by the firm of providing the most modern and up-to-date facilities for its patrons.

The fact that McCafferty's had transported in excess of $1^1/_2$ million passengers over a very busy section of the Toowoomba-Brisbane road without one serious accident testified to the serviceability of the buses used and the high standard of efficiency of its drivers.

The Queensland Railway Department was fortunate, added Mr Chalk, in having as its partner in the co-ordinated road-rail passenger service, a firm intent on providing the best possible standard of service. It had as its proprietor a man who was always ready to make suggestions to the Railway Department designed to improve the service available to persons travelling between Toowoomba and Brisbane.

Later, the co-ordinated rail-road service was given a boost when 150-horsepower stainless-steel rail cars were introduced between Helidon and Brisbane, with McCafferty's continuing to carry passengers by bus on the 12-mile Toowoomba-Helidon section.

The new £80,000 rail car, travelling on 'the smoothest line in Queensland' and stopping only at Ipswich, cut half an hour off the co-ordinated service timetable. In 1964 it took just two and three-quarter hours to travel from Toowoomba to Brisbane.

Fares were cut, too and the daily return fare was 37/6 and the Saturday and Sunday return fares were 29/6.

Those who made the inaugural trip as guests of McCafferty's Co-ordinated Bus Services and the Railway Department, as well as Lorna and I, were the Minister for Transport, Mr Chalk and Mrs Chalk, the former Minister for Transport and Leader of the Opposition, Mr J.E. Duggan and Mrs Duggan, Mr D.J. Kearney (Stipendiary Magistrate), Mr L. Liddell (president, Chamber of Commerce), Colonel J. Hooker (101 Wireless Regiment), Mr and Mrs R.W.P. Dodd, Mr and Mrs W. Glindemann, Mr and Mrs G. Rowbotham, Mr and Mrs W. Malone, Mr A. McCarthy (manager, Queensland Government Tourist Bureau, Toowoomba), Mr K. Jefferies, Mrs S. Mossetter, and Mr Kev Zimmerle, a representative of Falconer Motors.

In 1984, McCafferty's were operating four services daily from the Gold Coast to Sydney, via the Pacific Highway, and one daily to Melbourne.

Chapter 17

From an office to a coach terminal

(1986)

'In the early days, we used to put on special functions for our agents and some staff started playing up. I gave them a good talking to and told them that the functions were an opportunity to get to know the company's management and not to act silly.

On the next function night, I had given them all a talk beforehand and the evening finished around nine o'clock.

On the next day, Jack McCafferty was asked how the function had gone?

"Great night," Mac said. "Old Rambo gave them a 'tune-up' before they started".'

RAY MEDLIN

Headlines were made in the *Central Queensland News* on Friday June 6, 1986, to announce the opening of Emerald's new McCafferty's bus terminal. It had taken 11 weeks to construct the building, which was officially opened on August 8, 1986, by Mr Vince Lester MLA.

In the early days, Vince had been among our casual drivers, particularly during floods. McCafferty's used to use Vince's bakehouse in Clermont to drop off freight and Vince helped out when the company needed an extra hand at the wheel.

It had taken several years to gain the Emerald Terminal building including overcoming a dispute over a fire wall, between the terminal complex and a garage next-door.

I told the Shire Chairman, Cr Craig Edmonston, that the terminal represented an $80,000 investment. I had recognised the potential of the Emerald area many years earlier when I first visited the district.

I saw that Emerald could act as a hub for transport services, which could then service other towns on the Central Highlands.

Our company was keen to reinvest money gained in Emerald and was paying an annual wages bill of about $400,000. This was turned over a number of times in the town.

Emerald's population had increased because of the coal mines. In 1981, the shire had about 7,000 people, compared with 12,000 in 1994.

Ray and Laurie Medlin agree that the early days really were good old days when staff had more personal contact with passengers. They knew most of them, but as the company grew and the local population increased things got more and more impersonal.

Laurie says:

> *'We still know all the Rockhampton drivers. But, quite often if a Toowoomba driver pulls up on charter he has to come over and introduce himself.'*

Today, a large Kensington mango tree stands at the Emerald Terminal. It was planted on opening day – a day when the Medlins worked hard to ensure that everything would go right.

The company had agreed that its coaches would not drive directly into the terminal off a busy main street, but would enter around the back. Ray had a large sign made for the front saying

'Signs mean what they say' – Ray Medlin at Emerald.

'STOP. NO ENTRY', and he was not amused when a large car drove in ignoring his new sign. What happened when the driver – Ken McCafferty – failed to acknowledge the sign is recorded here by Ray:

> *'As you know Laurie and I were running the place as it should be run and we have one rule for everybody irrespective of who you are. If a stranger to town drives in the wrong way he gets one warning and doesn't do it again.*
>
> *I walked across to the big car as Ken wound down the window.*
> *"Can't you read?" I asked him.*
> *"Why?"*
> *I pointed out that he had driven past the big sign saying "STOP. NO ENTRY".*
> *"What will I do?" he asked.*
> *"Drive out, go round the back and use the proper entrance like everyone else."*
>
> *A few minutes later, the car was back at the terminal and as I walked across, another window wound down and I found myself looking straight into the eyes of Jack McCafferty. "Are we allowed to park here Rambo?" the deep voice asked with a touch of humour.*
>
> *And today, the name Rambo has stuck. It's an image I would like to go away but it does no harm against a driver who is a little slack in reading signs. He knows that when he drives into Emerald he has to have everything right.*
>
> *I believe that Jack McCafferty appreciated that I had stuck to my guns to get people to do the right thing.'*

Ray and Laurie are proud of their work and their loyalty to the local population. The Queensland flag flies high at the terminal.

Since McCafferty's have been established in Emerald, Laurie and Ray Medlin have encouraged local sporting bodies and school groups to charter coaches to distant parts of Australia.

Our company played a major part in servicing the developing coalfields of Central Queensland and the new towns as they were built.

The backbone to Emerald is the coal industry, and McCafferty's have held the contract to provide a coach service to the Gregory mine since 1980. There are seven air-conditioned coaches on this service working seven days a week. The mine operates 24 hours a day, seven days a week, with three shifts a day.

When the terminal at Emerald opened, the company had already been serving Emerald and the Central Highlands for 11 years, the previous $2^1/_2$ from Emerald.

Emerald Terminal in 1989.

In 1981, there were six late model air-conditioned coaches based at Emerald and these transported miners, who lived in homes at Emerald and Capella, to the huge Dampier-BHP coalmining venture at Gregory. These coaches operated at change of shift times, over 60km routes. To ensure smooth running, each coach was equipped with two-way radio, and had full Konvekta air-conditioning, fully reclining seating and fire-resistant curtains on the windows. Today, this contract still operates with seven air-conditioned coaches.

By 1986, there were 32 weekly services in and out of Emerald, from Blackwater to Mackay, and the new terminal had a staff of 11, including drivers.

The Emerald-Springsure feeder service began on Tuesdays and Thursdays. The 4.15 p.m. Emerald to Rockhampton service began, and the 8.15 p.m. Rockhampton to Emerald (Monday to Friday). Our company won the Toowoomba to Gympie licence in August 1981. A month after it started, this service was reported to be 'a winner breaking new ground'.

We continued to operate the Toowoomba-Gympie service until May 1985, when it was sold to Mr and Mrs Graham Henry.

From day one, the Emerald office adopted a high standard of dress and a photograph, which was reproduced in the *Central Queensland News* on Friday, June 6, 1986, showed Laurie (then

Lorienne Saunders) and a receptionist, Laurene Childs, wearing smart uniforms featuring a navy blue skirt, pink blouse, a McCafferty's scarf and blue vest for cooler months.

More recently, Laurie went ahead and introduced new uniforms for the female staff in navy and jade, and a remodelled scarf with the name 'McCafferty's'.

But, even with Ray and Laurie's strict code of conduct, there is always the time when schedules have to change because of outside factors. Sometimes coaches are held back at the terminal for 10 minutes to cater for railway staff whose train has been delayed, or if there is an urgent medical consignment from the local hospital.

Times are changing in the coach industry, as Laurie recalls:

> *'One of the good things about working for a company such as McCafferty's is that the boss rings us up in the morning.*
>
> *Mr Mac is marvellous. He appreciates honest answers and he considers some of his employees to be personal friends.*
>
> *Things have changed so much in coach travel since the early pioneering days. I often travel on the Rockhampton coach and nobody says a word. This wasn't so years ago.'*

The tidiness of the Emerald Terminal is a credit to all concerned.

Here again is another one of McCafferty's terminals capably managed with no problems, but when all the coaches meet there from Rockhampton, Longreach and Mt Isa via Belyando, the place is like Central Station. But, as Ray explains, everything is not straight driving:

> *'Sometimes Laurie and I run around in the middle of night picking up passengers missed by a coach and this shouldn't happen.*
>
> *There are now 46 services a week operating out of Emerald. The terminal staff start at 5.30 a.m. and the counter closes at 5 p.m. when the phone is switched through to the Manager's house.*
>
> *My pet hate is the people who ring up in the middle of the night and ask what time the six o'clock bus is going in the morning.*
>
> *Computers have speeded up the work after limited training. Our terminal staff received training on one day, from 11.15 a.m. to 2 p.m., to show them how to change over from manual manifests to computer operations.*
>
> *I am sure that older workers today are far more committed than young people entering the workforce. It is hard to get people to make a 100 per cent commitment to the job. There is no blame for things that go wrong – in the old days that was very different.'*

Ray and Laurie maintain an excellent garden at home, and they also tend the garden in the median strip in the street outside the terminal. They have won a chamber of commerce award for the best mature garden, come second in the tropical garden category, picked up the Vera Gibson Memorial Trophy for Civic Pride, and also gained a shield for the way they present the terminal.

Laurie has a delightful explanation for travellers who ask how Emerald got its name:

> *'In 1879, four Irish men camped on a property on a hill saw that a fire had burnt out the valley area below. After the rains came, the valley began to turn green again and the four men called it* **Emerald.** *The property on the hill became known as* **Emerald Downs.***'*

Our Central Queensland services were steaming ahead and we were also expanding into better facilities for travellers. McCafferty's formed an association with Viva Traveland to provide Round-Australia tours and we opened our own booking and travel office in Sydney. This office also served as a passenger and freight terminal for our express services.

We changed the colour scheme on some coaches to have our travel operations painted on the side, and with a large 'Viva' logo on the back windows. One coach carried a special registration plate: VAH (Viva Australia Holidays) 01.

The first Viva tour to Cairns was on May 8, 1981, with Gary Barnes in charge of 15 passengers.

McCafferty's provided the operating resources for three major tours operated by Viva that year. They were a 50-day Round Australia accommodated (four departures), a 23-day Red Heart tour (eight departures) and a 15-day Queensland Carousel to Cairns and the Barrier Reef (19 departures).

A multi-coloured glossy brochure featuring Viva/McCafferty's Australia tours was produced and distributed, coinciding with an extensive advertising campaign, at a total cost of over $80,000.

Charter work was big business for our company and vehicles were constantly rostered for long-distance runs, particularly on school educational tours to far-away places such as Darwin, Perth, Sydney, Tasmania and 'The Centre'. Groups such as pensioners, service clubs and schools were the biggest charter customers and the work extended from short distances around Toowoomba to anywhere in Australia.

Charter work represented about $1 million in revenue a year for McCafferty's and the company held well over $50,000 worth of camping equipment on hand for school and safari outings. We had sufficient tents, cooking equipment, sleeping bags and mattresses to outfit 11 Denning coaches at any one time.

We were one of the first Australian bus operators to break into the tour business after World War ll.

Our company was running about 50 tours a year, selling between 2,500 and 3,000 seats. On an average, we had 500 tourists in our coaches on any one day.

May to October were the months when the McCafferty's tour operation swung into action. There were up to 15 coaches away on tours simultaneously and, of course, the regular short and long-distance express services still had to be operated.

Our company was handling two million passenger journeys a year in addition to 3.5 million passenger journeys on the Emerald/Nanango operations. The company's vehicles were running up to 3.2 million kilometres on service routes a year and that didn't include tours and charters.

We called the Birdsville Races tour 'Australia's biggest safari', and by 1981 we were running direct to Birdsville, overnight where necessary. In addition to the 22 tonnes of equipment (including portable toilets) we had two professional caterers, nine drivers who doubled as cooks and eight other employees who were sent out ahead to set up the camp.

The idea was to get passengers into the swing of things as soon as they arrived at the race track, without the hassles of setting up camp.

We took 400 racing enthusiasts to Birdsville in 1981. Eleven of our coaches were used for the races with tours originating from Brisbane, Toowoomba, Gold Coast, Rockhampton and Emerald.

I was told that one woman, a veteran of the Birdsville races, had been criticised by her husband for returning home with bruises on her knees. She couldn't explain them so he said this was not the first time he had noticed them and he vowed to accompany her on her next outing to Birdsville and check out what was going on.

It turned out that while travelling on the coach to Birdsville, the woman made frequent trips down the aisle to the toilet and in the moving coach she struck her knees on the seats as she walked past. She had the bruises before she even reached Birdsville!

Often I look back on our early days when things appeared less complex and my views are shared by Susan Crossley:

> *'If something needed to be done in the early days everyone would get in and do it.*

Staff would stay back whenever a tour was going out and the exodus to Birdsville had to be seen to be believed. There would be some incredible scenes at the Toowoomba terminal. I'd be trying to mark people off on the manifest and direct them to the right coach. A number would have had a few drinks before they arrived and they completely disregarded our instructions and we would finish up with too many on one coach and not enough on another. There would be people on the coach, off the coach, around the coach and it was a nightmare until the drivers took off.'

Tours to places such as Birdsville were pioneering ventures, as Ron Crossley recalls:

'It was all hands on deck once we arrived at Birdsville a week ahead of the coaches. We carried the camping gear and food on two trucks, an old Bedford and a Ford F100.

The tent had to be erected in a perfect square so that good photographs could be taken from the air, and we had to dig the toilets and put up the showers.

Those shower facilities had to be seen to be believed. We hoisted a 44-gallon drum up a tree, filled it with water and let it gravity-feed shower roses in the showers. We put in a few posts and lined them with builders brown paper to separate the men from the women. But once the paper got wet you'd have the men poking holes through, and the women were doing the same thing.

For those who wanted a bath there was a hot water, free-flowing artesian bore and it was a very popular place to bathe with or without clothes.

Breakfast would be sausages, bacon and eggs, toast and tomatoes, and there was a 44-gallon drum full of potatoes on the fire at night time. People enjoyed eating them while they quenched their thirst.

The punters would camp on the wings of aircraft, underneath aircraft, in fact anywhere.

One year, Mr Mac flew out in the plane with the Japanese Consul and we were accompanied at the races by Mr Tom McVeigh. The Japanese Consul had a great time watching the horses and later seeing 'two-up'.

The buses left Birdsville on the Sunday morning, and arrived back at Toowoomba in time for work on the Monday morning. I think everyone learned a lot at Birdsville.'

We were now running local, long distance express, interstate, charters and tours, had a fleet of over 40 luxury coaches, and were well into associated activities such as the travel industry, with eight offices, terminals and depots stretching from Rockhampton in

Tucker time at the Birdsville Races. (1993)

John Osborne outside the Birdsville Hotel. (1993)

207

Tenth anniversary of the Dawson Valley Express. Jack McCafferty hands out promotional material on December 24, 1982.

Staff line-up in 1982 for a shot which could make a calendar.

Central Queensland to Sydney, with over 500 sales agents and depots in two States.

Our staff had now grown to 160, including 80 drivers, 12 mechanics, 20 travel office and administrative personnel and about 50 others.

Brisbane has always been a busy centre, and between March and April in 1982 no fewer than 27 coach-loads of Army personnel were ferried between Brisbane and Shoalwater Bay.

Our company opened its Beach House Office at Coolangatta in November 1984 when the rail line was electrified from Brisbane to Beenleigh, and McCafferty's were given a seven-year contract to operate the connecting coach service to Coolangatta.

The Department of Transport had received three applications from coach companies to operate the Beenleigh-Coolangatta road section of the co-ordinated service. We won against Greyhound and Skennars.

Transport Minister Don Lane told us that we provided most services, provided a cheaper fare structure and had the advantage of constant two-way radio control in coaches. The Minister continued:

> 'McCafferty's already operates a successful co-ordinated service, under contract to Queensland Rail, from Ipswich to Toowoomba.
>
> This service is known as the Toowoomba Metrolink and it is expected the new service will be marketed under similar guidelines and called the Gold Coast Metrolink.'

Beach House Coolangatta Office in 1984.

Shortly after the Minister's announcement, we placed an advertisement in the *Gold Coast Bulletin* and *The Tweed Daily News* seeking five experienced coach drivers to run the new service. They had to be residents of the Gold Coast.

That same year, we opened our Surfers Paradise Office at Imperial Surf with Ken McCafferty the sole office worker.

There was outright war among rival coach companies and Queensland travellers formed long queues to take advantage of a price-cutting war that slashed some long-distance fares by as much as 40 per cent.

The *Sunday Sun* on December 4, 1983, reported that 'The huge increase in the number of passengers using coaches is covering the cost of installing $15,000 video units in buses.'

The price war did tremendous things for the industry. People became far more coach-conscious. We had five coaches going to Sydney each day 90 per cent full and the *Sunday Sun* reported:

> 'Coach lines are coming up with new attractions to try to tempt travellers away from the trains and airlines and from each other.
>
> Non-smoking coaches, where travellers wrapped in a blanket going south can watch video movies from reclining seats, are some of the latest lures.

> *'While senior executives pay $106.90 plus taxi fares to go first*
> *class by plane from Brisbane to Sydney, coach travellers can do it*
> *for $25. And there are standby fares at $20. It takes an hour or so*
> *by plane and about 16 hours by bus.'*

The price war began when southern coach operators moved into Queensland using the Constitution on free trade to slash fares and create more services.

VIP Express was described by the media as 'The cut-price frontrunner'. Its passengers were reportedly queuing on a city footpath with luggage at the mercy of passers-by as they checked seat allocations. VIP Express, along with Deluxe Coachlines and Olympic East West Express, had to cross State borders to maintain the cut-price services.

In 1984, VIP Express was carrying passengers from Sydney to Brisbane and Melbourne for as little as $25, and to Adelaide for $50 and it was planning expansion into north Queensland and Western Australia.

A little earlier, in September 1983, Queensland's three major bus companies had started action to reduce their fares to combat VIP Express.

Ansett-Pioneer, McCafferty's and Greyhound had each lowered fares following discussions with the Queensland Transport Department.

McCafferty's had reduced fares from Brisbane to some centres by up to 25 per cent, but the average reduction was around 20 per cent.

Under the new fares, the journey between Gladstone and Brisbane varied from $36 (McCafferty's) to $40 (Greyhound) and $38.50 (Ansett-Pioneer). Under the old fares the same trip was priced at $42.50 for Greyhound and Ansett-Pioneer and $42.20 for McCafferty's.

Eleven years later, McCafferty's were in prime position with an array of services and destinations offered out of its Toowoomba terminal – the trip to Rockhampton cost $54, Sydney $60, Canberra $77, Townsville $111, Melbourne $117, Mt Isa $120, Cairns $130, Adelaide $135, Alice Springs $225, and Darwin $240. Concessions were available on most services for pensioners, students and children.

I celebrated my 70th birthday in 1984 and *The Chronicle* (Toowoomba) printed a special supplement outlining all McCafferty's staff inserted inside a huge coach wheel. In the hub of the wheel was a photograph of myself working at my desk.

Names around the hub included: Warren Eckhardt, Janelle Bruggemann, Gail Maree Kroh, Janet Tobin, Maree Schriek,

Suzanne Flohr, Susan Barclay, Lynette Woolridge, Sally Stedman, Deborah Schultz, Amanda Marsen, Dawn Needham, Sharon McGuire, Sheryl Anderson, Mark Smith, Anne-Maree Flohr, Susan Reinke, Stephanie Denham, Barbara Swan, Gayle Johnson, Paul Cleary, Thomas McErlean, Daniel McCartin, Harry Miller, Simon Rub, John Craig, Arthur Hunt, Graeme Bilesner, Ian Lavender, Neil Costello, John Ludlow, Susan Thompson, Helen Scarce, Douglas Lowe, Raymond Simpson, Kenneth Hayes, Iris Fletcher, Len Wallace, Gregory Fleming, Melinda Sauer, Adrian McDonald, Arthur Handley, Peter Harris, Ian Graham, Alan Gannell, Ronald Stevens, Stephen Winters, Lorienne Saunders, Stephen Rowsell, Stephen Crabtree, B. Jensen, Colin Paix, Margaret Goltz, Stevan Hammond, Raymond McGrath, Thomas Kelly, Neville Frohloff, David Hopper, Wanda Wilson, Vicki Flohr, William Bloxham, Christine Hance, Susan McPherson, Graeme Anderson, John Stimpson, Brian Franks, Richard Bertrand, Brian Hearne, Vincent Clarke, Malcolm Jackson, Peter Patzwald, Peter Biddle, Gerald Goodinson, John Green, Noel Wootton, Leisa Stewart, Terry Hayes, Melvyn Bundy, Neil Tucker, Vicki Turner, Noel Lavender, Colin Aitken, Ivan Verrall, Leslie Harvey, Lorraine Rowley, Barry Purdie, John Wilce, Barry McLennan, Anthony Fleming, Garry Laurie, Gregory Donaldson, Michael Smith, Geoffrey Bannerman, Nigel Macey, Daniel Flohr, Coral Daly, John Clough, John McCafferty, Rodney McCafferty, Kenneth McCafferty, Valma Flohr, Remy Giebeler, Gregory Oliveiro, Walter Emerson, Raymond George, Leslie Miers, Murray Jackson, David Marsden, John Fett, Janice Emerson, Dennis Densley, Edward Bignell, Stephen Cooper, Thomas Craig, Keith McKee, Noel Wooler, Angela James, Donald Ford, Brian Hayes, Adrian Nickols, Malcolm Williams, Milton Bielby, Alan Fink, Warwick Green, Leslie James, Bryce Rossington, Norman Wallace, Claude Mans, John Lacey, Helen Sutton, Sandra Sutton, Michael Harvey, Ashley Vidler, Shane Barbelor, Neal McDonald, Neil Laherty, Ronald Rohlf, Kenneth Muir, Gordon Marshall, Terence Richards, Brian McDougall, Terrence Clifford, Trevor Neal, Kevin Caffery, Kay Lee, Susan King, Melinda Bayley, Gregory Tetzloff, Rodney Chaffey, Robert Cunningham, Robert Gorle, Brian Henderson, Brian Hofmeier, Robyn Lloyd, Arnold McNicol, Victor Stevens, Timothy Johnes, Ian Graham, Reginald Purvor, Robin Lowther, Chris Yates, Raymond Medlin, Kimble Mayers, Donald Neaton, David Sauer, Ann Thompson, Sidney Schilling, Susan Swindale, Brian Carige, Gary Barnes, Christopher Carsas, Leonard Coombs, Phillip Finch, Leonard Fletcher, John Fletcher, William Hooper, Arthur Trevanion, Peter Smith, Alan

Ward, Neville Horan, Harold Grieshaber, John Ashwell, Thomas Cheers, Alan Maunder, Kevin Sullivan, John Fett, Keith Skinner, Coral Padget, John Wilson, Craig Wilson, James Buckley, David Darby, Neil Roberts, Mark Tobin, Ian Eiser, James Carr, Neville Dale, Peter Gleeson, Jack McCusker, Glen McMillan, Brian Richardson, Lyle Seng and Ross Baxter.

As well as the staff names, the front page of the feature included historic photographs ranging from a group on a Highway Holiday to me swinging a golf club superimposed against the Great Wall of China. It may not have been authentic but it certainly got the tongues wagging about McCafferty's.

Chapter 18

Melbourne and Townsville

'On many occasions Jack McCafferty would run out to a coach and place folding chairs in the aisle to accommodate extra passengers.

On the run to Rockhampton we used to carry half a dozen folding chairs. When we reached Wandoan there could be four seats left and ten people waiting for the coach. There was no such thing as a reservation – we just got the people on board the best way we could.'

GARY BARNES

When Toowoomba, with an estimated population of 75,940, celebrated its 125th anniversary in 1985 we began advertising 'McCafferty's – Queensland's Own Safety Conscious Coachline. Leave the worry, the tension, the escalating costs and the hassles of road motoring to us.

'Our drivers are always refreshed because we won't expect them to sleep on the back seat. In fact, we pay big money to rest our drivers in motels for YOUR safety. Over 45 years experience. You're in Good Hands.'

Despite my protests, staff always arrange a special celebration for my birthday. In 1982, a new Denning coach was added to the fleet with the insignia on front reading 'J.F. McCafferty', and with the personalised number plates 'JFM42'.

I wrote in the next staff newsletter, 'Thanks fellows, a nice thought, but one thing? Do I still have to pay for it?'

Our travel office manager Margie Goltz started with our company in January 1983, working in the accounts department at the Toowoomba Head Office.

This department was staffed by 12 who handled agents sales returns, as well as debtors and creditors.

After a short period Margie transferred to the payroll department. This was a very responsible task as it entailed handling large amounts of cash.

Margie recalls those days:

> *'There were 190 employees on the payroll when I started in this department. Times have certainly changed since then. I remember having to count all the cash delivered from the bank and distribute into pay envelopes. Sometimes this could cause frustration, as if we would have cash left over this meant that an error had been made and all payslips had to be rechecked.'*

After two years in the payroll department Margie began relief work in our Travel Centre. There were three Travel Centres, located at Toowoomba Terminal, Clifford Gardens Shopping Centre and Gatton.

To be a fully-accredited member of the International Airlines Transport Association (IATA), it was necessary to reach a certain target in airline books.

It took McCafferty's Travel only a few years to gain IATA accreditation, which enabled our company to issue overseas airline tickets. Aircraft were also chartered to take groups to Palm Island, Long Island on the Barrier Reef and to Central Australia and the Ord River.

We received the Sitmar Australia Wide Award in 1984/1985 for the largest sales of any travel agency in Australia and the top country sales. Our Toowoomba-based company had become the true specialist in cruises, offering a variety of cruises to popular destinations in the South Pacific and around the world.

I took 160 people including the entire Toowoomba City Council and other members of Darling Downs councils to New Zealand.

The Toowoomba Travel Office expanded again and this time it moved across the street to larger premises on the northern side of Margaret Street. They were formerly occupied by Bill Klaassen's Flying Dutchman Restaurant, and years earlier it had been Charlie Ivory's Billiard Saloon. I needed a higher profile to make the Toowoomba public more aware of travel opportunities – and I got it.

As mentioned earlier, the interior of the Toowoomba travel office had been decorated to look like the interior of a Boeing 747 Jumbo aircraft. The kerb-front travel office was fully accredited by IATA and handled all travel and tour bookings on an Australia-wide and world-wide basis. Sales staff had individual desks at which clients discussed their needs and made their bookings.

In 1981, our company was promoting group tours to USA, Japan, Britain, Greece and China.

Truckies refer to Queensland passengers travelling on our coaches through to Melbourne as 'Grasshoppers'. They travel through the night from Toowoomba heading south for Sydney, Canberra and Melbourne.

According to some truckies our passengers hop on the coaches in the middle of the night, enter service station restaurants and devour everything in sight.

A Toowoomba writer travelled to Melbourne on McCafferty's coach with the 'Grasshoppers' to check out the story. At the time there was a special fare of $50 Toowoomba to Melbourne. This is how the writer recorded the trip:

'The grasshopper story is not quite true and the passengers have as many laughs as the truckies.

Travelling by coach takes a lot of the hassle out of the long journey south and only the driver (sorry, coach captain) worries about tyre pressures and fuel.

One young fellow on board was leaving Toowoomba hoping to find a job in Wollongong.

There was a Toowoomba bank officer accompanying his father-in-law to an army reunion in Queanbeyan, and among the luggage in the hold was a large double box containing a wedding cake, marked with arrows "this way up", and destined for an address in Torrens, Canberra.

At Scone, we stopped while the coach captain helped change a flat tyre delaying a coach of a different line.

In cold Glen Innes, at one in the morning, pineapples were selling at $1.95 apiece, lettuces 80c, and tomatoes were $1.90 a kg.

The no-eating on the coach rule was in force so we didn't buy.

Toasted ham sandwiches and coffee for two cost $3.60 and there was a later stop at Doyalson, where we didn't really feel like eating a big meal. We chose a child's serve of egg, bacon, tomato, toast and tea with a bill for two costing $4.50.

Then, it was into Sydney with the view of the "coat hanger" and Joan Sutherland's place of special interest, and on into Kings Cross.

Three hours before the next stage to Canberra, Wagga Wagga and Melbourne gave us time to make the walk down to the fountain.

It wasn't night, but the weirdos were there just the same.

Of all ages, and of indistinguishable sex, they paraded the street.

Clothes ranged from tiger-skin leotards to skimpy mini-skirts.

There was one particular girl, about 20, wearing a lilac top and blue pants and with long blonde hair. Only when she turned her head and I smiled did I realise there was nothing to smile at. There was no expression in her sunken eyes. She was bombed out of her mind.

It was good to get back to the terminal and board the coach. Then, we sat back and marvelled at the coach captain battling the traffic along crowded Parramatta Road. The journey from Brisbane to Melbourne, which included numerous stops, took 28 hours.'

Our Sydney office was under stress again in May 1985, with the price-cutting war intensifying and affecting passengers travelling between Brisbane and Sydney.

McCafferty's single fare was $30, while our main competitor was offering seats for $25 with $20 stand-by.

With a wage increase of about $10 a week, and excessive increases in fuel costs from 36c to 40c a litre (approx 30%), there was no way we could carry on without cutting services.

Even with 40 passengers at $30 each, less agent's commission, it left the company with a $25 net fare. The gross return of $960 for a single journey of 640 miles – approximately $1.50 a mile, was a ridiculous return for a coach worth $250,000.

If there were only 30 passengers, the trip would result in a loss. Eventually, the problem was sorted out and we increased our share of the market.

Competition from VIP Express by way of the $25 fare from Brisbane to Sydney really stirred things up and encouraged a lot of people to travel by coach with the cheaper fares. McCafferty's were able to weather the storm, but only just, and when VIP folded, fares returned to a sensible level of up to $45 single.

Ann Barnes (née Harber) had already worked for nearly 10 years in Toowoomba before she joined us. She had been used to the large carpeted office of the Federal Member for Groom, Mr Tom McVeigh, before she moved to Townsville with her husband, Gary, who had been appointed McCafferty's North Queensland manager. She wasn't quite prepared for the heat and the change of office.

Now, more than 10 years down the track, her voice fills with laughter as she recalls the days when McCafferty's Townsville terminal was a tiny shop front in the Cat & Fiddle Arcade, with coaches loading on the footpath.

As there was no carpet on the floor, she and Gary obtained a piece of carpet from a vehicle and placed it at the entrance. They stuck up posters and the only phone was a small one on the wall.

Ann, who now enjoys an airconditioned office, reflects here on those first days:

'We took $40 the first day, and $70 the next and thought we were doing great. Then Gary went away on a trip – he had to do the "repping" of the travel agents to let them know that McCafferty's were now in North Queensland – and I was left to handle the office myself. I had never had any training and when Rockhampton driver Tom Craig arrived with the first service and handed me a passenger manifest I asked him what I had to do with it.

He told me that he didn't know but hopefully I'd find out by the time he'd parked the bus.

This was before the advent of computers and manifests were sheets and sheets of paper carrying passengers' names and destinations.

Firstly, every passenger's name had to be written on a card with a seat number and then the information was transferred to the Daily Service Records (DSR) pad. Copies had to be duplicated and forwarded by bus to onward destinations.

At times the manifest would have up to 140 passengers being carried in stages on the same coach travelling from Townsville to Brisbane and the information could be five days old before all the paperwork matched up.

Today, using the company's computer system, it matters little if say seat number one of the coach is used by five different passengers travelling between Townsville and Brisbane. The press of a button on the keyboard provides up-dates of seating for each stage of the journey.'

Seatbelts are now installed on new coaches, but in the early days the regulations were not so strict on carrying passengers in seats attached to the floor.

Gary Barnes, who started with McCafferty's on October 8, 1972, and gained driving experience out of the Toowoomba terminal before moving to Townsville, takes up the story:

'One memorable trip was on one of the early Gold Coast runs using a 49-seater coach. By the time we reached Labrador on the way home to Toowoomba, the number of passengers had increased to 65 and they were sitting everywhere, on the seat armrests and down the aisle.

Unfortunately, the coach broke down and another coach operator, Clarrie Skennar, stopped to assist. He took one look at the crowd on board and took off saying, "I don't think I can help you".

> *Eventually, a 45-seater coach was obtained from Brisbane. The passengers crammed inside and the coach made its way along the highway towards Toowoomba.*
>
> *It was when we were crawling up to the top of the Toowoomba Range with our heavy load of humans that I saw a police car waiting at the side of the road. "Oh heck, here we go," I thought and then a woman came down the aisle and asked me to stop. She explained that her husband was waiting to pick her up in his police car.'*

Gary and Ann had moved furniture into their small office and with the furniture came the kids – Kelli-Ann aged four and Natalie two. As the Barnes family didn't have close friends in Townsville they had no babysitter and so the children used to camp under the desk. Today, if you look underneath Ann's immaculate desk top there are some very youthful drawings.

A little later, the children took a great interest in the coach traffic and they were fascinated by an opposition coach company (Deluxe) whose drivers would roar past McCafferty's office. Natalie coined her own saying in answer to the noise: 'Hope your wheel falls off Deluxe'.

When I visited Townsville, young Natalie became an instant friend and she would walk up the street holding my hand. As a Deluxe coach went noisily past, she repeated her saying. I thought it was a great joke.

The day Deluxe went out of business, I rang up the Townsville office with a special message: 'Tell Natalie that the wheels just fell off'.

The demise of Deluxe Coachlines, which went into receivership in 1990, led to record bookings for McCafferty's.

We handled 10,500 passengers in one week, exceeding bookings for any week in the 50-year history of the company. The figures were unmatched even during the previous year's pilots' dispute or throughout Expo 88.

The increase in bookings was directly attributed to the demise of Deluxe Coachlines. Deluxe had been our main competitor and they carried the same volume of traffic in Queensland that we carried.

Later, we were able to purchase a purpose-built maintenance workshop in Duncan Street, West End, Brisbane, formerly owned by Deluxe. Our company paid $1.1 million at auction for the workshop, and Tony described the figure as a 'bargain price'. We were now forging ahead in Brisbane and North Queensland.

Hundreds of people lost their jobs and many coaches were thrown onto the market when Deluxe 'folded up'. The company,

Clarrie Skennar (left) and Jack McCafferty when McCafferty's took over Skennars operations on the Brisbane/Toowoomba/Roma and Charleville route and all their Margaret Street terminal equipment in March 1992.

with good equipment, had provided a fine service but had grown too quickly.

The industry also witnessed the demise of a number of other coach operators during this period. They included VIP, Sunliner, Greyhound, Pioneer, Casino 99, Trans City, Aussie Express, Intertour, Bus Australia and Skennars.

It was sad to see what happened to the famous Pioneer Services originally commenced by Reg Ansett. They got into financial difficulties and Greyhound took them over, and then found themselves in a similar situation. Although the names of Greyhound and Pioneer are still used, the present company is in no way connected with the original operators – except by name only.

Gary Barnes, who first arrived at Townsville on New Year's Day 1985, said problems really began when, by some error, his home phone number appeared in the Townsville telephone directory.

From then onwards he and his wife Ann got calls almost hourly throughout the night.

One of the worst calls was from a shiftworker who woke Ann up at 2 a.m. to book his holiday three weeks ahead.

On another occasion, Gary answered the phone at 2.30 a.m. to find an irate woman who complained that a coach had pushed her car off the road near Bowen.

Gary apologised for what had happened and then asked her where the incident had occurred and at what time. When she answered he explained that McCafferty's didn't have a coach running at that time.

She snapped back, 'No, no, I know it wasn't McCafferty's, it was some other bus but I just had to ring someone and yours was the only after hours number I could find in the phone book.'

On another occasion, a man flagged down a McCafferty's coach and paid for his ticket out of a four-gallon drum of money. It turned out that the passenger had just robbed a pub. Coach personnel at Townsville and Rockhampton combined their resources and the robber was detained while still seated on the coach at Gympie.

Crocodile stories abound in north Queensland and in the past McCafferty's have been involved, as Gary explains:

'There was the time that our Townsville terminal received a call to help return a stolen crocodile.

The two-metre croc had been taken from the Common in Townsville and dumped in a park at Hughenden.

A crocodile comes off the coach. Kelli and Natalie Barnes, of Townsville, whose parents Gary and Ann both work for McCafferty's, are pictured with the croc and a Wildlife Officer.

The Hughenden Police Sergeant rang McCafferty's and said it would be better if the reptile could be returned by coach to Townsville.

National Parks and Wildlife officers had secured the crocodile and he was in a bag when we arrived. We placed him in the aisle of the coach and drove speedily back to Townsville.

On another occasion a coach travelling from Rockhampton to Brisbane was carrying a most unwelcome passenger. Driver Alan Dagg was approached by one of the passengers who had great difficulty telling him that a snake had just climbed along the back of the passenger's seat.

The driver stopped the coach, opened the doors, and much to the relief of all passengers and Alan, the snake slid off the coach unaided.

Dogs are one kind of animal which are not allowed on board coaches – unless of course they are guide dogs for the blind or the hearing impaired.

During a trip north from Rockhampton, when the coach driver stopped to drop off freight near St Lawrence, he glanced up at the coach windows to see a dog looking down at him. The animal had been smuggled on board and then let out of a bag. He was taken off the seat and placed in a box in the luggage bay.'

Perhaps our oldest traveller to use a seat on a McCafferty's coach was Mr John Baker, aged 100, who travelled from Townsville to Mt Isa in the early 1990s. He travelled with his daughter and both were given free tickets and they had a great time in Mt Isa, where they were given an underground tour and Mr Baker was guest of honour.

Then our Townsville counter staff got another three passengers but they were not so prestigious.

Apparently, their ship had docked at Bowen and the three arrived at the counter in Townsville speaking little English but stressing that they wanted to see 'a big beach'.

Counter staff directed them to the local beach 'The Strand', but they returned a little later, saying 'big beach'.

Did they mean Airlie Beach, Surfers Paradise? However, when someone mentioned 'Bondi', there was a shout of recognition and they each paid their $120 fare and boarded a coach bound for Sydney.

Later, a Bowen newspaper arrived at the Townsville terminal and Gary Barnes noticed a story on three missing seamen who had jumped ship. He rang the police and the three were met by Customs officers on arrival in Sydney. They didn't have much time to see their 'big beach', which could have meant our famous 'coat hanger'.

Most travellers out of Townsville are locals, but slowly but surely the backpacker market is advancing. In the industry we refer to backpackers as 'FITS', Fully Independent Travellers.

Backpackers from across the globe rest in the Townsville terminal alongside signs that offer them the hire of a bicycle for $8 a day, or $2 an hour, and accommodation for $9 a night with a free city tour thrown in.

The terminal is in the Townsville Transit Centre, a privately owned establishment situated on the south-side of the city. It houses all express coach operators, and offers convenience to the travelling public, with backpacker accommodation on the second floor and shops and cafeteria on the ground floor. It's an easy walk over the river into the city heart.

According to Ann and Gary Barnes, today's backpackers watch every cent and only a few take advantage of the larger meals in the terminal's cafeteria, which at 1994 prices included roast chicken with salad and chips for $7.20, whole roast chickens $6.70 and 'Today's Special' Spaghetti Bolognaise $6.20.

Most backpackers travelling in north Queensland come from Europe and they don't like spending five cents more than they have to and have been known to ask at the cafeteria for hot water to recycle a teabag.

The backpacker passenger ticket market really kicked off about 10 years ago. It caused McCafferty's to rethink our original family-oriented bus company. It has seen the development and expansion of unlimited stop tickets.

In the early days, the backpackers were often looked down upon, as Gary explains:

> *'There was a joke going around when we first opened in the North. The opposition would carry the backpacks and we would carry the suitcases. We considered we were "up market and carrying real people".*
>
> *Today, the backpackers line up at our counter. They are carrying everything on their backs with billycans and knives sticking out of their packs.*
>
> *One morning, a young woman attending our counter couldn't lift the backpack belonging to a male backpacker. I asked the man, "What is inside?" "Food, just food," he replied.*
>
> *When an up-market backpackers' place opened in Townsville a couple of years ago it introduced very nice cutlery. Within a week all the cutlery had walked off down the road.*

> *On another occasion, Ann noticed a backpacker making his way down the street with a distinctive Northern Territory number plate hanging from his backpack.*
> *The manager at the Townsville Transit Centre had just lost one of the personalised plates off his Nissan Patrol.'*

A Finnish backpacker at Townsville said he had found out about our coach company before leaving for Australia. He said backpackers usually followed handbooks one was produced in England and the other in the United States. He had read about McCafferty's in the English publication and was delighted when he checked in at Melbourne and found that he could travel all the way to Cairns with five stopovers and for such a small cost.

Staff at Townsville and other terminals treat backpackers with respect, as Ann Barnes records:

> *'We have met some well-educated people among the backpackers who choose the sort of holiday they want.*
> *There have been some really nice ones. Seven or eight years ago they were a rough sort of backpacker. Now, they seem to be a far better type with girls teaming up to travel together and there are also lots of individuals.'*

Gary and Ann Barnes have seen great changes in the industry over the years and coach passengers today are more experienced. Among them are some really great people. There's much laughter among staff on McCafferty's counter at Townsville and the good humour extends to the lines of customers.

McCafferty's terminal at Townsville handled 1,080 people on an Easter Thursday without any hassle whatsoever. There are 35 drivers and 10 office personnel, and the terminal has five services a day each way between Brisbane and Cairns, two others serving the west in and out, and on Thursdays an extra service to Belyando.

Cruise ships, including the *Fairstar*, are now regular visitors to Townsville and day charters to Charters Towers are becoming increasingly popular. We also keep busy with charters all over the place.

McCafferty's have grown so large in recent years that it is increasingly hard for staff to know each other on a personal basis. It was much simpler in the early years. Now when I pay a visit to terminals in Townsville and other centres some drivers and staff are on shift work and it's impractical for everyone to gather together at the one time.

Townsville is forging ahead and Gary outlines some of the reasons for our success in the tropics:

'If anyone asks about the success of our operations in Townsville, I would say the number one factor is Jack McCafferty. The boss has done his homework and he is well able to read the industry and people.

McCafferty's is a caring sort of company, a family-oriented company, and this rubs off on staff in general. I think it is nice to be able to pick up the phone and talk to the boss if you have a problem, and not have to wait for memos to be processed or to deal with somebody at third-hand. If he says "No", it means "No".

It's amazing this far north that so many people come to the counter and ask about Jack McCafferty and say they know him personally.

People look at McCafferty's and see a company which is good, reliable and solid. A lot of other operators have flashed into the forum only to disappear. Over the years, McCafferty's has been a quiet achiever plodding along providing a service which people want.'

Manager at Townsville, Gary Barnes with his wife Ann and their daughters Kelli and Natalie in 1994.

When Gary and Ann started in Townsville 10 years ago, our opposition companies were buying 20 and 25 coaches a year. McCafferty's slowly eroded the competition and now most of the other companies have gone and McCafferty's are number one.

We have created a future in catering essentially for local people and we have worked out just where people in one town have an affinity with those in another and there's a great need for efficient transport between such towns.

Ayr and Ingham residents have a close affiliation with people in Bundaberg and there are many people travelling between Townsville and Toowoomba.

Today, people can travel by car, rail, airline or coach. Smaller towns like Innisfail, Ingham, Ayr, Bowen and Proserpine are well served by McCafferty's. They are great little towns and very prosperous places.

Among the regular passengers travelling between Townsville and Bundaberg is an architect who prefers a seat on the night service. He enjoys having a good sleep and being refreshed for his work in both centres. "I wouldn't travel any other way," he told Gary.

There are also a lot of people from the coal mines as well as army personnel and their families travelling through the Townsville terminal.

For McCafferty's there's money in short-haul sections and on occasions no fewer than 130 or more passengers have been booked in stages on the same 45-seater coach travelling from Mackay to Cairns.

Freight too is increasing all the time, but there's one period in Townsville when staff would rather be on holiday. It's from the middle of November till Christmas Day and known locally as 'Mango Madness'. Gary could see the potential for mango freight when he first arrived in Townsville. For the record he tells what happened:

> *'Some years ago, I suggested that McCafferty's should move into the mango freight market to help people in Townsville send boxes of mangoes to their friends down south.*
>
> *The service was advertised as "Mango Magic", and in one year the freight bill for mangoes out of Townsville, travelling in the freight compartments on McCafferty's coaches, totalled $50,000.*
>
> *As well as being excellent Christmas presents, the mangoes also pay the bills for some locals who have a mango tree in the back garden. They often call in pickers to harvest the crop and the proceeds from the sale of the fruit pay their rates.'*

Gary Barnes hand picks his drivers. He said to be successful an applicant needs to be a safe driver with a good track record and must be responsible behind the wheel. Then he should also have a pleasant personality and be good at public relations.

"Quite often we get good drivers who can't really handle people," he said.

Gary and Ann, who married in 1976, form a great partnership in the coach and travel industry. Ann has strong views on travel offices:

> *'In Townsville, we hope that the image people get when they contact our office is that they would want to travel with us. We try hard to be friendly and we let people know that we are genuinely interested in them.*
>
> *We follow the boss's example by assisting the public. If a person has a genuine problem, even if you can't help them you should try to understand their situation and take an interest in that person.'*

Gary Barnes has little time to think of the old days, but his office is lined with photographs of coaches travelling through dusty and muddy roads. He continues the story:

> *'During one trip through floodwaters at Biloela, the Don River had burst its banks and our coach got through with the bow wave of the water half-way up the windscreen.*
>
> *I used to go on 49 and 52-day tours around Australia, but it was on a smaller 14-day tour to the Barossa Valley that I lost a passenger in unusual circumstances.*
>
> *On the last day of the tour we were at Port Macquarie and heading home to Toowoomba with about 28 passengers. We stopped at the Big Banana in Coffs Harbour, and by now all the passengers were used to returning to the bus on time.*
>
> *We climbed back on board and I called out "Everyone here?". Voices called back, "Yes, take it away Gary".*
>
> *Then ten kilometres up the road, a fellow walked down the aisle and said, "Gary, I think you've left my wife behind".*
>
> *When I asked him jovially if he wanted me to return and pick her up or keep on driving he replied, "I suppose we'd better go back and get her".'*
>
> *Fifteen minutes later she was back on board and she was ropeable. I told her not to take it out on me but on her old man. He'd been sitting alongside her throughout the trip – that was until Coffs Harbour.*
>
> *I have driven with a number of Members of Parliament as passengers on McCafferty's coaches, including Tom Burns and Ed Casey.*

> *In the early days, I used to do the Toowoomba to Rockhampton run six days a week and have the Sunday off in Rockhampton. But it never seemed like a day off. The boss would ring up and say "While you're in Rocky give that coach a greasing and a wash, and take it out to where people will see it".'*

Gary estimated that for 32 weeks out of 52 he was away on tours. Now, he and Ann are together 24 hours a day, and the Townsville terminal is open 19 hours a day, starting at 5.30 a.m.

How entertainment for the public using coaches has changed over the years is outlined here by Gary:

> 'I love the coaches and the industry and it's in my interest to make sure our terminal is running properly. Whenever a new coach comes into the yard I like to get behind the wheel, but my favourite is still the Landseer.
>
> The other day I came across an old Bingo set which I used on the round Australia tours. Those were the days when we used to play all sorts of games to keep passengers amused and occupied on long stretches of highway. We'd have talent quests and skittles down the aisle using a ball to knock over cans.
>
> Today, drivers just put on a video and hope that the passengers will be entertained.
>
> Each coach carries two videos which are selected by a company in Brisbane as being suitable for family audiences.'

Watching videos night after night may not be everyone's cup of tea, but sometimes in the past it was necessary as Ann points out:

> 'When videos were first introduced on coaches, I would go to the local video shop and take out a selection. Then, Gary and I would sit up late into the night to make sure that the videos didn't have explicit language and were all right for family viewing.
>
> We got more sleep when the video library opened in Brisbane and guaranteed that the videos supplied had all been approved for general exhibition.'

When you're sitting back watching a video on a coach today, spare a thought for the terminal managers and their families, who had to sit through dozens of videos in the early days to select ones suitable for family viewing.

But even today the choice is not easy, although equipment has improved since the first video monitor was installed in coach No. 307 in February 1988.

On one Sydney to Melbourne coach, a traveller was very disappointed when he asked for a one-day cricket match to be screened during the journey and the driver couldn't oblige.

On another trip, a passenger complained that the film *On Golden Pond* was pornographic, although it had been passed as suitable for general exhibition.

The most popular videos are westerns and good comedies, but most drivers agree that the younger passengers will watch almost anything.

The videos help passengers to pass the time but they can be a nuisance to the drivers. On rainy nights, drivers on some coaches, get a reflection on the windscreen of the interior of the coach behind them. Drivers won't put them on in these conditions.

As well as videos, our coaches are equipped with tape decks and the drivers usually provide their own tapes. Gary Barnes prefers country and western music but admits that it is not to every passenger's taste and he usually takes along a selection of instrumental music.

The aim is to keep the volume under control so that it doesn't annoy the passengers.

The Hervey Bay-Pialba area became included on the Brisbane-Rockhampton service, and when Stewart & Sons, Bundaberg, opened a coach terminal and restaurant in mid-1985 we were the first operator to start using these facilities.

In 1985, we advertised Dreamworld Tours and on our new Brisbane service the chance to win a return trip for two to Singapore flying Singapore Airlines.

Our company was also conducting Round Australia Tours, 50 days and 49 nights (including 87 meals) ex Brisbane and Sydney from $3,640 twin share. It was described as 'A leisurely holiday seeing the best of Australia. From Sydney and Brisbane to Cairns, then across to Karumba and the Gulf Country. Thence to Alice Springs and Ayers Rock, Kakadu, Darwin, Lake Argyle and Broome. Across the Nullarbor to Adelaide, Mt Gambier, Melbourne, Canberra and back to Sydney and Brisbane'.

The 1980s also saw more spectacular expansion in long-distance express services. More coaches were acquired and more drivers employed.

We had 70 buses in 1985 and our workforce totalled 200. A licence was granted from Brisbane to Cairns with two services daily each way, and today five services a day each way operate very successfully.

I have a saying about the service industry I love so much. It's "If you're in business, and particularly the service business, you should have enough confidence to trade under your own name."

And that's the case with my own company – after all, the name is seen right around Australia every day of the week.

When I seized the opportunity to move into servicing the too often forgotten outback areas some critics said even I would not be able to provide a reliable service to the bush and make a bob or two. Dogged determination won out, and when the coaches 'went bush' for the first time the country was put in touch with the city on a regular and reliable basis.

Our next move was for a service to run from Brisbane through Toowoomba to Melbourne via the Newell Highway.

In May, 1985, we were advertising an all inclusive two-day tour of the Gold Coast for $49. It included a visit to the newly opened Paradise Centre and a cruise on the waterways as well as a visit to the Seagulls Entertainment Complex. The second day included experiencing 'One of the most beautiful days of your life at Dreamworld'.

McCafferty's were already well established on the Gold Coast and the Metrolink service from Toowoomba to Ipswich was proving popular with the travelling public. Up to 125 services were operating weekly and a similar trend was showing on the Brisbane/Beenleigh/Gold Coast service.

We were operating both these services in conjunction with the Queensland Railway electric city train system.

Chapter 19

Giving the passengers a better deal

(1986-1990)

'On one occasion Jack boarded the coach I was driving and said in a loud voice: "Guess what I've just done. I've bought 200 tickets for Johnny Cash down in Sydney."

I looked skywards and thought, "He's flipped his lid." But, then Jack put a couple of adverts on Channel 10 and he sold every ticket.'

TONY McCAFFERTY, GENERAL MANAGER

The Brisbane terminal was relocated into the modern Roma Street Transit Centre in 1986. Specially built for all long-distance coach services, and both intrastate and interstate rail services, it was one of the most progressive moves ever made in the long-distance coach industry.

In 1986, I announced that we would spend $1 million on improving services for coach travellers in and out of the Central Queensland area. My company had enjoyed having a presence in Rockhampton since 1972.

McCafferty's were building two luxury coach terminals, one in Rockhampton and one in Emerald. Both would be air-conditioned and the Rockhampton terminal would have a snack bar, and Emerald would have a lounge area.

Big Al's, on the corner of Brown and Linnett Streets, would undergo about $500,000 worth of remodelling for the Rockhampton terminal.

McCafferty's old premises in Rockhampton were sold to Keppel Island Cruises, but the terminal would still be available for

231

Christmas 1986 – from the left: Jack McCafferty, Ken McCafferty, Mick Manteit, Ron Goodenough, Coral Probst (née Tame), Otto Fittkau, Clive Fletcher, Steve Cooper, Bill Fett, Les Miera, Kay McCafferty, Rod McCafferty, Jack Warnecke and Ken Toombes.

passengers wanting to be picked up or dropped off on that side of town.

Other features of the upgrading were express services and Australia-wide tours.

I told the *Morning Bulletin* (Rockhampton) that more Australians were wanting to see their own country before they went overseas and McCafferty's coaches would provide for this with the launching of new tours throughout Australia

A daily service each way from Brisbane to Melbourne via the Newell Highway began in 1987. Three years later, our company moved into 205 Victoria Street, West Melbourne, and coaches were arriving and departing at the Spencer Street Coach Terminal. McCafferty's Melbourne Terminal was officially opened in 1989.

When the Wrest Point Casino opened in Tasmania, we organised visits to the Melbourne Cup and then flew patrons to the casino on day trips from Melbourne for around $200 per person.

Tony McCafferty bought a $2 casket ticket in January 1986. He was later watching an evening TV news program when he heard his name read as the winner of the $50,000 major prize.

He then had a sleepless night because although he goes by the name Tony, his real first name is John so he wasn't certain that he'd won the prize until he made inquiries on the next day.

He had just moved to a new house and the prize helped pay for home improvements.

Establishing new services sometimes meets opposition as a former staff member pointed out:

'When Jack started the inland route to Rockhampton some of us thought he was crackers.

Only two men and a dog would want to travel, but it was at a time when they were pulling up the railway lines, and he might have picked up the vibes.

Jack McCafferty's brain is going the whole time. He has to be down at the terminal to know what is going on, who is going on the coach and what kind of customers are travelling.

In Brisbane, it's amazing the number of people who come in wanting a discount or a refund and they say: "I know Jack McCafferty and if you don't do the right thing I'll dob you in."

Quite often they don't realise that they may be speaking to other members of the McCafferty family.

At the Brisbane Transit Centre, as well as running coaches to Sydney, Cairns, Gold Coast and Toowoomba, McCafferty's Terminal provides a wide range of other services, including courtesy coaches for Tangalooma Island Resort, and the transfer of visitors from Brisbane Airport to various hotels and motels in the city and the coastal areas.

At nearby West End, a contract cleaner cleans 14 coaches every day, ensuring that McCafferty's high standards are maintained at all times.

There is a great deal of loyalty among McCafferty's staff.

People feel they are working for Jack. He is not aloof or remote from others. He makes it his business to know their first names, and they feel that they are part of the family.

Jack goes round most of the staff socials, and he puts in an appearance. People feel they are worth something because he turns up at the show.

When they brought in the $17^{1}/_{2}$ percent loading for holiday pay, Jack thought it very unfair and said, "That's it, no more Christmas parties unless the staff pay for them themselves." And, I believe, that's how it remains today.'

Drivers are often away from home at Christmas and this causes problems, as former driver Mick Manteit explains:

'I was often away for six weeks over Christmas. In December, Jack would have me working the southern end of tours in Sydney, and when I headed back to Toowoomba I would meet another coach say

at Warwick and we'd swap driver's seats and in no time at all I'd be back in Sydney.

I never had a Christmas home for 11 years.

My wife and mother-in-law complained and asked me if there was anyone else who could work over Christmas.

Finally, I actually arrived home for Christmas and everyone was so pleased. Everything went well, until I was called out on Christmas Day to do a trip to the Bunya Mountains. I didn't get home until 11 o'clock that night and any popularity I had enjoyed earlier had disappeared.'

I was invited back to the Toowoomba City Council in 1986 as one of 14 former aldermen who received medallions as a token of appreciation of their service to the city. The function was recorded in *The Chronicle* (Toowoomba):

'At a function where the primary purpose was to recognise the community's debt to former council members, Mr McCafferty turned things around with his generous praise for the present Mayor (Ald. Clive Berghofer) and aldermen.

"In view of the time and effort you put into civic affairs, there is small recompense," he said. "When you compare Toowoomba with some of the other cities of Queensland, you are certainly underpaid and over-worked, and no doubt about that".'

Today, the name McCafferty is perpetuated around our company's home city – Toowoomba. There's McCafferty Park in Tourist Road, the main route to Picnic Point, where I operated my very first bus. McCafferty Park was opened in 1964, when the park amenities were handed over to the city by the East Toowoomba Jaycees. The park's name is featured on a plaque set in a basalt wall, in front of a free-form concrete playground structure called 'The Monster'.

There is also McCafferty Street on the western side of Toowoomba.

I was proud to be named as a Queenslander of the Year Finalist in 1988. The nomination was for my contribution to the development of Toowoomba and my work in introducing regular transport to people of the outback and Central Queensland. As Mayor of Toowoomba for nine years I had actively promoted the city's general development and tourism.

In 1987, the company installed a $1 million computerised passenger booking system, and in 12 months we had a 40 per cent increase in revenue. Tony McCafferty explains:

A Denning Landseer coach.

'While new coach services contributed to the increase most of it came about as a direct result of the new computer system.

When the new Canon equipment, installed by Matrix Office Systems, of Toowoomba, began operating in October 1987, the benefits were immediate with bookings being handled in seconds and an immediate overview of all reservations available country-wide.

The system has been described as "the biggest local area network multi-user in the world".

Bookings were being received at the rate of 1,500 a day and these also included multiple reservations for couples and families as well as return journeys.

A total reservations staff of 10 manned the terminal between 4 a.m. and 9.30 p.m. every day to take bookings from members of the. public and from agents throughout the Eastern states.'

The two new A200SX processors were joined by a third machine. All information relating to reservations was stored on these machines and it took just a few seconds for an operator to display details of each booking, which could be traced either by the name of the passenger or by the booking number.

The system searched out all bookings made in a certain surname and displayed them alphabetically according to the Christian name initial.

Bookings could also be traced from other directions such as departure point and destination, the date and the route number.

Bookings were now being made from our 54 computer terminals stretching from Cairns to Melbourne, and the details entered from these points were assimilated almost instantaneously.

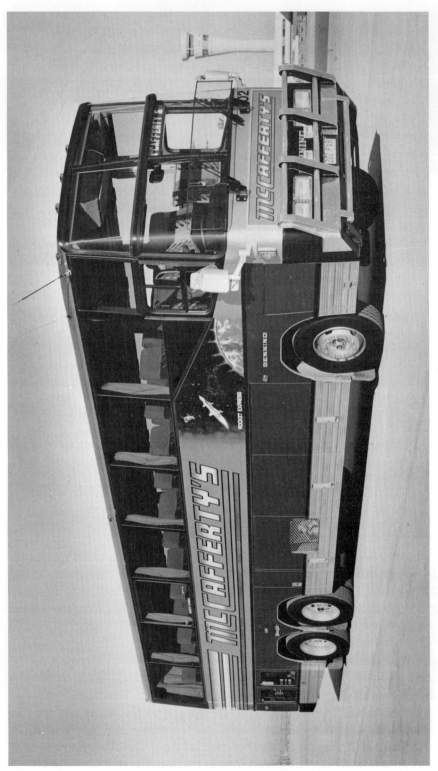

A high-deck coach in 1988.

The system would not accept further bookings for a coach that was already full, just as it would not accept a multiple booking if the number of available seats was not enough.

The three processors, which each provided full access to the system should the others be closed down temporarily, also stored details of bookkeeping and accounting and allowed a complete overview of operations, from the spare parts inventory to where each coach was at any time.

It became possible to see which coaches were using more oil or fuel than others, indicating the need for repair or servicing and, on the financial side, running costs were always available.

The system monitored and adjusted tables of figures, which provided on-going information such as the cost of fuel per kilometre or how much the cost of a driver was per kilometre. It was then possible to obtain the average cost per coach per kilometre and to make accurate cash-flow projections.

Included in the accounting system were payroll details, as well as those of debtors, creditors and the stock of spare parts at the Taylor Street workshop in Toowoomba, where initially $1,000,000 worth of spare parts were carried.

It became possible to produce graphs in colour to illustrate different figures and compare aspects of the business.

Around 1,200 agents were also serviced through the system and kept supplied with timetables and tickets.

In 1988 on the domestic scene, tickets could be purchased on coaches travelling from Toowoomba to Darwin, via Mt Isa, for $221, to the Gold Coast $15, Rockhampton $45, Townsville $75, Cairns $88, Sydney $35, Melbourne $80, and to Brisbane via the Metrolink $10.20.

Chapter 20

Quicker services to the Gold Coast and Cairns

'Our staff work to ensure that McCafferty's continue to provide a level of service that not only meets the expectations of our customers but that surpasses their expectations.'

JOHN OSBORNE

Twenty years after it started, the Toowoomba to Gold Coast service improved greatly with the completion of the Logan Expressway Toll Road in 1989.

During busy holiday periods as much as one hour was now saved by avoiding Garden City and travelling by the Logan Expressway. Although it cost $4.50 for a coach to go through the toll road, it was money saved in distance and time.

The route was so popular that in 1984 we introduced three direct coach services daily between the Gold Coast and Toowoomba.

McCafferty's had also opened other services to travel from Sydney to Melbourne direct, then Melbourne to Adelaide, Adelaide to Alice Springs (commenced August 31, 1989) and Alice Springs to Darwin (commenced August 18, 1989), and Darwin to Mt Isa, linking up with the Mt Isa to Townsville run. In addition new offices were opened in Adelaide, Alice Springs and Darwin.

Dalby came in for special attention when the State Transport Department in Queensland deregulated licensed passenger services in 1989. Our coaches had been operating through Dalby for 17 years on the Rockhampton service but had been denied the rights to service Dalby residents prior to deregulation.

February 14, 1989 and the delivery of the 100th Denning coach. Ted Rolls, General Manager of Denning, is on the left with Jack McCafferty, Tony McCafferty, Miss Julia Buckle and Mrs Sharyn Wessling.

Under the legislation no vehicle more than five years old would be allowed to start the service, and it had to be air-conditioned and equipped with toilets.

The company was able to comply with all the new requirements and began picking up and setting down passengers travelling from Dalby to Brisbane and Brisbane-Dalby.

At the same time our company was permitted to carry passengers between Toowoomba and Brisbane on a direct run in opposition to an operator who had enjoyed a monopoly for more than 40 years.

The most northerly McCafferty's terminal in Queensland is still the one at Cairns. Opened in July 1989, it is a far cry from some years earlier when coaches had to park outside an agency in Shield Street.

Today, the smooth-running coaches pull into the Cairns Terminal at the Trinity Wharf Centre, where former coach driver Stephen 'Steve' Briscoe heads McCafferty's team of seven, including three who drive between Cairns and Townsville.

Although Steve did the same run for several years before he became manager, he is still getting used to the foreign accents of

Manager at the Cairns terminal Stephen Briscoe in 1994.

many passengers and the variety of freight that moves through Cairns.

Booking in live crocodiles causes raised eyebrows, but as long as the crocs are properly secured they find a ready place alongside the boxes of live fish and the day-old chickens in the luggage compartment.

There are also consignments of live mud crabs and oysters destined for the busy restaurant trade.

The Cairns terminal opens at 6.45 a.m. and closes at 6.45 p.m., and when Steve is not at the counter, or answering one of four phones, he could be taking part in one of his favourite hobbies such as gymnastics or water-skiing. This is how he sees his job:

> *'Cairns is a most important tourist destination and there's now a growing trend among young Japanese tourists to come out to Australia on their own instead of on escorted tours with Japanese speaking guides. There are also many backpackers who travel north to the city from popular centres such as Airlie Beach.*
>
> *Staff on the counter at Cairns have adopted a caring attitude, showing lots of patience for travellers who sometimes have a limited knowledge of English.*

240

> *We work hard to ensure that people – Australians and international travellers – return to our coach services. With the development of the new casino and other building projects the tourism market can only continue to grow.'*

It is this patience and care that have paid off with Cairns now rivalling Brisbane as McCafferty's major centre of activity on the company's balance sheet.

By 1994, Cairns was the fastest-growing office in the network as far as revenue was concerned. Overseas tourists, particularly the Japanese, dominated the market, and some motels were charging $4 for a stubbie of beer and $10 for a Snowball cocktail. Closer to the waterfront, the price for a milkshake was $3.50.

The 1988 World Expo in Brisbane was a tremendous shot in the arm for tourism. It was one of McCafferty's most successful years, especially for the Gold Coast to Brisbane Service.

Things were really hopping and I wanted the coaches to turn round as quickly as possible. The more trips, the greater the service, and the more money at the Surfers Paradise Office. I went out on to the street and watched a coach being loaded. When another coach arrived I decided to take a more active role and stood on the footpath directing people to get on board quickly for the trip to Expo.

According to one observer, I was filling one coach fast. Enthusiasm then got the better of my actions and I called out that the coach was about to leave and began escorting people from the footpath to the coach.

Two little old ladies walking on the footpath were confronted by me waving my arms and shouting that everyone should be on the coach. They took my advice. Some time later, when the coach arrived at a suburban railway station, they admitted to the driver that they didn't want to go to Expo and anyway they didn't have any tickets. It took some time and patience to get them back to where they had started.

In 1989, we were informed by New South Wales State Transport that restrictions had been lifted on all interstate coaches to pick up and set down anywhere along the routes in New South Wales.

This allowed McCafferty's Brisbane/Sydney services and Brisbane/Melbourne services to carry passengers between any New South Wales towns, provided they were travelling further than 40 kilometres from a main town.

Our company commenced its 50th year of operations on April 1, 1989.

Lorna and Jack McCafferty at the company's 50th anniversary celebrations.

McCafferty's had increased its size to include 80 of the latest Denning Queensland-built coaches, with 160 coach drivers and a total staff of more than 300, mostly employed in Toowoomba.

Our Marketing Department arranged for the Australian Broadcasting Corporation to take an active part in the 50th anniversary celebrations by having 4QS/QW broadcasting from our Toowoomba Terminal on April 1, and giving the function wide coverage in South-West Queensland. There was a huge crowd at the terminal and the ABC also conducted an 'on air' competition with the prize of a trip for a family of four to anywhere on McCafferty's network.

The Toowoomba to Brisbane licence now allowed McCafferty's to offer alternative coach travel from Toowoomba to Brisbane, either by Metrolink or by direct coach service. Altogether, our company was offering up to 15 services daily between Toowoomba and Brisbane. The direct service cost $12 single, and was slightly dearer than the longer service.

The Brisbane Transit Centre service to the Gold Coast was operating, and restrictions had been completely lifted on the Townsville to Mt Isa service.

Previously, McCafferty's had been operating a daily daylight service on this route to the Threeways (Tennant Creek), Northern Territory, to connect with services to Alice Springs and Darwin.

We had not been allowed to carry passengers at intermediate stops between Townsville and Mt Isa, because Greyhound and

Ted Rolls of Denning is on the left with Jack McCafferty and Tony McCafferty. This photograph was taken on April 1, 1989, when Denning presented the company with a plaque to mark its 50th anniversary.

Pioneer had the monopoly on this route. Now McCafferty's could pick up and set down anywhere between Townsville and Mt Isa, and an extra service was started three times a week each way overnight.

Restrictions were also lifted on the Rockhampton to Longreach service, where Greyhound had enjoyed a monopoly.

We began a six times a week service each way from Rockhampton to Longreach on Monday, April 24, 1989. There was a special through fare from Brisbane to Longreach of $80, and Toowoomba and Dalby to Longreach cost $70.

We were also now able to carry passengers travelling between Mackay and Longreach through Emerald instead of having to travel down the coast and out from Rockhampton, a saving of hundreds of kilometres in travel, time and money.

Passengers were able to leave Mackay at 7 a.m. and arrive at Longreach at 5.30 p.m. on the same day, and travel through some of the most exciting scenery in Queensland – sugar cane country, mining, graingrowing, the gemfields area and the Western Queensland cattle and sheep country to the famous Hall of Fame at Longreach. A service that offered a round trip through

Blackwater, Rockhampton, Sarina and Mackay also began on Monday, April 24, 1989.

The Sunshine Coast route licence was granted that same year for a service operating from Brisbane to Caloundra, Maroochydore and Noosa.

Restrictions were also lifted on the service between Wallangarra, Stanthorpe and Warwick. Any coaches travelling to Toowoomba or Brisbane and McCafferty's services to and from Sydney could now pick up and set down anywhere on this route between Brisbane, Ipswich, Toowoomba, Warwick, Stanthorpe and Wallangarra.

The Goondiwindi to Brisbane route was also deregulated in 1989 and we were able to pick up and set down passengers between Brisbane, Toowoomba and Goondiwindi.

We set up a new Marketing Office in February 1989 in the New Zealand Insurance office complex in Russell Street, directly across the street from our Toowoomba Terminal. John Osborne joined McCafferty's and moved in with a staff of two who were already on McCafferty's staff. One staff member despatched tickets and timetables and the other worked as his secretary.

I admit that I wasn't in favour at first of some of John's new ideas like telemarketing, nor were some other members of the senior staff. However, it has proved itself a winner in recent years.

Today, Marketing has a staff of seven and two part-time personnel. Two of the full-timers are professionally trained

Marketing staff – Therese McCarthy, Tania Moloney and Jason Judd.

telemarketers, who are actively engaged in contacting all of McCafferty's agents on a regular basis as well as carrying out customer surveys. John Osborne takes up the story:

> 'We were the first coach company in Australia to introduce telemarketing in late 1989. I had read how it was being used to good effect in the United States and realised that in Australia too there were problems with the growing cost of having representatives on the road, and the need to more frequently service agents.
>
> We have adopted a combination of face-to-face representation and telemarketing. We now also use telemarketing to check the level and standard of service. Customers, who have returned home from a trip, are selected at random and asked a series of questions, which are designed to check that the level of service provided meets their expectations.
>
> This has become a real winner for the company.
>
> Customers are even asked about the labelling of their baggage and encouraged to make suggestions as to how the company can improve its service. Among the suggestions, which have already been considered, are the introduction of new services and details of how they can operate.'

Marketing sends stocks of new unwritten tickets to about 1,600 travel agents.

We have to provide enough tickets to meet agents' sales. Keeping up supplies of timetables is always demanding, but this has been streamlined and through our initiatives we print special one-service timetables for distribution by agents. These are particularly useful in cities such as Sydney and Melbourne where there is a high volume of passengers on certain routes.

Now we are entering an era where we have the responsibility for promoting McCafferty's services into travel agency networks in New Zealand, United States, Canada, Europe and the United Kingdom.

We set ourselves a strategy early in 1993 to enable people living in those countries, and who wanted to travel to Australia, to be able to pre-purchase McCafferty's tickets before leaving their country. This facility will be widely available by 1998, and, in the past 12 months, some 700 travel agents in New Zealand have been provided with direct access to McCafferty's Reservation Centre in Toowoomba on a toll-free telephone line, seven days a week.

We have linked with major wholesalers and retailers who are now featuring McCafferty's Express Coach Services as a product that can be purchased by someone who walks in off the street and wants to travel around Australia.

Regular mail-outs are sent to large wholesalers and retail outlets in overseas countries and McCafferty's work closely with the Australian Tourist Commission and the various State tourism overseas offices.

The name McCafferty's and its services are getting better known overseas. Our company is represented at the Australian Tourism Exchange, one of the largest travel expos of its type in the world. Organised by the Australian Tourist Commission, it enables McCafferty's to deal in face-to-face presentations with overseas operators.

On the domestic scene, the most successful publicity campaigns have involved using TV and newspapers simultaneously. Australian TV game shows such as *Wheel of Fortune, The Price is Right* and *Family Feud* have been used since late 1992 to publicise McCafferty's through travel prizes.

In February 1990, John Osborne successfully negotiated a month-long promotion with a Melbourne hoteliers group and Syme Newspapers. This promotion brought together several different newspaper groups with a combined readership of four million people in 38 Melbourne suburbs. It was the first time that a promotion involving opposition newspapers had ever been organised by our company. The 16-day campaign involved the publishers of 38 major suburban newspapers in Melbourne.

At the same time, the company was placing emphasis on the development of preferred product arrangements with large travel agency groups such as Traveland, UTAG, National Australia Travel, American Express and Harvey World Travel.

John sees considerable benefits by being linked to travel agency chains because of their large advertising campaigns, they are well known and the volume of sales is very high.

Since John Osborne joined McCafferty's there has been a sharpening and strengthening of the company's corporate image and the way in which we service our network of travel agents. Now, there is consistency of presentation, everything is in set colours, set design and set format.

The corporate image has been reinforced with McCafferty's pens and watches, McCafferty's caps and T-shirts. Our male staff now wear specially designed ties. The design of the ties was upgraded again in 1990. They were dark navy to match new epaulettes and feature gold and white stripes and the McCafferty's insignia.

In June that year we were using the slogan "Make it McCafferty's" in an advertising campaign that publicised the

Brisbane to Toowoomba coach fare as $12, and same day return fare only $18.

Reservations from around the world are now within our reach, as John Osborne explains here:

> 'In recognising the importance of our agents, Marketing staff guarantee same-day service for orders and we have introduced initiatives to show agents when stocks of tickets or printed information run low.
>
> There is consistency in the presentation of our product. We've really gone back to the basics in terms of marketing, and place a lot of attention on the "little things".
>
> We're moving into a whole new era with the company – very soon McCafferty's will be taking reservations from all round the world.'

John was responsible for the introduction of the first ever series of travel magazines on our coaches in Australia in 1991.

Some of our earlier promotional travel material put out by enthusiastic McCafferty's travel staff makes interesting reading.

It stated in part: 'There isn't a place on the planet that's out of reach of McCafferty's.

'. . . if it's a yak trip in the mountains of Nepal, a frolic in Fiji, or a straightforward cruise through the Coral Sea, McCafferty's can meet the tallest travel order.'

Accredited by the I.A.T.A. and the A.F.T.A., McCafferty's 15 travel consultants can, at the press of a computer key, map out an itinerary to any speck on the globe.

A same-day service to provide a speedy delivery of tickets, timetables and other material to McCafferty's agents began in 1990.

In the week leading up to Easter 1993, one of the Marketing Department's staff, Amanda Farr, packed 213 orders.

Macintosh desktop publishing equipment had been introduced in our Marketing Department about two years earlier and all the timetables and other promotion material were prepared in-house as 'camera-ready' art. This resulted in considerable savings in typesetting costs.

Many of the promotions arranged in the Marketing Division stem from requests for support from newspapers, sporting bodies, schools, shopping centres, travel agents, police, defence forces and show societies. Most of the requests seek support in the form of donated travel to be used as a prize, and each request is examined to see if the company should be involved.

What has to be decided is if the 'free' travel price will return to the company sufficient value in advertising at the venue of the function, and just how much advertising literature is going to be printed and distributed.

Marketing decides whether promotional ideas should be developed, as John Osborne outlines:

> *'Suppose we have a new service, and a school in that area approaches McCafferty's to support their 75th Anniversary Celebrations. We would directly reach a large number of people, and would have the opportunity to introduce them to our company, and alert them to the benefits of coach travel as well as our parcels and freight service.'*

The Marketing Division handles about 100 promotional requests a month.

Among the promotions that paid off with useful publicity was when the company became involved in a promotion organised by the Queensland Government Travel Centre and the Victorian Football Association in conjunction with the *Sunday Sun*.

The football association, in an effort to promote their competition, offered a series of prizes to the Gold Coast. McCafferty's provided four return tickets from Melbourne to the Gold Coast.

In 1991, our company promoted Toowoomba's annual September Carnival of Flowers by displaying colourful decals on the back of our coaches. With some 70 coaches displaying these decals, an invitation to visit the Garden City's annual event was extended from Cairns to Melbourne on a 24-hour basis. Toowoomba Events Corporation manager Gary Mears described the sponsorship as 'tremendous publicity offering continuous promotion'.

That same year, I was selected for inclusion among a 'Proud to be Australian' display in a shop window during Toowoomba's carnival.

Our company won an award at the Toowoomba Chamber of Commerce Business Awards presentation evening in 1989. The popularity of McCafferty's win in the trade section was shown by the applause from the audience of 500. The awards attracted 60 nominations and I received the plaque from Queensland Premier Russell Cooper.

When McCafferty's won the Queensland Tourism Award in the Tourism Transportation section in 1991, John Osborne was there to receive the 'Tourism Oscar' on my behalf. It was presented by

QTTC Chairman Peter Lawrence at a glittering presentation evening attended by 650 people at Jupiters Casino on the Gold Coast.

John Osborne was reappointed to the National Board of the Australian Tourist Industry Association for a second term in April 1994. As well as being a director of the national tourist authority, he was also appointed Chairman of the Queensland Tourist Industry Association.

John served on the Toowoomba City Council as an alderman from 1976 until the March elections in 1994, when he stood down from office because of his work commitments at McCafferty's.

In 1989 I announced that our company had a commitment to buy a minimum of 10 new coaches each year as part of an on-going fleet replacement program.

While in Europe I examined various types of coaches, and I felt that the Denning coaches purchased by McCafferty's were equal to, if not better than, any of the coaches on the road in Europe.

In 1994, a new Denning Landseer coach cost $450,000, compared to the old Jumbo that had a price tag of $72,000.

Over the years, passengers have noted several colour changes to the livery.

McCafferty's began with coaches painted black with a gold band, then moved to red, white and blue on the Bedfords. (The company added its first Bedford Comair coaches to the fleet in 1963.)

The next change was to pale blue all over, and then to white with a magenta strip around the waist, before changing to silver coaches, and in 1989 – for the 50th year – we painted a Denning coach with two-tone gold. We took it to the Sydney Bus Show, where it won the 'Bus of the Show', and gained many favourable comments. Four of the new gold coaches were ordered initially, at a cost of $360,000 each, and gold remains as the principal colour today.

The first gold coach was delivered in September 1989, and was given the number '50' and personalised number plates that read, MCC50.

The day after it was delivered, the coach was decorated with live flowers and, with Paul Wilkes at the wheel, it was in the Carnival of Flowers parade in Toowoomba. Paul did a fine job waving to the crowd, but best of all was his salute to the Governor of Queensland, Sir Walter Campbell, as the coach passed the official dais.

Anniversaries are always good for promotional work. The Boss pictured with coach number 50 on the occasion of McCafferty's Golden Anniversary in 1990. Note the attention to detail, which includes the number plate.

Above: The Cessna 402C Business Liner sweeping along the coast. (1982).

Below: McCafferty's Citation jet, purchased in 1993, and pictured at Townsville.

Above: A special display for the company's 50th anniversary.

Below: An artistic reproduction of one of the successful series of coach models.

Many people, even those not connected with our industry, remarked on the choice of the golden colour for the coaches. They said it gave the coaches a regal appearance – not too colourful, but very distinguished looking. Our company uses two-tone gold, with clear over gold base, and it costs $8,000 to paint each coach and add the necessary decals.

The first service operating via Toowoomba, Miles, Charleville, Blackall, Barcaldine and Longreach to Mt Isa, began on August 11, 1989. The Mt Isa Terminal is operated by Campbells Coaches. It's next-door to the Brothers Concordia Club on the Barkly Highway.

The new Toowoomba to Brisbane Express Service in 1989 opened up an alternate way of getting parcels to and from Brisbane on regular daily services at a nominal charge.

Throughout McCafferty's network, parcels and freight were carried at reasonable cost, on a terminal to terminal basis.

McCafferty's negotiated a special deal with the RACQ in 1989 to help stranded motorists. Under this arrangement, a motorist who was a member of RACQ Plus, and whose car broke down, could continue his or her travel with McCafferty's.

Within days of the new service being announced, it was used by a family on a holiday to North Queensland. The total value of their travel was $600.

Melbourne Cup luncheons, parties and raffles among staff – often won by the boss – remain popular features of our company life.

McCafferty's Social Club, headed by Margie Goltz and a band of other enthusiasts, arranged a night for staff and families at the James Cook Tavern in Toowoomba for a State of Origin match. The rugby match was televised on two big screens and 75 staff turned up, including five from the workshop and a number of drivers. It was a great night with plenty of raffles.

Earlier, Margie had helped organise a hat party knowing that I would wear my usual pork pie hat. Staff were rather taken aback when I entered the room wearing a devil's hat with two big horns.

Janelle Leaman has also helped organise many Christmas parties and she recalls the fun we have:

> 'One typical Christmas party in Toowoomba on November 25, 1990, featured Festhaus Frolics at Durans Nightclub, with the Bergendorf Oompah Band. This, the golden anniversary Christmas party, was billed as "an evening of dancing, singing, surprises and lots of laughs".
>
> There were some really great parties. We would invite bank and other business people, people from Dennings, the police etc. All

staff and their partners would also be invited. There was lots of fun, raffles and give-aways and Mr Mac always made a speech.'

As part of our 50th anniversary celebrations in 1990, we produced complimentary bookmarks that were distributed to library patrons in Bundaberg, Rockhampton, Mt Isa and Cairns. Each bookmark featured this limerick:

> *I love our giant sunburn country,*
> *from the outback to the seas,*
> *Although it always seems so hard to go,*
> *almost anywhere you please.*
> *But there is a name to get you there,*
> *in comfort and with ease,*
> *It's the same name that always has,*
> *the name's McCafferty's.*

Library patrons were encouraged to write their own limericks and to send them to McCafferty's.

Some Christmases stand out more than others and for a variety of reasons. In the coach industry we do everything possible to avoid accidents and breakdowns. When they happen it is traumatic for the people involved and those manning phones hundreds of kilometres away.

Janelle Leaman looks back to one Christmas that we will never forget:

> *'The worst Christmas staff encountered was the one which followed the news of a serious coach crash in New South Wales in 1989.*
>
> *It was the last working day before Christmas and we had organised Christmas drinks. Then, we heard about the Kempsey crash and office staff were crying and everyone thought of Mr Mac. What was it going to do to him? We were so upset, we couldn't look at each other. We were part of the family and we were all hurting. Safety was always one of his big things. It rocked the whole company and even now I really get upset when a flashback appears on TV.'*

The first person to hear of the crash was the Operations Manager in Toowoomba, Murray Jackson, who was alerted at 4 a.m. and had one of the most difficult days in his working life. He found out as the day progressed that the first report that no one had been killed was sadly wrong and in fact the crash claimed 35 lives.

We have a loyalty among staff that is the envy of many other companies.

Janelle Leaman is a prime example of that loyalty and she explains her feelings this way:

> *'I have liked working here ever since I started. Sure enough you have your bad times and you get upset with people. But you enjoy working with these people. It's a family company. Mr Mac is a fine gentleman and I have great admiration for him. He is well respected and I'd love to have his brain and memory.*
>
> *He expects the best from everyone. He gives 100% and in return he expects the same from his employees. It is a very nice company, old fashioned in some ways but with ethics.*
>
> *Sure enough Mr Mac may be a thorn in a lot of people's sides, but he has to make the decisions. He doesn't suffer fools gladly. He expects the best from everybody. Mrs McCafferty is always in the background and occasionally staff see her visiting the office.*
>
> *After 12 years with the company, I left to have a baby girl. Today, I am back as a part-timer working two days a week in Marketing.'*

Older staff and former staff still talk about the company's 40th anniversary celebrations when we held a party in a pavilion at the old Toowoomba Showgrounds. We got a person from Cobb and Co, who did the camping tours, to do the catering. He did a 'camp cook' and served up beef stroganoff, and it was a very enjoyable occasion for many people in the travel industry.

In 1990, our staff took to their hearts a seriously ill 17-year-old American boy whose wish was to see Australia.

He and his family were flown to Australia to spend nine days touring the country after the American Make-a-Wish Foundation and McCafferty's Coaches joined forces to grant the boy's wish.

The youth, Eric Haughee, had life-threatening spinal muscular atrophy, which had confined him to a wheelchair.

He said before returning home that the visit to Australia had been fantastic. He had been for a helicopter joy-ride, held a koala and half-held a kangaroo.

Later, McCafferty's staff were saddened when news came through that Eric had died some time after returning to the United States.

On April 4, 1990, McCafferty's commenced two new daily services between Brisbane and Charleville (Services 191 and 192). It was the year of the Charleville floods and our staff were among many who donated items for the flood victims. Our company provided free travel for volunteer workers and carried freight to assist flood-devastated families.

Wally Emerson recalls some times in the floods:

One of the hazards drivers face in Queensland when the rain does come down. This was the scene at the Rockhampton terminal in 1990 when traffic came to a standstill and the river peaked at 9.3 metres.

> *'People depended on us to get the bread and stuff through in the floods. One night coming back from Rockhampton in the floods I was at the wheel for 24 hours. I remember having to spend three Christmases in Rockhampton. We carted everything in those days. It was the first time many people in the inland had received daily papers and a regular mail service.'*

Is there anything McCafferty's don't carry? We handle newspapers, magazines, mail, urgent motor and agricultural parts, vaccines, blood samples, seed samples and cans of film for cinemas. For a while, our coaches were also carrying gold from a mine at Cracow near Theodore – hundreds of thousands of dollars worth of gold samples travelled in mail bags from Theodore to Brisbane.

However, one driver refused to drive with the gold on board because he claimed he needed more security. Just where was the gold kept on the coach? Wally Emerson remembers:

> *'We used to throw it in a bag underneath all the mail bags. One of the hassles with the mail was at Mount Morgan, where the postmaster would never unlock the gates for us, and we had to lift the big bags of mail over the fence.*
>
> *In those days we carried more mail and freight than passengers.*

> *We had engine heads for D9 Caterpillar equipment and headers,*
> *and they were so heavy we had to lift them out on corn sacks. When*
> *the harvest was on we used to get spares, including huge tyres, out*
> *to the farmers.'*

The freight business across Australia is growing and to coach companies it's worth millions of dollars.

McCafferty's carry many unusual items including coffins needed at short notice, day-old chickens, cotton bale samples from Emerald to places like Moree or Brisbane and mangoes from north Queensland.

On one occasion we received a letter of thanks from the Bundaberg District Tourism and Development Board. It praised McCafferty's for the tremendous assistance given to the Board throughout the year for freighting their regional tourist information guides to various destinations. The Board thanked the coach drivers and transit offices who really did the 'hands on' work in shipping their many bundles of books around the country.

Chapter 21

Humour and a few awards

(1991-1992)

'I was working behind the Toowoomba Reservations counter in 1991, and I couldn't believe my eyes when mega-star Mel Gibson strolled into the terminal to ask directions. I promised not to reveal the star's identity to any other customers in the terminal or his destination, and in turn I received Mel's autograph for my scrapbook.'

SHANE WESSLING

But working in Toowoomba Terminal is not without humour. There was the cold winter's day when one of the male staff arrived at work wearing pantyhose and shorts – he was given short shift and sent home to change. From then onwards his nickname was 'Pantyhose'.

On another occasion, an agent phoned in to tell staff that an 84-year-old woman had just booked her 104th trip with McCafferty's. The woman was given a complimentary ticket from Caringbah to Brisbane.

McCafferty's at Surfers Paradise met a demand for a variety of tours in 1991. There were over the counter sales of tickets for a number of companies including Sunshine Coast Coaches, Intercoaster to Sunshine Coast, Kirklands, Lindsays, Murrays (Canberra and tours), Surfers Paradise day tours, Sunstate day tours, Grahams Coaches, Captain Cook Cruises to Sydney, Great Western Cruises, rail tickets to Brisbane suburbs, as well as packages to Movieworld, Dreamworld, Sea World and Wet'n'Wild.

As well as needing the best computers, McCafferty's telephone network was being stretched to the limit. In December 1991, the

Ready to board the coach in Toowoomba for a journey to Brisbane for the official opening of Southbank.

company installed a new $30,000 Telecom switchboard, with 16 exchange lines and 60 extensions. Hopefully this will take the company through to the year 2000.

I have been keeping one eye on the clock for years and it usually pays off.

When Alf Probst was driving a coach to Brisbane for the opening of Southbank in July 1992, there was a bang and there was one very flat tyre.

As Alf and John Osborne and another helper moved in to change the wheel, I too came forward, but I didn't have any tools in my hand – I just had my watch. 'Not bad,' I said when the new wheel was in place. 'You've done the changeover in 12 minutes.' I later gave them an honourable mention in the staff newsletter.

That same year we purchased Skennar's services from Brisbane to Toowoomba, Brisbane to Roma and Brisbane to Charleville, and four late-model Denning coaches. Business was growing in Brisbane, and over Christmas 1992 Brisbane had 64 extra services and there were 80 additional ones in January 1993. McCafferty's Brisbane Terminal also handled 39 per cent of all express departures and 57 per cent of all local departures.

One of our company's busiest periods was in July 1993, when nearly 100 extra coaches were chartered to cope with all the work.

The three Johns in the boss's office in 1992. John Francis (Jack) McCafferty (seated) with son John Tony and grandson John Paul.

It was a bonanza for many private operators who were normally having a quiet period and then found their coaches in demand.

In December 1993, our Brisbane terminal despatched 24,300 passengers and handled 123 extra divisions, giving a total of 1,100 services out of the terminal in the month leading up to the Christmas break. Daily phone calls peaked at 1,357!

The US Navy was in Sydney, and an American serviceman got lost in the big city. He called into McCafferty's terminal at Kings Cross and asked the attendant in uniform what naval ship he was serving with. The staff member quipped back 'HMAS McCafferty's'.

Among honours that have been accorded me are the Order of Australia Medal, which was awarded in the 1992 Australia Day Honours for my services to the community and the coaching industry, and the 1992 Queensland Tourism Industry Award for the Most Outstanding Contribution by an Individual.

Jack McCafferty with the individual tourism award in 1992.

McCafferty's won the tourism transportation section in the Queensland Tourism Awards in 1991. Pictured with the citation and award are John Osborne (National Marketing Manager) and Tony McCafferty (General Manager).

Finalist in the 1992 Toowoomba Chamber of Commerce Business Awards, sponsored by NZI Insurance. Jack McCafferty is pictured with Therese McCarthy.

When I received the OAM, I also got a congratulatory letter from the Queensland Premier, Wayne Goss. After offering his personal congratulations, and those of the Government, Mr Goss went on to say that 'this honour is a fitting recognition of your service to the road transport industry and tourism'.

The medal was presented to me by the Governor of Queensland, Sir Walter Campbell, at Government House, on April 10, 1992.

I received another accolade from Father James Byrne of the Sacred Heart Church in Toowoomba that same year.

It was during a speech of thanks to Lorna and I for hosting Father Byrne and about 40 others to a day at Brisbane's newest theme park – South Bank.

Father Byrne said that Toowoomba and its community benefited in many ways as a result of having me as one of its citizens. He said I had done much for Toowoomba when Mayor, and as a business leader. I was one of the greatest ambassadors Toowoomba had ever had, and many of my activities had benefited the city in a direct and indirect way.

In March 1994 one of our coach drivers – Ronald Alfred Leschke, of Marsden – received a bravery award from the Governor General, Mr Bill Hayden.

Queensland Transport Minister David Hamill (centre) about to present a bravery award to McCafferty driver Ronald Alfred Leschke, of Marsden, in 1994. Tony McCafferty is on the left.

The award was for Ron's actions when an armed man threatened passengers on a McCafferty's coach on September 15, 1992.

Ron placed his safety in jeopardy to protect his passengers from the armed man on a Cairns-bound coach out of Brisbane.

Ron was the driver of a coach that was subjected to a hijack attempt by the man, who was armed with a hunting knife.

He was directly threatened by the hijacker but was concerned for the safety of his passengers who were being repeatedly menaced by the armed man.

Despite the increased danger to himself, Mr Leschke turned the steering wheel of the coach violently to throw the hijacker off balance. A passenger struggled with the man and was able to disarm him.

An 18-year-old Toowoomba man was later dealt with in Maroochydore Magistrates Court on charges of kidnapping, being armed in public so as to cause fear, and unlawful assault with intent to kidnap.

Chapter 22

The best is yet to come

(1993)

'On one occasion, I pressed for better manners when answering the phone. I addressed a special message to all staff members using our phones: 'Please be mindful of answering your calls in a courteous, bright and cheerful way. You never know who could be on the other end – it could even be me!'

JACK McCAFFERTY

I was concerned over the astronomical phone bills that arrived at my office early in 1993. I was asking myself if all these calls were necessary and how we could prune some costs. It was important to retain our competitive advantage.

I wrote in the staff newsletter: 'Just a reminder – watch those phone calls, don't use the phone unnecessarily. Don't waste paper – apart from being costly, it is no good for the environment – and wastes trees! Wherever possible use a small piece of paper, especially for notes, or the other side of paper that has already been used.' Care is needed in not making files too unwieldy.

I have always remembered a motto adopted by the large British retailing giant Marks & Spencer, which was 'If in doubt, throw it out'. After deciding that paperwork was becoming cost prohibitive, that company decided to simplify, eliminate and throw away unnecessary paper. This included making unnecessary photo copies (the old: 'I need four but I'll get five just in case'). In two years, Marks & Spencer managed to do away with two million forms weighing 105 tons!

The best year for our company at the Birdsville Races was 1993, when we took 300 passengers out in seven coaches with no mechanical problems and only one puncture.

Clem Cheers was 'Camp Captain' with the McCafferty's contingent, a job he had enjoyed for a number of years. Attendance was boosted by the RACQ, which had given McCafferty's a two-page write up in their magazine *Road Ahead*.

There were 5,000 people at the races, and over 400 light planes were parked at the aerodrome – a record. I dropped in with the Citation Jet on its way to Alice Springs and parked beside Dick Smith's Citation – the only other jet there. The airport committee must have made some money that day – $10 each for every passenger arriving by plane.

I had a talk with Dick Smith which resulted in McCafferty's providing coaches for the Dick Smith Innamincka Mission restoration excursion. The tour was mentioned in Dick Smith's *Australian Geographic* magazine. Six coaches were ordered, with a program of camping out and real bush tucker.

We took out advertising space in *The Chronicle* in the home city of our headquarters. It coincided with the Chamber of Commerce Business Awards.

It stated simply: 'We've come a long way since we started our first coach service in Toowoomba over 50 years ago. But no matter how much we grow, no matter how many different towns and cities we travel to, we'll always think of Toowoomba as our home.

'More importantly, we'll always regard the people of Toowoomba as our friends, and we'd like to say a big thank you to all of you.

'We thank you for your past support and look forward to being of service in the future.'

Our company now had an annual turnover in excess of $40 million, our coaches were travelling 30 million kilometres a year, and consuming 10 million litres of diesel fuel.

The cost of a tyre had risen to $550 and each tyre was expected to cover about 300,000 kilometres.

Coaches were costing us $400,000 each and could be expected to be replaced after six years and completing three million to four million kilometres, depending on which route they operated on. We had 530 employees and paid $1 million in wages each month, and we now had 100 coaches with the introduction of 19 Landseer Coaches, which had been added in 12 months.

Easter 1993 was extremely busy with McCafferty's transporting more than 25,000 passengers in one of the company's largest logistical exercises.

No fewer than 120 additional services were organised to cater for the traditional Easter rush. Our entire fleet was on the roads in Queensland, New South Wales, Victoria and South Australia. The most popular service at Easter was the Brisbane to Cairns run, which had five services running in both directions each day.

McCafferty's became the top privately owned coach business in Australia when it launched its new direct service to Sydney and Adelaide in December 1993. We used 360-horsepower fully air-conditioned coaches, complete with video and toilet facilities.

The claim was correctly based on the thousands of passengers carried as well as the range of services offered.

Our nearest competitor was Australian Coachlines – a conglomerate of three companies – Greyhound, Pioneer and Bus Australia, headed by Chairman Sir Llewellyn Edwards. (Australian Coachlines changed its name at its annual general meeting in November, 1993, to 'Greyhound Pioneer Australia'. It announced that it had 180 coaches, travelling 50 million kilometres annually and carrying 2.5 million people. In June, 1994, Greyhound Pioneer was weighing its options for a capital reconstruction and seeking capital from a British investment group.)

Our Toowoomba-Sydney-Canberra-Adelaide service had been introduced after extensive market research coupled with demand from travel agents.

This service enabled travellers to join a coach at the Toowoomba terminal at 9 p.m. and arrive in Sydney at 1 p.m. the next day, then leave for Canberra two hours later and arrive there at 8.05 p.m. The coach continued to Adelaide, arriving at 12.45 p.m. the following day.

From Sydney, the service passed through Mittagong, Goulburn, Canberra, Yass, Wagga Wagga, Leeton, Griffith, South Hay, Euston, Mildura, Renmark, Berri, Blanchtown and on to Adelaide.

In 1993 my family business had recorded a 20 per cent increase in passengers over the previous 12 months, and with more services opening up over the next six years to the turn of the century that growth would escalate.

We were now servicing all mainland states and territories in Australia, except Western Australia, but even here I believed that with proper planning we could open up a Nullarbor service to Perth to complete our national network.

Our company's services and facilities far exceeded those being offered by coach firms in the United States.

When I travelled from New York to Key West in Florida, the coaches on that route were 18 years old and not as up-to-date as ours, while the facilities at depots and terminals were shabby and run-down. The American industry has been ravaged by industrial disputes.

In 1993, our company entered another stage of computerisation when staff stopped writing out cheques manually, and let the computer do the job.

Our mail expands daily and we receive many letters of appreciation from passengers. One example, which is typical of many, was included in the staff newsletter in 1993 and is worthy of inclusion here:

> '*I recently travelled from Darwin to Alice Springs with McCafferty's and write to thank you for the excellent service. I commend you on the two drivers who impressed me with their efficiency, politeness and attention to passenger comfort. Both drivers are great ambassadors for the company and the company should consider itself very fortunate to have drivers of this calibre. I have lived in Alice Springs for 25 years and travelled to Darwin with an opposition bus company on this same trip and the service of McCafferty's ran rings around them.*
>
> *My friends and I travel quite extensively by coach and have done for many years, and I can assure you that McCafferty's will be our Number 1 choice from now on.*
>
> *Well done and please keep up the good work providing a much needed and much appreciated service to and from the Centre.*'

Tony and I flew to Alice Springs to look at the company's operations in June 1993.

'People are flying here in droves but they still have to get around in a bus to see the centre of Australia,' I told a reporter from the *Centralian Advocate*.

I was amazed at the difficulty of landing at Alice Springs, where airport authorities expected two days' notice of an impending arrival. This is the first time we had struck this. We had difficulty landing there. Talk about car parking space problems – it's getting that way with aeroplanes now.

The secret of a successful business is 'to have a heart and soul in it – someone who is dedicated to it'.

I paid tribute to the assistance given by the Northern Territory Tourist Commission when our company was doing its research before opening an office in Alice Springs.

I think what encouraged us, more than anything, was the fact that there was only one company operating in Alice Springs.

People always want an alternative service to select from, and I have always accepted competition. I think it really keeps businesses going.

I believed that by moving into the Northern Territory our company had 'picked a winner'.

After the agents had experienced four weeks of our service with Landseer coaches, dedicated coach captains and on-time schedules, they all welcomed us with open arms. Even agents who had not been accredited were chasing us to become agents.

Our new Northern Territory services were launched by the Northern Territory Minister for Tourism, Mr Barry Coulter, in Alice Springs on Tuesday, May 4, 1993.

There were 10 paying passengers on the first run from Adelaide to Darwin on May 20, and 10 were booked on the run in the opposite direction.

Six weeks later, we had full coaches operating out of Darwin on the Alice Springs-Adelaide route.

We picked the right 16 drivers in Adelaide to operate the service. Being experienced Central Australian drivers played a big part in the success of what was a very expensive operation. Congratulations went out to Kel Davis, the Area Manager in Alice Springs, Terry Murphy the South Australian Area Manager, and Juan Block, the Darwin Area Manager.

In the first 12 months of operation of the Northern Territory services more than 50,000 people travelled with McCafferty's to the Top End.

The new Townsville to Northern Territory service began on May 28, 1993. Drivers at the Mt Isa terminal were by now working on UHF Channel 34.

I was now looking forward to introducing a daily service from Alice Springs to Ayers Rock and connecting with the Darwin to Adelaide service.

Kel Davis was directing passengers arriving at McCafferty's Alice Springs terminal to the Gap View Motel, where Ross Paddon was looking after motel and backpackers' accommodation.

Kel did an operator's accreditation course at Yulara in 1994.

It was necessary for us to become a licensed operator, enabling the establishment of our daily service to Yulara. McCafferty's became a fully accredited operator for the Ayers Rock Resort area.

Werner Sarny, owner of the BP Travel North, became McCafferty's main agent in Katherine, and their promotions officer and marketing manager Sylvia Wolf had her hands on all the local tours and accommodation.

With the opening of Alice Springs, the Townsville Transit Centre terminal had taken on a bigger workload. Gary Barnes was one of

McCafferty's longest-serving employees, with more than 21 years' service.

'I am very impressed with the way in which Gary runs the show,' I wrote in the staff newsletter. 'Everyone knows what they have to do and goes about it in a businesslike fashion. The system works very well. There is one thing about Townsville operations – we never had any problems with them.'

Townsville had to lease the office next-door to its booking office, previously occupied by Brolga Tours, to handle the increased freight.

The first high tech two-way radios were installed in our coaches early in 1993. It cost $250,000 to install the equipment on 92 coaches and the supplier was Mr Derm Guerin, of Comtel, Toowoomba. The ramifications of the equipment were explained at the time by Tony McCafferty:

> *'This new "state-of-the-art" equipment enables drivers to communicate at long distance on a coach-to-coach basis, as well as from their coach to the major terminals in Queensland, New South Wales, Victoria and South Australia.'*

The new two-way network was also to prove a boon in the Northern Territory, where it made it easier for drivers and operational staff to relay current information on road conditions and highway delays.

The new technology updated equipment installed 40 years earlier.

With the old system, there were a lot of black spots when travelling near mountains and tall buildings and the new equipment overcame this. The old system also had only a limited range between coaches, depending on the terrain.

The new equipment enabled drivers to be warned to divert around an accident on their route and to update their manifests en route to pick up last-minute passengers.

In October 1993, the new UHF radios proved their worth by averting a major road accident.

Arthur Hunt, on Service 142 (Cairns to Brisbane), picked up a message from a semi-trailer driver informing him that there was a large injured beast lying in the centre of the south-bound traffic lane, just south of the Kunwarrara Road House.

Arthur immediately contacted the Service 141 (Brisbane to Cairns) driver John Geddes and told him of the position. Between them, and with the help of passengers from both coaches, they managed to stop north and south-bound traffic while they dragged the beast off the road — preventing a motorist smashing into it.

I was still receiving an odd letter of complaint regarding the conduct of some drivers, especially when dealing with young women, so I gave them a blast in the staff newsletter. I told them: 'If you value your job, my best advice is be careful, and don't leave yourself open for anybody to make a complaint against you. Always be attentive to your driving – passengers notice irresponsible driving and they get concerned – and rightly so. I have just received a letter referring to a "cowboy" style of driving.'

We purchased our first jet aircraft, a $1,000,000 nine-seater Citation from Melbourne Jet City in February 1993.

Tony did his endorsement on the spacious aircraft in Melbourne, and this included three hours of written work and three hours of actual flying. He went on to complete more than 100 hours and became captain in command of the aircraft.

He flew the jet from Toowoomba to Brisbane in 10 minutes. On another flight, Tony and I took seven media representatives for a 'dry' run from Toowoomba. In no more than an hour, they were whipped down to Surfers Paradise at 515km/h at 4,000 metres, then along the shoreline north to Mooloolaba at 300 metres, past the Glasshouse Mountains, and back home to Toowoomba.

About that 'dry run', one journalist wrote '. . . tea and sandwiches were served before take-off, but the Citation boasted no flight attendant and no bar. But then, nor do McCafferty's coaches.'

Tony was doing the company flying and another pilot had taken on the charter work, and the charter charges were about $1,800 an hour, depending on a number of variables.

By 1994, courier delivery vans were on the road sporting flash new metallic reflective signs 'McCafferty's Parcel Express'. Our company's vans and those of the couriers promoted a very professional image in the business areas of Brisbane. At the same time, couriers and agents throughout the network started to promote the service and sell pre-paid freight labels at an enormous rate. By May that year, the West End Depot manager, Les James, had a complement of eight mechanics on duty, which enabled him to get vehicles serviced in minimum time.

McCafferty's survived the record floods early in 1994 in the Central Highlands area around Emerald, Capella and Clermont.

Ray Medlin recorded over 18 inches of rain at his home within a week. The company suffered the longest delay in services since it started in the area over 20 years earlier. The road from Clermont to Emerald was closed for nearly two weeks. Even the buses could not service the mine area.

One coach, travelling from Clermont to Rockhampton, was caught in the floodwaters and as a result the engine was damaged to the extent of nearly $20,000.

Some of our coaches cover fantastic distances, unthought of during the early days of gravel roads. Monthly figures never cease to astound me.

In April 1994, one coach (No. 309), which had travelled the most kilometres of the whole fleet during that month, had covered 35,590km and had used 12,055 litres of diesel fuel.

No. 309 started the month doing a Brisbane to Charleville return, a one-day charter in Brisbane, and then left for a journey to Darwin and back via Sydney and Adelaide. Back home for a two-day complete check and maintenance service at the Toowoomba workshop and then off again to Sydney, Adelaide, Sydney, on to Brisbane, up to Cairns and back, another trip up the centre via Adelaide, then back to Brisbane to finish the month doing a Hervey Bay return and a nice, easy Brisbane to Gold Coast return. The coach carried a total of 1,042 passengers during the month.

Early in 1994, Queensland Transport decided to conform with all other State Transport Departments and allow 'two-up' drivers – something that we had been suggesting for years. This meant that two drivers would be able to travel on the same coach, one sleeping in a registered sleeping compartment, while the other was driving and then changing over when required.

Although two-up drivers had been approved in 1994, as this book goes to press we have not been officially advised that we can use this system.

'Two-up' drivers in the early days were often referred to as 'Dad's Army', and McCafferty's first introduced the system on interstate services in December 1979. A reunion for 'the boys in Dad's Army' was held at Wivenhoe Dam in February 1993.

The 'two-up' system had proved itself on the Brisbane to Sydney run via the New England Highway. Drivers could have their rest and turn round quicker, and instead of being away five or six days they could be home in two. Initially, the first six Landseers, from No. 101 to No. 106, were fitted out with bunks and the company also used a couple of the older Denairs. Seats were removed to build the bunks, but with coach No. 107 onwards, coaches came with the bunk built in across at the back, behind the toilet and above the engine. According to one driver:

> *'It's noisy, but when you lie there for a while you hear the beat of the motor going constantly and you soon fall asleep.'*

On services like the Mt Isa run, 'two-up' driving is ideal for that situation, all the way from start to finish.

In the early days, there was keen competition on the Mt Isa run between McCafferty's (the newcomer) and Greyhound.

'How many did Greyhound go out with tonight?' asked one of our bright young counter staff.

'Oh', I said, 'they went out empty.'

'Well, that's not bad,' smiled the staff member. 'It makes our 26 look pretty good.'

Then, after a few seconds silence, I spoke again, 'Greyhound didn't go at all tonight'.

In 1994, the women working in Administration controlled over 1,500 working accounts, and the Reservations Department was bursting at the seams.

Like any big business, staff can often become frustrated when simple requests for equipment seem to take ages to be answered. Reservations Manager Craig Wilson recalls what happened in one instance when counter staff took delivery of a new tape dispenser:

> *'We had been waiting for the tape dispenser for a long time, and when it finally arrived, the shining new maroon-coloured equipment held pride of place on the counter at Reservations in Toowoomba.*
>
> *Three staff were at the counter when a male passenger, who had dozed off, missed the 3.05 p.m. Metro. He was so incensed that he picked up the tape dispenser on the counter and threw it at the door behind us. It shattered in pieces on the ground. We couldn't believe what had happened and one of the staff quickly cleared the counter in case he threw anything else.'*

I believe in moving with the times and keeping up with technology that wasn't around when I started in business. In April 1994, my photograph appeared in a computerised photographic exhibition in Toowoomba. Taken by Michael Dooley, it featured me standing inside a modern coach smartly dressed, wearing my traditional hat and jacket.

The colour photograph was one of more than 50 specially taken in Toowoomba by members of the Society of Advertising, Commercial and Magazine Photographers.

The photographs featured in the *Dawn to Dusk in Toowoomba* exhibition. All of them had been produced using film scanners and desktop computers, as well as digital cameras using compact discs instead of film. A set of copies of the new age photographs was sent to Takasuki, Toowoomba's sister city in Japan.

Chapter 23

Strengthening the Kiwi connection

(1994)

McCafferty's made history on April 30, 1994, in making what was believed to be the first international flight from Toowoomba aerodrome. Sales and marketing staff from McCafferty's Express Coaches left in the company's Citation jet for an overseas sales tour of New Zealand.

'History is being made in Toowoomba with somebody taking off on an international flight,' I explained to the media.

The party included Lorna and I, daughter Kay, General Manager Tony McCafferty, National Marketing Manager John Osborne and agency sales representative Tania Moloney.

The Citation Jet headed out of Toowoomba and our group reached Norfolk Island two hours later, where we stopped overnight. On the next day we headed for Auckland. We spent three days "selling McCafferty's" at a travel agents' function we had organised and which was attended by 150 New Zealand travel agents.

We also visited Wellington, where our team spent two days, and then had another day in Christchurch before flying home.

It was our company's first overseas sales tour targeting the New Zealand independent travellers' market.

The Fully Independent Travellers (FITS), who were significantly coach travellers, were coming to Australia in unprecedented numbers.

Twelve years earlier, in 1982, we had completed arrangements with Mt Cook Airlines (NZ) to be their general sales agent in Queensland. McCafferty's Friendship Tours to New Zealand using the Mt Cook Service were launched.

In 1994, McCafferty's adopted a five-year strategic plan to move into the overseas market, starting with New Zealand, then the United States, the United Kingdom, across Europe and North America.

Eighteen months before the Citation jet's visit to the land of the long white cloud we had established a toll-free line in New Zealand, allowing agents in New Zealand to book coach travel for clients before they arrived in Australia.

The two-way flow of tourists across the Tasman has seen some strange side effects. On one occasion during an agency business session, John Osborne was surprised as he started to give Margaret Bennett of Go Australia Travel Bureau, New Zealand, a spiel on McCafferty's Margaret interrupted to say her cat was named 'McCafferty's'.

She explained that a friend had brought the kitten to her home at a time when she was studying McCafferty's literature and timetables, and so Margaret thought what better name than McCafferty's?

When John returned to Toowoomba he mailed off a McCafferty's sticker, which was later placed on the cat's sleeping box!

On the more recent trip, the marketing and sales team visited agents in Christchurch, Wellington and Auckland. It was seen as a necessary step in following up opportunities outlined at the Australian Tourism Exchange in Sydney in June 1993. It also strengthened the contacts our Marketing Department staff had developed when visiting New Zealand to take part in various Australian Tourist Commission and Queensland Tourist and Travel Corporation trade shows.

Aviation has played an important part in the success of our company's operations, as Tony McCafferty explains:

> 'I don't know just how we managed before we had the aircraft. With our service operations in such a large area we can hop in the aircraft and within minutes or hours be in conference with our staff or suppliers.
>
> We have used the plane to take mechanics and parts to coaches stranded by mechanical faults as far away as Alice Springs and the North West coast. We have also used it to ferry coach drivers at the end of their shifts from places such as Tamworth, Kempsey and Broken Hill on normal services, tours and charters. It is a most useful and essential part of our business.
>
> In three days, we can have functions with our agents in places like Adelaide, Mildura, Griffith, Wagga Wagga and Canberra.

*Regular airline schedules don't allow you to stop off at places like
Griffith and Wagga.*

*McCafferty's are increasing their market share at the rate of 25
per cent a year and the revenue is going up – a reflection of our
focus on service.'*

Early in 1994, I set off with my sales team in the Citation jet to
visit key agents around Australia. On the last leg of our journey we
left Sydney at 3.40 p.m. and arrived back in Toowoomba 50
minutes later.

Using the Citation, we covered some 12,500km in just 10 days
and made personal contact with dozens of our company's top
agents and met our various area managers and staff. We had also
inspected all McCafferty's terminals and offices and discussed
future requirements and met potential employees.

All this could only have been achieved with the use of our jet. It
enabled us to be more flexible with our timing and also to use to
advantage the mobile phone – which I consider to be one of the
most significant advances in the world of communication. It didn't
matter where we were, our mobile phone was beside us, enabling
us to give quick answers to problems and make on-the-spot
decisions. What a great era we are living in now. Time and tide
wait for no man and we at McCafferty's are not letting grass grow
under our feet.

In an industry like ours with a large network, a jet plane is not a
luxury if it is used wisely, it is a necessity. For us to have used a car
to complete all our visits it would have taken more than a month,
and costs of accommodation and meals would have been
astronomical. With the jet it took just 10 days.

I have always maintained an interest in air travel, and when I
was Mayor of Toowoomba in 1963 I was on board the first flight by
TAA from Brisbane to Oakey Airport, when Toowoomba's first air
mail service was introduced. The mail was carried by TAA from
the first day of operation of the airline's new Darling Downs
services. McCafferty's were appointed TAA's general sales agent
on December 1, 1981.

Tony and I believe that there are exciting times ahead for the
coach and travel industry. Tony predicts that McCafferty's will
become more entrenched and recognised as the leader, surpassing
other Australian coach operators in patronage and revenue in the
next few years. He continues:

*'We have a splendid fleet of modern coaches. The secret of our
success lies in our slow consolidation, the build-up of a strong asset*

base, recognising cost effectiveness, and only employing coach drivers who have a good track record.

One thing that can annoy me is a staff member who doesn't take sufficient care.

In a large workforce occasionally you may get a driver not taking necessary care, and we take a pride in our coaches. If he hits a bull on the road then he could cause $20,000 damage. Years ago we drove on far worse roads and in unsophisticated coaches yet we usually avoided such accidents.'

My daughter, Kay Elliott, remembers the early days of motorised coach travel in Australia with great fondness. She began work in Toowoomba when she was 16 and now works at the Surfers Paradise terminal.

She and the other staff at that terminal have a gift of good humour that makes them among the favourites of the travelling public.

They recall excellent days in the beginning. Life was simpler and the people who travelled knew exactly where they were going and why, and it was mostly on the Metro in those days. Kay continues:

'Basically, you let difficult customers have their say. Take a few deep breaths and then sift through to use a little psychology.

People used to know what they wanted when they bought their tickets. Nobody talked of suing anybody and if something went wrong, then it was a nuisance and just one of those things and people still smiled a lot.

There was a wonderful Korean guy who came into Surfers Paradise when McCafferty's were using Shop 1 in the Cosmopolitan Building, on the Gold Coast Highway, and Sydney coaches had to pull up on one side of the road. He got out and went for a drink, but when he returned the coach had left and he was absolutely distraught. He was totally lost. He couldn't believe the coach had left without him.

I said, "All right, I'll get my car and we'll pick up the coach down the road."

Staff used the two-way radio and stopped the coach at Burleigh Heads, but before he got aboard the man asked for my name and said, "I will remember you".

He returned to the terminal a couple of months later and asked me for a photograph. I'd just picked up some new ones from the photo shop and although puzzled I gave him one. He returned again later and presented me with a beautiful sketch he'd made from the image on the photo.

Other passengers have returned with boxes of chocolates and they often send cards from remote places and countries overseas.'

The worst day in Kay's working life was when floods occurred and the roads were cut between the Queensland border and parts of northern New South Wales.

A leading footballer, whose marriage had broken up, was anxious to spend time with his girlfriend in Brisbane and he put his two children on the coach to join their real mother in Byron Bay.

Police stopped the coach because of the flood waters and it had to return to Brisbane. When McCafferty's called the footballer to explain what had happened he shouted down the phone that he didn't want the children returned to Brisbane and the coach just had to get through to Byron Bay.

His language got more and more colourful. Kay and the others on the staff were appalled and then he put his girlfriend on and her language was even worse.

Kay was holding the phone away from her ears when one of our drivers came into the terminal and saw what was happening. He took the phone from Kay's hand and said just a few words to the man and woman and replaced the phone back on its stand. He advised the staff never to speak to that couple again.

Life on the Gold Coast is never dull. On another occasion, two druggies came into the terminal and with difficulty asked for tickets to Beenleigh.

The slightly-built woman weighed only about four and a half stone and she had a large black hat pulled down, and a long black sweater also pulled well down. On her feet were long black boots. Her male companion was 'off with the fairies'. It was while swaying from side to side that he accidentally collided with his girlfriend and staff watched as she fell in slow motion to the ground. Then she opened her great big eyes, looked up at him and said in a little girl's voice, 'You knocked me down'.

A driver came in and took one look at the couple and said, 'They're not booked on my coach are they?' 'Yes' replied Kay. 'Just get them out of here.'

Gold Coast staff had another unusual experience when a Vietnam veteran lost his cool over an incident involving money.

When he arrived from Beenleigh late that night, he offered a $50 note and the driver said, 'I haven't any change – you'd better go to the office'.

There was a crowd at the counter, and staff noticed that this man was getting more and more agitated. Then he suddenly yelled out, 'I'm going to come back here with a gun, I've got a gun and I'm going to kill the whole lot of you.' People just moved sideways out of the office and Kay was left at the counter.

Although she holds a black belt in Tae Kwon Do, Kay was extremely frightened but she managed to calm him down and he left the terminal. She rang the police and told them about the incident. Even today she is still not sure if the man was carrying a gun.

Staff at Surfers Paradise have also had young girls arriving at the counter who claim that they have been molested.

They listen with a sympathetic ear to their stories but also run a professional eye over the appearance and dress of their potential passengers. If the women are dressed provocatively in very short shorts and scooped-down tops, staff make their own conclusions; they know that most young women don't want or need to travel on coaches dressed like that. We moved across the road to the Surfers Paradise Bus Station in 1992 and six months later we had 22 coaches daily Monday to Friday, and 25 coaches Saturday and Sunday. In one month, these services carried a total of 19,086 passengers, and the terminal had also undergone a facelift with the bays being repainted and water blasted to remove grease and oil stains.

On occasions McCafferty's staff have to question the name on a ticket to check if the right person is presenting it at the counter. However, on one particular occasion, the conman didn't even bother to present a ticket to Kay, who outlines what actually happened:

> *'The young, attractive man just turned up at our terminal and introduced himself as a company driver who needed to go down to Sydney to return with a coach. As he was wearing a coach driver's shirt our obliging staff found him a seat.*
>
> *But, then on a second occasion, he got a bit too cocky and dropped his guard. When he returned to the same terminal an observant staff member noticed that although he was wearing the correct shirt and shorts, he had joggers on his feet – something not allowed by the company.*
>
> *The suspicious staff told him that no seats were available on the Sydney run, but he said he would stay and wait for the driver. "Which driver is it tonight?" he asked. "George ———," the staff member replied. "Oh, he's all right, I'll check with him when he arrives."*
>
> *When the official driver came in, the man got out of his seat and called out, "Hey, George, how you're going, can you fit me on tonight?"*
>
> *"Who are you?" George asked. "I've never seen you before in my life. No, there's no room on the coach."*

Moving through the countryside on the gold Denning.

> *The man left the terminal in a hurry and although staff never saw him again the police did. They found he had his own wardrobe of shirts stolen from different coach companies and an appearance in court ended his travelling days.'*

New security checks were quickly introduced by our company to prevent any similar occurrences.

In 1994, our coaches were covering two and a quarter million kilometres each month. It was taking at least four days to re-engine each vehicle after about 1.5 million kilometres.

As mentioned earlier we receive many letters complimenting us on our customer service. Another example, received from a Lockyer Valley businessman in 1994, is reprinted here with the permission of the writer:

> *'I have much pleasure in compiling this note to you in order that you can be made aware of the extra care and dedication shown by your staff to my mentally handicapped son, Glenn, when unexpected circumstances dictated that he travel to Gisborne, Victoria, alone, on one of your coaches.*
>
> *Glenn, who is aged 34 years, is an adult in every way except for his mental disability. He is very quiet and requires only minor supervision.*

I rang your booking office at Toowoomba at approximately 11 a.m. on Saturday, January 1, 1994, and received excellent advice and courteous attention from a very pleasant young lady. I booked Glenn on a seat on the Melbourne-bound coach to Gisborne, departing 4.40 p.m. that day.

Following the advice given by the female booking officer, at the point of departure, I spoke with your driver, Neil Zischke, and advised him of the position re Glenn and requested that, if he had the time, would he supervise Glenn with regard to meal stops etc. This he willingly agreed to do.

Because of the obvious concern and the agreeable attitude of your driver, I returned home both reassured and satisfied that my son was in safe keeping.

The following morning I received a phone call from your driver, Neil Zischke (ringing at his own expense) requesting advice as to the breakfast that Glenn would eat, for Glenn, on occasions, refuses to communicate.

Then again, when the coach had reached Gisborne, I received another call (again at the driver's expense) from the second driver, Gordon Marshall, advising that the coach had arrived at Gisborne and Glenn's sister was not there to meet him. As well as making enquiries at the Service Station Depot, they remained at the depot for a longer period than was required. Then, some five minutes later, a second call from Gordon Marshall advising that contact had been made and Glenn was handed over.

I would like to convey to you the appreciation that both my wife and I have for all the staff concerned, firstly the Booking Officer, secondly the Reception Officer who wrote the ticket and was obviously informed of Glenn's disability, and finally, but certainly not least, the two drivers, both of whom went to extra lengths to see Glenn safely to Gisborne.

I feel that in this day and age, small business can far outdo the larger businesses in both service and attention. How gratifying to discover such a large business as yours gives both service and attention, has employees who are obviously proud of their skills (and justly so), and who are prepared to give just that little bit more.

Congratulations!

I would be more than pleased if you could, in some way, officially thank these fine employees and people who have been such a credit to your company.'

The writer added that in future any employee of McCafferty's who called at his business would be given free coffee, and a discount on any purchase.

Not all the letters about our coach service come directly to McCafferty's. Many appear in the daily press. The following is an example that was in *The Chronicle* (Toowoomba) on August 3, 1993:

'My 18-year-old daughter travels frequently between Brisbane and Toowoomba for a course she is presently doing.

Last week just prior to the bus arriving in Brisbane I found the regular person that normally picked her up from the bus stop was not available to do so. I wish to sincerely thank McCafferty's for all their help in organising transport for her and the coach driver who refused to leave her on her own at a deserted bus stop in Brisbane, waiting until her taxi arrived.

It is nice to know that there are still people who care enough about the well-being of others.'

Chapter 24

From the driver's seat

'I tell you driving coaches is far better than when I worked as a truck driver because you get more rests.'

MICK BATCHELOR, COACH DRIVER
AND FORMER TRANSPORT DRIVER

Driver Don Johnson doesn't drink and doesn't swear, and he's known as 'the Reverend'.

An experienced school bus driver, he has been driving with our company for $3^1/_2$ years.

When he began handling Denning school buses, he had strict control of the passengers. Today the scene is rather different and driver Don Johnson tells of feeling the sting of unruly students:

'Drivers now have problems supervising students and getting them to behave on school buses because of the more liberal regulations. The students get away with a lot now and many know they can get away with it too. We drivers have to be careful what we say to passengers.

You can't pay women compliments any more and I feel that is rather sad. I remember one woman who boarded my coach and had perfect teeth and a really beautiful smile. When I told her that she had a beautiful smile she snapped back, "Are you trying to get off with me?".

I was just paying her a compliment but it went wrong. Now, I think twice before I open my mouth.

There was another time when I had an Islander student who travelled regularly between Ayr and Townsville. She was also clean, tidy and neatly dressed and I would have loved to have told her how smart she looked, but then I thought of the other occasion and said nothing. It is sad really that men can no longer pay a compliment to a person of the opposite sex.'

When you talk to Don about the Emerald terminal he smiles. 'It's the way to learn, when Laurie has a go at you,' he said. 'In fact, it's a great company we work for and every coach has its own history.

The one I was in today used to belong to Clarrie Skennar (Skennar's Coaches). We have to keep the coaches moving, if they sit idle in the yard they are not earning any money.'

Another among the long list of McCafferty's drivers is Mick Batchelor, based in Mackay. He's been driving for 10 years, including seven on the service between Emerald and Mackay. One of the services we provide is to drop off parcels at mail boxes along the road.

Mackay is among the key areas in our network. This region is the centre of large potential tourist growth in the Whitsunday Passage – plus the wealth of the sugar cane industry. John Mansell is our major sales agent there, and today with his modern terminal he is a dedicated McCafferty's agent and one that we greatly admire for what he is doing for the coach and tourist business.

On March 23, 1994, John Mansell was presented with a certificate acknowledging him as McCafferty's top selling agent with sales of $1.5 million for the year. The presentation was followed by Press and TV interviews.

By 1994, our Sydney office at Kings Cross was heavily overtaxed. People who expected the office to be fully-serviced with showers and toilets were disappointed to find it was just a booking office. The office was also being flooded by freight.

While McCafferty's senior executives were working on plans for an actual terminal, staff were recommending that passengers should use Bay 13 Eddy Avenue, at Central Station, which had every facility available including cloakrooms, toilets, waiting rooms, refreshment rooms, phones, taxis and lockers.

In conjunction with the Sydney City Mission and other church groups, we have used our Kings Cross terminal to help to reunite runaway children with their families. Seats were provided on coaches to transport youngsters back to their home towns.

Our company suffered one of the biggest disruptions to its services during the disastrous bush fires in the Newcastle and Gosford area in the first week of January 1994.

When I later visited McCafferty's Sydney office I was amazed at the huge pile of bushfire-relief cartons stacked in the front of the office.

When office staff said they had been told that it couldn't be moved till the following week, I rang the manager of the St Vincent de Paul Society and explained that there was a major problem and the cartons needed to be removed immediately. Within the hour, the manager and another man were at the office and the problem was solved.

Above: Launching seatbelts for coaches in Queensland. Rod Hood (left), Transport Minister David Hamill and Jack McCafferty.

Below: Jack McCafferty with one of the first coaches in Queensland fitted with seatbelts. (1994)

The drivers' reunion at Wivenhoe Dam in February 1993. Back row: Ray George is on the left with Greg Fleming, Harold Grieshaber, Alan Ward, Tony Green, Keith McKhee, Lyle Seng, Arthur Fotheringham, Lester Baguley, Nev Carr, Jack McCafferty, Gordon Marshall, Brian Hayes, Ian Lowe, John Fletcher, Ian Dawson, Danny McCartin, John Williams (obscured) and Jim Pearson. Second Row (left) Clive Fletcher, Stan Wallace and Stan Burton;

McCafferty's Sydney office staff worked long hours during the bushfires, which destroyed many homes.

Our staff, under the leadership of Manager Robyn Bright, coped with the late coaches admirably. Coaches had to be re-routed around the fire areas and McCafferty's received a lot of praise for keeping their services going. Communications were a major headache for those fighting the fires, and those driving coaches.

While staff at the Sydney terminal worked long hours to assist passengers, our drivers used their own mobile phones to make it easier for Toowoomba Operations to organise coach movements.

We gain encouragement from passengers' letters and the following one pays tribute to one of our drivers:

> 'Recently my two young daughters, aged 14 and 12, travelled to Brisbane on one of your buses and returned to Sydney, commencing their return journey at 7.30 p.m. on Friday, January 7, at the height of the New South Wales bushfires.
>
> They reached Doyalson the following morning, but were unable to go any further because the F3 was impassable. Their bus and some others went back to Newcastle for the night and during the next day (Sunday) were given a sight-seeing tour of Newcastle – finally arriving at Parramatta at about 9.15 that night. Why am I telling you this? Because the behaviour of your driver Mr Geoff Bannerman was exemplary. He treated our daughters as his own and allowed us and members of our family to have access to him by mobile phone at any time of the day.
>
> I couldn't speak too highly of Geoff and indeed other drivers in your fleet.'

The Northern Territory Tourist Commission promoted the world's first legal Cannonball Rally from Darwin to Alice Springs in May 1994, and it seemed a good way of promoting our company in the Territory.

We entered the rally with Tony McCafferty nominating his 1980 Jaguar XJS V12, with John Osborne as co-driver.

There are no speed limits on Northern Territory highways which are constructed wider than many other highways. The entry fee was $7,500, but regarded as good value considering the amount of publicity the race generated in the media and particularly on television.

Tony is no stranger to car racing. In 1989, he entered a time trial meeting at Lakeside organised by the Ferrari Owners Car Club. Driving the only automatic at the meet, Tony set the fourth fastest time of the day and the fastest time by a Jag.

Preparing Tony's Jaguar for the Cannonball run from Darwin to Alice Springs in 1994. Tony McCafferty is on the left with John Osborne.

However, the Cannonball Race was a far tougher challenge. The six-day race involved a field of 140 high-speed cars.

In one section, a 137.2km stretch from Erldunda to the Mt Connor Lookout, our Jaguar, called the Cannonball Cat, averaged 191.51km and finished just 24.23 seconds inside its allotted time.

Earlier, the car had developed a problem with the air-conditioning, which affected the electrics, and coming into Alice Springs on darkness there was a vibration at cruising speed which caused some concern.

Our team mechanics, Peter Knihinicki and John McCafferty, worked on the car throughout the night and by 7 a.m. the car was once again running perfectly.

Four people died on the third day of the event when the leader, a Ferrari F40, left the road and slammed into an official checkpoint vehicle. The driver of the $750,000 Ferrari, Japanese dentist Akihiro Kabe, and his co-driver, Takeshi Okano, were killed as well as two race officials.

The incident brought a 'cloud of gloom' over what had been a very successful event.

When I heard of the fatal accident, I got in touch with the McCafferty team. I told them to keep the Jaguar running on four wheels and not to take any risks with the 500-horsepower machine.

A tremendous amount of effort had gone into the preparation of the car. For months mechanics had been working on every mechanical part to ensure that it would put up a first-class performance.

The Toowoomba workshop mechanics Peter Knihinicki and Peter Gleeson had put hundreds of hours into it, and to ensure that it did perform, Peter was riding and sleeping with it all the way to Darwin.

Peter and John McCafferty jnr (Tony's son) had accompanied the Jaguar to Darwin in a 6/8 tonne International Pantechnicon. Gary Barnes (Townsville) had joined Peter and Tony as another relief driver to handle the pantechnicon, which was used to enhance McCafferty's freight operations after the race.

McCafferty's benefited considerably from the publicity and firmly established itself as a reliable and credible operator in the Northern Territory region – and not only in Australia, but also in overseas countries where TV coverage of the event was shown.

The event was extremely popular in Katherine, Alice Springs and Tennant Creek.

People in the outback don't see fancy cars that often and it was a real eye-opener for them.

We were especially pleased when our Jaguar finished in the top 10.

Tony McCafferty's Jaguar was renamed the Cannonball Cat for the race down the centre of Australia.

When Tom Craig started with our company there were only two drivers. Now there are several hundred. Tom has firm views on his choice of drivers at Rockhampton:

> *'In 1994, I am selecting drivers who have a good appearance and manner and with no tattoos. If male, they must be clean shaven. The next test is to take the driver out on a coach and to see if he or she can drive.*
>
> *They have to handle a coach worth a quarter of a million dollars, and that vehicle and its passengers must be in safe hands.*
>
> *On the whole, a country lad makes a far better driver than a city type. He's a different person all together and brings to the company a different attitude. Country drivers are not as arrogant as some of their city counterparts.'*

Rockhampton Terminal now has 14 permanent drivers and four casuals. Gavin Lucke is Assistant Manager.

Manager Ray Shaw insists on having pleasant counter staff who are cleanly dressed and able to handle computers.

But it is strange, that in the world of computers coach drivers still favour old-fashioned full-face wristwatches.

When the company made available staff watches in 1990 they came from Schaeffer-Timex with a clock face – not digital. However, in keeping with modern trends the watches didn't have a winder, but were fitted with a battery. They cost $30 each and came with a 12 months warranty. Each watch featured McCafferty's logo in blue on a white face and had a black leather band.

As well as the other staff, Rockhampton also employs five permanent cleaners and one casual, and coach passengers are asked to observe some rules to help keep the coaches clean.

Drivers allow screwtop soft drink bottles which don't spill, but they don't like drinks in cans, hamburgers, or fish and chips.

There are occasions when some passengers need to eat for medical conditions such as diabetes. They need to be able to nibble on a sandwich, and then there are the sight-impaired travellers who have the 'no dog on board' rule waived so that they can be accompanied by their guide dog.

A woman passenger with her guide dog often travels north to Cairns. Her big, black dog sits near the front seat with the woman and never moves throughout the trip.

McCafferty's Rockhampton terminal is exceedingly busy, with 17 coaches in and out on the busiest weekdays, and on a Friday night, five 45-seater coaches are handled within 45 minutes.

Our coaches can't compete against subsidised railway travel in Queensland, which provides free trips for pensioners and railway staff. However, the coaches do get a spin-off, particularly with people who travel by train from Rockhampton to Brisbane with their free pass and then board a coach to complete the section from Brisbane to Toowoomba or interstate.

Passengers who go missing are always a matter of concern. On one occasion, two people going from Rockhampton to Gladstone booked in but never occupied their seats. Staff made efforts to find them before the coach left, but they never turned up. Were they picked up by someone else?

And then, there was another occasion when Ray Shaw did a head count on Service 145 and found that he had one person too many. He went back down the aisle and did a recount – the extra head belonged to a big teddy bear occupying a full seat.

And that's not the only teddy bear story. I hear a lot at 'head office'. On one occasion a teddy bear was handed in to lost property, and when it was unclaimed one of our female staff took pity on the bear and provided it with a seat in her office. She also improved its attire, gave it a pair of sunglasses and even a can of Coke was placed alongside in case it became thirsty.

She was enjoying her new toy until two other staff members hatched plans to kidnap the teddy bear. They stayed back and removed it when she had gone home.

It was placed in a carton and sent on a trip around the network with a series of instructions. Ransom notes were sent back to the Toowoomba staff member who had befriended the bear saying that unless she made tea for all the staff in her section, one of the bear's paws would be returned on a McCafferty's coach. The teddy bear also sent back postcards saying he was enjoying his trip. Eventually, the teddy bear finished up at Mt Isa, before the prank ended and he was returned to 'Lost Property' in Toowoomba.

Then there was the time at Bundaberg when a cat broke out of his box underneath a coach and the driver just caught him by the tail as he was about to escape from the luggage compartment.

Staff at Rockhampton say computerisation has helped to reduce the paperwork. It's a far cry from seven years ago when they had to work out everything manually.

On one occasion at Proserpine, a driver looked on with disgust as the wind took control of his eight-foot long manifest and unrolled it out across the footpath!

Computerisation has taken the hazard out of placing passengers on seats in coaches. Down the track will be computerised tickets, written on the computer and printed out at point of sale.

At the Rockhampton terminal, McCafferty's staff are on duty from 5.30 a.m. till 9 p.m.

The terminal prides itself in giving service, and in 1994 it received the Central Queensland and Southern Region Tourism Award.

If there is a need for minor maintenance while a coach is in Rockhampton the company turns to Whites Auto for tasks such as replacing radiator hoses, brakes and fan belts. All major work is sent south to the company's Toowoomba workshop which includes a large shed purchased from TNT Rocklea and moved to the Taylor Street site. An idea of just how busy the Toowoomba workshop is can be seen from the throughput figures. From January to April 1991, staff in Toowoomba carried out no fewer than 500 programmed maintenance services on our fleet of coaches.

Chapter 25

Knowing names and faces

'You have to watch your speed on the western roads. You can't swerve suddenly with a coach and you have to hold a straight line, unless the object is a horse or cow. Being on airbag suspension the possibility of a roll exists there if there is a sudden change of direction.'

LEO SMART

I am still waiting to meet some of our new drivers but I keep an eye on their performance. As mentioned earlier, it is a tall order with so many very busy coach schedules.

Leo Smart is one of the drivers based at Rockhampton and this is how he sees his work as a driver:

'My wife Muriel and I have never met Jack McCafferty. I don't mind my nicknames of "Get Smart" (from the TV secret agent program) or "Smartie" (from cheeky school children), and I enjoy driving coaches between Rockhampton and Longreach.

I gave up driving concrete trucks to drive for McCafferty's. I had also had experience with Biloela Coaches.

A lot of people think it's great to have a big shiny truck, with massive bullbars and big headlights, but you have to pay for it, haven't you?

I started doing casual work for McCafferty's about 18 months ago. I did a run to Townsville and a whole new career opened up.'

'Get Smart' lives up to his name. When he was selected to drive a Queensland orchestra around Central Queensland in 1993, he went to town on the coach, polished all the chrome work and even put shoe polish on the tyres. Everything was shining, and then to Leo's horror, the air-conditioning packed up and the musicians said it could affect their instruments, which were on the coach baggage racks.

A new coach was brought in but Leo didn't have time to polish its tyres. He took 34 people to centres including Blackwater, Emerald, Clermont, Dysart, Moranbah and Mackay.

The orchestra had a truck following with their heavy gear and stage equipment, but smaller instruments like trumpets, clarinets and violins were carried on board the coach.

Children came from all over with violins and other instruments to meet the orchestra and take part in workshops, and concerts at night drew audiences of 180 to 200 people. The tour was a great success.

Leo continues:

> *'I have vivid memories of the drought and driving to Alpha, Jericho and Barcaldine.*
>
> *Just before the drought broke, it was nothing to see pigs out on the side of the road looking for something to pick along the edge.*
>
> *Graziers had sheep and cattle grazing in the "long paddock". One night, I was travelling from Barcaldine to Longreach with students on board going back to school. The kids were counting the kangaroos and we saw 20 that night.*
>
> *Some coaches have five-speed gearboxes, some of the Landseers have seven gears, while others have six.*
>
> *I like the coach I was driving today – number 284. She pulls well. She has a V8. You get to know all the coaches, the goers, the mediocre and the "dogs". But you can buy a brand new car and get a "dog". McCafferty's drivers often refer to some of the older coaches as "Dinosaurs".*
>
> *I must say I like driving the gold Landseers, the colour has taken off with the public. The Landseer in grey looked smart but the gold looks better.'*

When he begins a coach journey, Leo interrupts conversations to advise passengers about the coach. He turns on the public address system:

> *"Good morning folks. All hear me at the back? Welcome on board McCafferty's Service 81, Rockhampton through to Longreach and all intermediate ports. My name's Leo and I'm your driver on the way out today and I'll be doing the return service tomorrow.*
>
> *'For those of you who may not have travelled with us before I will quickly point out the main features of our coach. We are equipped with a rest room. It is located at the rear of the coach on your left as you go back. The rest room is equipped with a chemical toilet and please use only the tissue provided. You will also find a wash basin there and the paper hand towel there is a little too much for the toilet and will block it, place it in the receptacle provided.*

Immediately outside the toilet you will find a drinking fountain equipped with paper cups in a dispenser. Underneath that area you will find a rubbish bin for larger objects.

'Going down the coach, immediately above your seat area you will find your air-conditioning vents, which can be adjusted clockwise to open them and anti-clockwise to close them down. You will also find your reading-light switch is located in that same area. Your seat is adjustable with the flick of a button located in the arm rest, and you may find a foot-rest which folds down from underneath the seat in front. If you wish to use it, just give it a pull with your toe and it will pop down, push it back the same way. You will find a motion-sickness bag in the envelope of the headrest in front. However, if at any stage during the journey you feel a bit sick please come up and tell me and we'll pull the coach up and maybe a walk around outside will make all the difference. This is a non-smoking service, however, there will be times during the journey when I am unloading freight and passengers. If you feel like a cigarette and you jump off please let me know that you are leaving the coach. It is your responsibility to make sure that you are back on the coach when we leave. We're going to have a meal break today. The first one is at Emerald. We should be out there at two o'clock. ... If you have any queries or problems along the way please come up and see me about them – things like if the air-conditioner is too cold or not cold enough, the video's too loud or not loud enough please come up and tell me and I'll make the adjustment up the front. Once again welcome on board Service 81. Sit back and make yourself comfortable and enjoy your journey. Thank you.'

Leo Smart's address over the microphone is fairly typical of the introduction to coach travel given by our drivers. Some prefer a shorter version and sometimes drivers create problems.

On one occasion, a passenger was using a tape-recorder on a coach and happened to be recording when the driver was speaking. She sent me a copy and I was appalled.

I couldn't believe any of our staff would talk like that to customers. It just reminded me of a camp commander shouting out the rules to prisoners in a concentration camp. We now keep a record of any misdemeanours or complaints against any staff, and if the complaints get too frequent the evidence may be there for dismissal.

Early in 1994, my company introduced a seven-minute video. The video featured the story about McCafferty's and explained the features of the coach, including seat adjustment, toilet and air-conditioning.

In the early days, there were different ways of helping passengers feel at ease. Mick Manteit relates his experience:

> 'I had a technique in the early days of McCafferty's to get passengers to sit back and relax. You know they would sit in their seats wondering what sort of a fellow the driver was.
>
> I would stop the coach outside the depot and tell the passengers what we would do that day, where we would have meals and encourage them to get to know each other.
>
> I told them to feel safe because I wanted to return home safely too. I said I had a wife and six little children at home and I loved every one of them. As I was the first fellow up front I would be driving carefully and they could sit back and relax. It worked wonders although I did exaggerate a little – I only had one child at home.'

Today our drivers are on the road on so many different routes, as Leo Smart explains:

> 'Yesterday, I did the run out to Capella, the day before that I was in Townsville, a fortnight before that I was on charter. We all do the Brisbane run out of Rockhampton to Townsville, Longreach, Clermont, Moranbah, and the service to Emerald.
>
> McCafferty's drivers are an institution, especially in remote areas.
>
> We are as institutionalised as much as the mail man or the flying doctor. People come up to the coach looking for freight and ask you for information such as "what is the road like behind you"?
>
> Freight is a big part of the service, people rely on McCafferty's to have their freight on board. Many passengers, particularly those in the cattle and grain industries, get to know the drivers by name.
>
> One fellow out west always has some fillets of fish for the McCafferty's driver. I'll bet you today that he will give me $20 on the way out to Longreach to get a cask of Moselle, a packet of Drum tobacco and a packet of cigarette papers to bring back for him tomorrow. It's then that he will tell me to help myself to the filleted fish.
>
> These people are our agents and should we break down they are the first to help organise a tow or anything else we might need.
>
> The run from Rockhampton to Emerald and on to Longreach is one of the "cream runs", and you can wind down a bit, unlike the coastal runs when you have to think a great deal about freight.
>
> We get some interesting passengers. I've had one woman who thought she had gone into labour, and a number of other men and women who have awoken from a deep sleep and thought they had gone past their stop.

I was about to leave West End in Brisbane on one trip when I saw in the luggage compartment what I knew was a coffin. The manager told me that I had an extra passenger on board – but I realised later that it was a joke.'

Then there was the day when a 'parcel' from Cronulla was accepted for Service 102. The consignor was a funeral director and the 'parcel' measured about 6ft 6in by 18in by 18in. The superstitious driver refused to go near the bin where the 'parcel' had been placed.

Many of the more usual boxes consigned out of Sydney contain live fish for the pet store market.

Loving couples can pose problems on a coach, if they become too loving.

On one occasion, our man was in the driving seat when he was approached by a woman who was upset by seeing a couple down the back making love.

'Yes, they are definitely making love,' she said. 'They've got a blanket over them but it is getting so vigorous we keep seeing flesh.'

The driver pulled up the coach on the roadside and walked down the aisle to where the man and woman were seated. He asked them to cool their ardour and to respect the presence of other passengers. They spent the rest of the trip looking out of the window.

On another occasion, a driver had to stop the coach when a man came forward and said there was a fellow at the back 'shooting up'. He thought he was a druggie, but it turned out that the man was a diabetic and was using insulin.

Dealing with drunks is never easy. Leo Smart outlines the problem in Rockhampton.

'I agree with other drivers that drunks, especially on the night run from Rockhampton, are a real problem. Every now and then one of them gets past you and when you reach Dingo or Duaringa, they are flagged out and you can't get them off the coach. You can't lift them, they are a dead weight.

I turn off the coach video at about 10 p.m. and also leave the radio off overnight. While the passengers sleep I switch over to my personal Walkman and play my own tapes, while keeping an ear on the 'two-way'.

The 'two-way' stays on the truck channel 40, but I usually use the headphones so that if any bad language comes over, the passengers miss out.'

We are in the era of new-age technology, but sometimes it causes a real headache, as one of our most experienced drivers explains:

> 'I still remember the Melbourne-bound coach which had just left Goondiwindi when an alarm went off. The driver made an emergency stop, but was bewildered because there were no alarm lights showing anywhere. The cause was a passenger who had recently boarded the coach and who was sitting just a couple of seats behind the driver chatting away on his mobile phone.
>
> Then there was the night a driver from the north came into Toowoomba well behind schedule and was very agitated. He had finished getting passengers and freight off the coach when a man's voice asked, "Why were you late?"
>
> "What's it got to do with you?" replied the driver, who didn't recognise the owner of the voice.
>
> "I run this show," replied Jack McCafferty.'

McCafferty's ended a 47-year-old tradition on Monday, August 23, 1993, when we stopped picking up passengers at the Toowoomba Railway Station for its Metrolink Service. All Metrolink services began departing from the Neil Street Terminal, because of traffic conditions and the changing lifestyle of customers.

With the extension of the electric rail from Ipswich to Rosewood in 1993, we introduced a Gatton to Rosewood service, connecting with the electric train to Brisbane. It followed closely on the heels of a new daily service introduced from Dysart and Moranbah to Mackay, operating Monday to Friday.

In December 1993, we were ready to start the new co-ordinated service from Helidon and Gatton to Laidley, Grandchester and Rosewood to connect with the new extended electric train running between Ipswich and Rosewood.

Two coaches would be used on the seven Helidon-Rosewood daily services each way Monday to Friday, and five services each way Saturday and Sunday and holidays. Two services would operate each way between Toowoomba and Rosewood.

I had noted predictions that there would be a dramatic increase in the local population over the next few years with the University of Queensland Gatton College more than doubling its number of students.

We had our foot in the door and students were now being provided with our new service right into the college grounds.

Electronic ticket machines, linked up to the railway computers, were installed in each coach by the railway.

By February 1994, the new co-ordinated service was 'firing well'. In fact, it had far outweighed the expectations of the Railway Department and McCafferty's. Originally the contract provided for a 22-passenger bus, but we had to introduce a 45-seater coach, because of the increased demand for the service.

When we were contracted for this service, one of the stipulations was that we had to provide for wheelchair access. In the first two months of operation we received only one request. Any passenger using a wheelchair has to advise our company 24 hours in advance so that we can arrange a taxi.

In 1994, I spearheaded McCafferty's to be the first coach company in Australia to introduce enterprise bargaining for its drivers and cleaners with outstanding success. The new award provided an aggregated rate for our drivers and yardmen (cleaners) that suited the particular conditions of the coach industry and the State Transport Department.

The award broke new ground in enterprise agreements in the industry because it applied a loaded rate, instead of the weekend overtime rate, for the 24-hours-a-day, 7-days-a-week nature of the industry.

Mick Manteit looks back on the time when he received his pay packet containing a much lower amount than paid to drivers today:

> *'In the days when McCafferty's began, some drivers only wanted their pay envelopes but some of us did more for our money. We wanted the business to succeed. We stuck with Jack and whatever we could do for the business we did. We always tried to improve things and make it successful.'*

McCafferty's Express Coachlines never stop still. On Friday, April 15, 1994, the company launched one of its newest services to link Adelaide, Darwin and Alice Springs to Ayers Rock.

The fare for the journey from Alice Springs to Ayers Rock was $70 for adults, and from Ayers Rock to Adelaide $135. This service was a vital factor in assisting the growing tourism industry in the Northern Territory. It introduced reliable and economical access to many areas not serviced by other public transport.

It was a year in which McCafferty's were offering a huge network of services across the country, and the shorter routes were also not being neglected: no fewer than 14 services daily were taking shoppers and business people into the heart of Brisbane from Toowoomba.

Chapter 26

Looking back on tours

'Jack McCafferty's charisma is the secret of his success in getting people to go on organised tours – when other operators were saying that everyone wanted to do their own thing.'

WENDY McCAFFERTY

When we organised our big New Zealand tour with 140 people back in 1966, no one else was doing such a thing. And yet McCafferty's were also doing flying trips to Central Australia. Years later, in 1994, a Sydney company was flying to Alice Springs and Longreach and people thought that it was something new.

Then there was the time when our first big overseas tour to Japan and Hong Kong took off in 1968. The group were so proud of their badges, which were written in Japanese, but in Hong Kong we were advised to remove the badges. 'It is too soon after the war,' we were told. 'Please do not wear them here.'

McCafferty's pioneered bus tours to Central Australia in the mid-1960s at a time when no one else was interested.

Every 12 months I take a touring party overseas. I've taken about 30 at the last count. Recently I returned yet again from England, Scotland and Ireland, after visiting North America, and in other years it has been to Europe, Canada, Singapore, Taiwan, China three times, South America twice, South Africa twice, Japan four times and Thailand six times. I like to travel. I enjoy travelling, I don't get bored because I like seeing things and studying people.

I'm an avid reader and writer and take notes while on tour. On return from one overseas trip I outlined the attractions of a number of countries and added a footnote: 'If you are an alcoholic – go to Europe and you will soon be cured as drinks are frightfully expensive!'

Since leading my company's first overseas Goodwill Tour in 1966, I have taken many hundreds of Australians to New Zealand, Fiji, America, South Africa, Europe and the Far East.

I have travelled to practically every corner of the earth. In fact, I'm a proud member of the exclusive Inter-continental Club – having been to every continent.

Wendy McCafferty sees it this way:

> *'In 1993, Jack went with a tour to Canada. He doesn't know or care that other operators are saying that group tours are dead. He is still doing escorted tours. He just puts an advert in the paper to say he's going and he fills the seats. He defies all the odds. I've known tours being sold out even before the adverts got into the paper.'*
>
> *Jack made a statement 20 years ago that he could see the day when New Zealand would be part of the domestic air service. When this occurred there would be no need to board an international flight to visit New Zealand. People thought that he was mad, but now this is happening. He has always been ahead of his time.'*

Occasionally you hear something about yourself from members of your own staff – sometimes its good and sometimes it's otherwise. The following is an example:

> *'Staff have learned much from Jack McCafferty. Through him and the company our whole horizon has been broadened.*
>
> *He encourages us to get in and have a go. He has an aura, but it is not forbidding. He is always one in the crowd.*
>
> *We would fight in the office, sometimes I would win or he would win but he never held this against me.'*

Travel to me is always exciting and I have had many opportunities to escort international tours which have been organised by our Travel Centre. Our Travel Centres certainly have grown over the years, today boasting a staff of 10. Seven in Toowoomba and three in Gatton.

Margie Goltz makes this comment on recently organising a tour to the United Kingdom and Ireland:

> *'This tour that departed in July 1994 was one of our most successful. During the planning stages we anticipated 20 passengers travelling. With Mr Mac leading this tour and with his constant push for making things successful the tour departed with a total of 48 passengers.*
>
> *The tour was valued at $5980 per person and this proved that even though times were tough the fact that Mr Mac was the tour leader made it successful.'*

Among the passengers who enjoyed that trip were my daughter Kay, and my wife Lorna, who had this to say:

'We've sort of got used to going overseas. From one trip to another, people say where are you going next? It's like being on a roundabout in public life, once you're on it you find it hard to get off.

We took 48 people on this trip, and we had 57 once before on a world trip.

Jack loves being with people. He has great enthusiasm. I don't think there is anyone like him.'

Also enjoying the flight with us overseas was my long-time friend Darcy Dukes:

'I was also among the passengers and it was a great trip. One of the best things is that I had many chances to talk with Jack McCafferty.

He is an unusual sort of man, always alert and aware of things. He is far removed from the worlds of failed entrepreneurs Alan Bond and Christopher Skase, who blotted their copy books over money. Jack told me that he is not particularly interested in money. As long as he can keep the place going correctly, straight and honest, then money will never be a problem.

Jack makes no secret that he has operated for quite some time without the assistance of a bank. This is at a time when some other companies are not running right. If a company can survive without the assistance of a bank then it speaks volumes for the capacity of the man.

He is always on the look-out for ideas. I remember sitting with him in an arcade in a community centre far away from Australia. There was a little coffee stall, with one person standing in it and people all around. After a few minutes, Jack said, "Do you know that thing is a very good money spinner. They have sold so many cups of coffee in so many minutes, and maintenance is practically nil. I'm thinking of putting one of them into the terminal in Toowoomba."

He was 9,000 miles from home and still thinking about something that could make a bob. He sees things that others take no notice of.

When we pulled into a place in Ireland there were 40 coaches lined up in one bus park. Our passengers set off to visit a large church, while Jack went along to the coaches and began chatting with the drivers. He was busy asking about the various models and checking out their faults. He laughed when he found that some of the coaches had plastic at the front and said they wouldn't last long with the kangaroos in Australia. The coaches in the UK have heating systems but no air-conditioning.

Early each morning, when he is on tour, you can find Jack in the foyer of the hotel reading the morning paper. He also receives an information fax from his staff in Australia every day to keep him abreast of the local news.

> *He is not interested in money but I know he wouldn't spend five bob unless he was getting value.*
>
> *On the way home from Europe we were three hours out from London when the head steward came to my seat and said, "Mr McCafferty has requested that you be taken up to the flight deck." Jack knew as a pilot I was interested and I later asked him how he got me on to the flight deck? "Oh," he grinned. "The head steward's wife is one of our booking agents at Gosford".'*

To make tours successful it is essential that passengers are kept informed at all times to ensure that their holiday is enjoyable and hassle free.

Margie explains why McCafferty's Tours are always successful:

> *'Some of the advantages of travelling on our tours are that we provide an informative film presentation on the destination we are visiting. Prior to the departure of the tour we have a luncheon with all the passengers and representatives from the airline and tour company.*
>
> *The representatives give detailed information on various aspects of the tour. This includes information on the type of clothing, climate and currency. By doing this our tour passengers have a complete understanding and knowledge of the tour they will be experiencing.*
>
> *In many countries it also pays to cover up any tattoos.*
>
> *Visas too can be a problem. Some countries are strict and if one question on the application form is not answered then there could be a major delay.*
>
> *Many times, injections against disease are not necessary and McCafferty's Travel advise people going overseas to check with their general practitioner.'*

Among the most favoured domestic destinations in Australia are the Queensland islands, while many Toowoomba people have a close affinity with Tasmania.

We launched our Tassie-Connection service in July 1994. It is a unique Australian coach travel service, which includes travel throughout Tasmania, a fare on the Bass Strait ferry, and then connection to the Melbourne McCafferty terminal for onward travel throughout the company's national network.

People also love New Zealand and many older people prefer the quietness of Norfolk Island.

McCafferty's Travel Agency provides a special service for honeymoon couples. The most favourite spots in the 1990s are the

An agents' function when McCafferty's began operating in Adelaide in 1991. John Osborne is on the left with Jack McCafferty and Sandra Boode.

Pacific islands, including Fiji and Vanuatu, and Queensland offshore resorts such as Dunk Island.

Champagne and flowers are placed in the room for the usual stay of seven nights. It costs around $1,000 a person and this is great value when you realise that a good unit at the Queensland resort islands costs between $600 and $700 a week.

Another venture, which has really taken off, is the mystery night and the mystery flight. This is where a person pays around $109 and nominates a day when he or she would like to take a mystery flight. Passengers can stay overnight, for up to two nights, before returning. Normally, if they have an overnight stay they are advised of the actual destination of the mystery flight on the day before leaving so that they can pack the right kind of clothes.

The $109 works out as a major saving on, say, a return flight from Brisbane to Sydney, which is normally $530, or Brisbane to Melbourne, $772. This type of flight, which has a minimum time guarantee of three and a half hours, is very popular, especially with people who have not flown before.

At Christmas, more people now buy mystery flight vouchers or travel vouchers as gifts for their friends and relatives. The vouchers are also popular as wedding anniversary presents.

McCafferty's staff were again busy in 1994 making hundreds of crepe-paper decorations for another spectacular float for

Presenting tickets for a mystery flight won in a Carnival of Flowers competition in 1994. The winners, Mrs I. and Mr S. McGuire, of Toowoomba, are receiving their tickets and being congratulated by Jack McCafferty and Anthony Kuster of McCafferty's Travel.

Toowoomba's Carnival of Flowers procession. Some 480 real flowers were also added to the float on the day before the actual parade.

In 1994, when some people in Toowoomba wanted to turn the city's transit terminal into a shopping centre, I said Toowoomba was nearing the critical population figure of 100,000, when public transport usually becomes a worthwhile proposition. Maybe it is time to re-think on buses for regional cities and to consider a fleet of individually owned minibuses, travelling whatever routes they desire. This could get people back on to public transport.

Our door-to-door Parcels Express Service had been operating since 1993, when Cathy Kirk was busy in Sydney and Melbourne arranging couriers to handle the freight. This system was in addition to our depot-to-depot parcel system.

A year later, the freight division in Brisbane introduced navy blue Sloppy Joe jumpers bearing the printing: 'McCafferty's Parcel Express'. They were being snapped up at $16 each.

'Good morning – McCafferty's – Coral speaking', is the voice you get on most days from our switchboard in Toowoomba. Coral Padget has been with us quite a while and now her contribution to this book makes interesting reading:

> *'I joined McCafferty's when they opened the Neil Street terminal 15 years ago. I began on counter sales and moved through the ranks*

to the switchboard and spent two years as training officer, the latter role now taken on by consultants.

But in those earlier years, I did an intensive 'Train the Trainer' course and trained McCafferty's staff throughout the network from Cairns to Melbourne. Later, in April 1993, the training program was taken over by Ray Parnell. Staff training resulted in letters of complaints about staff falling to just a trickle.

There were some unusual items among freight in the early days, everything from tractor parts and chickens, to live chooks, puppies, goldfish and fingerlings. The goldfish, which were originally packaged in plastic bags, are now transported to pet shops in polythene boxes.

There was one consignment of cockerels which woke all the passengers up at dawn as the coach was driving through the Armidale district in New South Wales.

*Rural women used to wait for their **Women's Weekly,** and they and their husbands would stand at their gates to pick up newspapers and magazines.*

Between Toowoomba and Rockhampton there was often more freight under and inside the coach than passengers, and even today mail is still one of the most important items of freight.'

In 1980 McCafferty's coaches carried Australia Post mail to all towns between Rockhampton and Clermont, but eventually the coaches couldn't handle the increasing volume, and by 1984 it was carried by large truck.

There is also a considerable amount of lost property, which includes pillows, blankets, glasses, towels, hats, jackets and coats, shoes, umbrellas, transistor radios, personal items, wedding and engagement rings and earrings. Cleaners often find wallets and purses lodged down the backs of seats, along with credit cards, pension cards, passports and watches. One wallet, handed in recently, contained well over $1,000.

In storage are bags full of clothing as well as jumpers and hats left behind on school trips.

We go to a great deal of trouble to find the owners of lost property, but it's often an uphill battle.

An example of this was when a woman rang to say that she had left her cardigan on a coach. When a staff member rang back to say it had been handed in, the lady said, 'Well, when are you going to deliver it?'.

On another occasion, a woman rang up a McCafferty's terminal and said she had lost a very expensive French bra.

'I was wearing it when I boarded the coach, but I didn't have it when I left,' she said. 'I would like it back.'

A quick check revealed that it had been thrown out with the rubbish, but it was relocated after a search and returned to the woman.

Any unclaimed lost property items are sent to the head office in Toowoomba, where they are held for a period of time. They are then disposed of in the most appropriate way with items regarded as having value being distributed to the St Vincent de Paul Society, Lifeline and the Salvation Army.

Coral Padget tells how she never loses her cool while working on the McCafferty's busy switchboard:

> 'You need patience. I go with the flow and the only thing that gets me wild is when people swear. I say, "Listen, if you swear at me again I will hang up", and that's just what I do.'
>
> I know what it's like to be left stranded when you miss a coach, but it's no use screaming at me over the phone, you're not going to get anywhere.
>
> To work the switch properly requires a good knowledge of the network.
>
> Callers who want to travel to destinations not serviced directly by McCafferty's own coaches are switched through to the travel office. Many travel enquiries are received for destinations across Australia and overseas.
>
> Sometimes people will ring up and say, "I want to book a bus". I then have to ask them where to?
>
> You also get the ones who ring up and ask, "When's the next bus?"
>
> My switchboard at the Toowoomba terminal has over 50 lines, as well as the 008 numbers from our agents across Australia.'

The Toowoomba switchboard is manned from 8 a.m. till 5.30 p.m. when calls are night-switched to reservations until 9 p.m. Terminal staff come on duty at 4 a.m., and reservations staff at 5.30 a.m. But over the Easter and other holiday periods the phones are manned 24 hours.

As well as using the phone system, Coral also works a fax machine and a photocopier. She always shows me respect and knows that I like my tea without sugar, and have no time for coffee. Her office is close to mine and she makes many observations:

> 'All mail received at the terminal is taken upstairs and opened, stamped and put in baskets for Mr McCafferty to read before it is distributed to other sections.
>
> He is a man to be looked up to. Each day he goes for a walk around town to soak up the atmosphere and get a breath of fresh air.

The new Reservations Section at the Toowoomba Terminal.

One of my most amusing experiences occurred when I was working at the front counter with Ray George.

A woman and a man came in for a trip to Brisbane using the coach-rail Metrolink.

When the man asked for two tickets to Brisbane, I asked, "Single, or return?" The woman grabbed the man's arm, glared at me and said, "We're married". So I just handed over two single tickets.'

On the Thursday before Easter 1994, we had more than 120 coaches on the road, including some provided by sub-contractors.

The only headache was from one of the sub-contractors whose alternator had packed up on his Mercedes-Benz at Warwick, enroute to Sydney. He was six hours late arriving in Sydney, and there was plenty of flak from the disgruntled sporting team that had been due in Sydney at 9 a.m. and didn't arrive until the afternoon.

Customer service remains top priority with our company and this is emphasised time and again in McCafferty's internal newsletter.

One item, worth repeating, was headed:

'Remember Me? ... I'm the customer'

- I'm the person who goes into a restaurant, sits down patiently and waits while the waiters do everything ... but take my order.
- I'm the person who drives into a petrol station, would never think of blowing the horn, but waits patiently while the attendant finishes tuning his mate's car.

- I'm the person who goes into a department store and stands quietly while the sales people finish their little chit-chat.
- I'm the person who rings a company and is asked 'please hold the line'. When I finally speak to the non-apologising operator I never get upset.
- Yes, you would say I'm one of the good guys. But do you know who else I am? I'm the person who never comes back, and it amuses me to see you spending thousands of dollars every year to get me back when I was there in the first place – and all you had to do was **show me a little courtesy!**

In 1994, we launched a new quarterly in-coach magazine, which was 'up market' to our original publication. The full-colour, 42-page magazine, *Travel Time,* features articles on Australian tourism destinations and tips on coach travel.

The first edition looked at outback Queensland stations, Toowoomba, the Matilda Highway, the Canberra Festival and attractions in South Australia. It also profiled McCafferty's, with a special feature on the first 50 years, the routes and services offered, maintenance of the 105 coaches in the fleet, and proposed network expansions.

1994 was also the year in which our company featured prominently in the Queensland Tourism Awards

McCafferty's Express Coaches won the Tour and Transport Operators category at the awards ceremony in Townsville on Saturday, July 30. In its 54th year of operation the company was carrying more than two million passengers a year.

It was the second time the company had won the Queensland Transport Award, while two years earlier I had won the most outstanding individual contribution award. National Marketing Manager John Osborne made the following comment:

> 'This year's award (1994) recognises the company's dedication to service.
>
> I see it as recognition of the efforts by our team of 550 employees to provide a high level of service. In particular our reservations staff, counter staff and our drivers, who have the most direct contact with our customers.
>
> Equally, the result recognises the work of our cleaners and mechanics maintaining the fleet of 105 coaches.'

Chapter 27

Keep looking forward

'When Jack celebrated his 80th birthday, staff turned themselves inside out by hanging up balloons and making the occasion so successful. They are all part of the company and Jack regards the staff as his friends. He has never been interested in making money. It has all fallen into a pattern. He is one of the most generous men you can find and has been a wonderful provider.'

LORNA McCAFFERTY

We have a great staff and this is how one staff member views our company:

'Over the years, the company has developed a "family atmosphere" among its staff, who have a commitment to serving the public. They consider coach passengers not as numbers on seats but as "members of their extended family".

Mr Mac's working day starts at 7 a.m. in the nerve centre of our company's headquarters in Toowoomba, 132km west of Brisbane and the regional capital of the rich Darling Downs.

He is a familiar figure, dressed in a suit and pork pie hat, and standing behind the counter and chatting to passengers leaving Toowoomba in the early hours of the morning. Although his son Tony has long been General Manager, Mr Mac still enjoys working alongside his staff and meeting the public. He speaks to the staff, the drivers who come in from other centres, and the passengers who are leaving the terminal.

Later, after the first coaches have left for their destinations, Mr Mac returns home for breakfast, but he is back at his desk by 9.20 a.m. to attend to the mail, answer calls and meet visitors. He drives back home for lunch at 12.30, returns promptly at 2.30 p.m. and goes home for dinner at 5.30 p.m. each night. Then he returns again to the Toowoomba Terminal to check out the night-time arrivals and departures. This is a routine, as rigid as one of his coach timetables, which goes on each week, unless he is relaxing during the occasional weekend at his unit at Surfers Paradise on Queensland's Gold Coast.

*On his 80th birthday on Friday, March 11, 1994, his wife, Lorna, presented him with 80 red roses. The Toowoomba daily newspaper **The Chronicle** referred to him as "Queensland's grand old man of tourism". The occasion was marked by a party which, despite protests from Jack, involved a large gathering of staff, family, friends and the public at the McCafferty's Coach Terminal at 28-30 Neil Street, Toowoomba.*

Jack McCafferty – founder, managing director and inspirational force behind the company for 54 years – was toasted in champagne as he cut the large birthday cake. His usual favourite drink is Chivas Regal blended Scotch Whisky with a dash of water – but only one a day.'

Toowoomba's Mayor Alderman Ross Miller was among the big crowd at my birthday celebrations. He congratulated me on my birthday and my business achievement in building the company into a national icon that also promoted the city of Toowoomba. He said I had put Toowoomba on the map of Australia.

I told the guests that the success of McCafferty's had been achieved through the love and support of my wife who had put up with me for 55 years. Either I am easy to get on with, or she puts up with anything.

Over the years many tributes have been sent to McCafferty's about the company and the service it provides. The following is one of a number of works set to rhyme.

A Queensland Pioneer
by Kathleen Eleanor Kirkby

To the pioneers of Queensland, we owe our deep respect,
And Jack McCafferty is there, together with the best.
For he opened up the outback, when they said 'It can't be done!'
Jack, with his foresight, started up, his golden country run.

Beginning in the forties, when life and times were bad,
With one small bus he ventured out, a vision that he had.
From one small bus, to a hundred plus, he's built an empire grand,
And now his name lives evermore, throughout this vast brown land.

From the humblest of origin, to international fame,
The coaches of McCafferty's are now a household name.
Of Queensland and of travel, there's none that can surpass,
The coaches of McCafferty's are of the better class.

I take my hat off to him, as he moves from strength to strength,
And his coaches glide by silently, across Australia's length.
For the courage and the foresight, of this gutsy, self-made man,
Who had a dream and persevered, and carried out his plan!

And to Jack's trusty workmen, who toil away each day,
To make the coaches safer, as you journey on your way.
Dennis Densley runs the workshop where only the best will do!
For the name of Jack McCafferty, is riding there with you.

A number of times over the years I have been asked where the name McCafferty came from?

Well, a few years ago, I did a bit of investigative work to determine its origin.

Apparently, McCafferty comes from the Gaelic Mac Eachmharcaigh, meaning steed and rider. The family is a branch of the MacGuires of Fermanagh, who were renowned in battle and won themselves many an honour in their country's history.

The townland of Ballymacaffrey near Fivemiletown, on the Tyrone border, marks their homeland in Ireland.

The coat of arms includes a white horse and a knight in complete armour; and according to historians the white horse is not a symbol liberally used and indicates that this would be an ancient and noble family linking itself far back in history.

There is strength in using McCafferty's name on the coaches.

When a family member had the audacity to suggest changing the name, I snapped back: 'Listen here, if you are not game to put your name to the product don't bother being in the business. I've put my name up front and we have to do the right thing by the people. If you want to hide behind a company then go and do it – but don't try and do it here.'

It has paid off. Passengers give our company plenty of feedback and, if a staff member doesn't do the right thing, then they write to me.

Today, my office in the modern terminal at our Toowoomba headquarters is heated and air-conditioned. I enjoy life in Toowoomba, the home of Australia's major floral festival – the annual September Carnival of Flowers – and we've invested a lot of money on land and buildings in the city.

I'm a practical person and haven't much time for astrology. In fact, astrologists despair in finding out that I am a Pisces, and they tell me that I don't conform to the Piscean pattern of 'a person who doesn't move around very much!'

How things have changed in coach travel as now, in 1995, we enter our 55th year of service to the travelling public. At the latest count we, as Australia's oldest coach company, have 600 employees and 105 luxury coaches, and are running 1,000 regular scheduled services throughout all mainland states and territories, except Western Australia.

Gone are the 'bone-shakers' that transported our grandparents across the country. They have been replaced by modern super coaches. There are now five daily services between Brisbane and Cairns, one between Melbourne and Adelaide, one between Alice Springs and Darwin, nine between Brisbane and the Gold Coast and Brisbane and Toowoomba, four between Brisbane and Sydney, and other services including those out west, making convenient stops along the routes.

Tourists from overseas who arrive in Cairns can tour the city then head down the east coast, taking the time to enjoy the tropical islands of far north Queensland, visit towns such as Townsville, Mackay and Rockhampton, on the way down to Hervey Bay, all in the comfort of the coach.

If tourists are looking for rugged country, McCafferty's will deliver them out west, along the Matilda Highway through Longreach to Cloncurry and even to sample life on an outback station in Charleville, Barcaldine or Winton.

Yes, coaches have changed much since the days of 'The Challenger' at Toowoomba's Picnic Point. Today, our largest coaches are 14.5m long – the longest coaches allowed on the road in Australia. Each can seat 52 passengers in comfort and has wide panoramic-view windows, so passengers can enjoy the sights outside the coach.

The early 1990s saw a complete reorganisation of the Queensland Transport Act, when the Government introduced a type of performance contract with accreditation to operators who met the stringent requirements of the Act.

Coaches used on Express Services were limited by age and had to meet all safety requirements, with seat belts for all coaches built after July 1, 1994. This was when longer coaches with increased seating was allowed.

The first two new extended 52-seater coaches were added to the fleet in 1994 – one by Austral Denning and another by Motor Coach Australia. These were the first two delivered from an order of 15 new coaches to be delivered by the end of June 1995.

On February 23, 1995, the Lord Mayor of Adelaide (Henry Ninio) opened our new terminal at the Adelaide Transit Centre.

Breakfast for business executives and heads of government departments in Toowoomba. Jack McCafferty is on the left with Queensland Premier Wayne Goss, Ms Flint and Les Lewis (Queensland Transport).

In May 1995 West Australia will be added to our network, making McCafferty's a complete national coachline covering all Australian mainland capital cities with connections in Tasmania using Redline Coaches.

There's no short cut to success. It's hard work and determination, that's my motto. Sure I've gone through life and I've made some mistakes – a person who never made a mistake never made a success did he? And if you don't make the same mistake twice you have learnt by it.

In 1994, McCafferty's Express Coachlines recorded a record turnover of $50 million, an increase of $10 million on the previous year's record. In the 12 months, our company carried more than 2.2 million passengers, which was a 20 per cent increase on the previous year.

We had also increased our national market share to around 42 per cent, and the increase in turnover had been achieved without increasing fares. The first of 15 new 14.5m stretchliner coaches, costing a total of $7 million, were ordered for delivery, and 122 new staff members started work during the year.

Chapter 28

Looking ahead and some thoughts on business

A lot has been written into the history of McCafferty's over the past 55 years and no doubt a lot more will be written in the future – not by me – but hopefully by Tony and my family and others.

I can see plenty of areas for expansion.

During this exciting era I have always had, in the back of my mind, the thought of developing a modern Transit Centre and headquarters for a company that has over the years become nationally known. This would be a tribute to the place that gave me the opportunity of making history for Toowoomba.

As a private company which does not have shareholders' money to play with, we have to watch our finances and expand accordingly on a priority basis. We own the present site, which is ideal for such development.

I now believe the time has arrived when we should proceed with the Transit Centre – worthy of the City of Toowoomba – to usher in the 21st century.

The ideal Transit Centre should comprise ground-floor accommodation for the coaches, with lounge and ticketing offices. The next floor could be used for off-street parking, the third floor for McCafferty's administration office, and floors four to 11 could include a hotel with bistro and entertainment section overlooking Queen's Park.

What an ideal location right in the central business district. At present our terminal has a continuous flow of 'passing through travellers'. A project like this could cost $20 million.

I visualise great scope for development not only for Australia and Queensland, but also for Toowoomba to capitalise on further tourism expansion. However, this can only happen if we have the facilities such as a modern hotel to cope with it, and one with a nucleus of a Transit Centre to stimulate it as a busy centre.

Whether this is undertaken by a developer in association with McCafferty's or privately undertaken remains to be seen – but my wish for the future is to see it eventuate.

In Conclusion

You can see by this historical record what has been achieved over the past 55 years and you may well ask yourself how did all this happen?

Well, I can tell you – it wasn't easy!

At 81, I still put in a 12-hour day, getting up at 5.30 a.m. and relaxing at night with a little TV and reading, particularly books on travel.

When am I going to retire? When I can no longer get about and think.

I've enjoyed every minute in the coach business even though I have had my 'ups and downs'. My philosophy is 'If you enjoy doing what you are doing, it will be a success.'

In my opinion the first and foremost prerequisite essential to success in business is to have a plan and aim to achieve it. To do this you have to plan ahead and protect yourself if things do not turn out as you expect them to do.

While I describe myself as a 'loner' I did things that I thought were correct, most importantly 'acting with honesty', and this is a key ingredient with any success story that any private operator can achieve today.

In my life I have travelled to all parts of the globe – by air, ship, train and coach. I have met many important and influential people in my worldly travel and I have taken notice of the way they operate and have learnt from them. Sure I have made mistakes, but from any of my mistakes I have always consoled myself with the old proverb – 'The man who never made a mistake – never made a success'.

When opportunities do come, after deep consideration I study them from all angles and when my mind is made up I go for it – always remembering another favourite proverb of mine 'Procrastination is the thief of time'. Don't hesitate!

Whatever history I have helped to write and what achievements I have created in my lifetime there are similar opportunities if you look for them today.

I was born in 1914 at the start of the First World War. When I reached school age after that war nobody worried whether you went to school or not. As a result I only had a primary school education and two years at high school with very little scholastic achievements.

Then came the Depression years of the 1930s and there were thousands unemployed and no work. For me I started to sell warm milk with a horse and cart and this was when I planted the seed for future expansion.

Following this with the 'Big Time', owning a bus service in 1940, which saw the start of the 'King of the Road'.

The rest of the story is included in this book – covering a period of two world wars and leading up to the 21st century.

During this whole exciting period I never at any stage had any thought of making a pile of money. I was always content with having enough funds to support my family and being able to pay my bills. I was content with this and the result was a buildup of assets and funds and providing a national coach service for the millions of passengers we carry each year. I get a lot of satisfaction from 'doing the thing right' and 'making people happy'.

To achieve this I can tell you it has taken a lot of determination. Believe me, the philosophy is 'right is might', 'hasten slowly,' and always remember 'Rome was not built in a day'.

You don't need to have high academic qualities to be successful today – but it helps.

And, no, I didn't have anything given to me 'on a silver platter'. Whatever I bought in my early days it was always on time payment or Bills of Sale – but I always met my commitments and never had any possession repossessed.

Finally, my advice to anybody starting a new business today is don't be afraid to put your name up front. Don't hide behind a phoney, flashy name. If your product is good, show the public that you stand behind it and don't be afraid to advertise – but do it wisely.

Over the years I have been blessed with relatively good health and I've been fortunate to have enjoyed a good relationship with my wife and family and we have all made big sacrifices.

Dick Eversen, the man who assisted me with our radio advertising campaigns in our early years, sums up my wife's support this way:

> *'Lorna McCafferty is a wonderful woman who has supported Jack in all his endeavours and that is why he has been so successful.*
>
> *He has achieved something in his own life time. Jack has a wonderful staff and family who are working for him and his family will carry on.'*

And, now I'll let Lorna have the last word:

'Jack will never retire. He will die with his boots on. I don't want him to take it easier. I like to see him doing what he wants to do. I think he is motivated and he has disciplined himself. He is a loner.

He gets up at the same time each day and he comes home for breakfast and lunch. He likes good, simple food. In the morning he starts with orange juice and cereal and then enjoys bacon and egg or scrambled egg, or sausage.

Jack is like a gramophone record: No matter what people say or how he is criticised he just keeps on going.'

McCafferty's Staff List
– July 27, 1994

Abell, Noel Leslie
Abernethy, Robert Ross
Alden, Jenifer Monica
Allanson, Jason Scott
Allen, Rebekah Anne
Anderson, John Michael
Anderson, Tony John
Andrewartha, Natasha Kim
Angus, Malcolm Paul
Antaw, Gregory John
Armitage, David
Ashton, Paul Jonothan
Atkinson, Judith Sarah
Atutahi, Susan Mary
Augostis, Nicholas Michael
Baguley, Lester John
Bain, Robert William
Baker, John Edward
Bannerman, Geoffrey Robert
Barclay, Edward Thomas
Barclay, Susan Maree
Barker, Barrie Alexander
Barling, Debra Mary
Barnes, Ann Maguerite
Barnes, Gary Franke
Bartlem, Robert Frederick
Batchelor, Maurice John
Batham, Debra Annette
Batley, Geoffrey Ross
Batley, Peter Frederick
Baxter, Ross Harold
Beasley, Mark John
Bell, John Philip
Bellingham, Richard Eric
Bendall, Theresa Mary
Berry, Gary John
Biles, Leslie Allan

Birse, Lyndsay Scott
Blacka, Douglas Michael
Blatchford, Elizabeth Grace
Block, Juan Allan
Boath, Erin David
Boath, Kenneth David
Bogileka, Cheryl Ann
Boland, Michael David
Bonaventura, John Samuel
Bonell, Andrew Marshall
Boswood, Sandra Elizabeth
Bowden, Penny Ronalde
Boyce, Cameron Dean
Boyce, Jennifer Anne
Brain, Andrew
Bray, George Winston
Bray, Philip Keith
Brebner, Donald John
Bremner, Alexander David
Bridgford, Jonathan Vance
Briscoe, Stephen Robert
Britton, Glyn Maxwell
Britton, Peter Malcolm
Brosnan, Susan Melissa
Brown, Justin Conrad
Brown, Michael Thomas
Brown, Paul Augustin
Brown, Robert George
Brown, Terence Colin
Brown, Vicki Maree
Buckingham, John Gregory
Buckley, Barry James
Burrows, Michelle Kathleen
Burton, Stanley Wayne
Bussell, Leisa Jane
Butler, Dean
Butterick, Ian John

Byron, Monica Maree
Callow, Robert Raymond
Cameron, Kevin George
Campbell, Anthony Wayne
Campbell, Catherine Jeanette
Campbell, Deann Marie
Cardiff, Sheree Nicole
Carey, Darren James
Carless, Lesley Patricia
Carroll, Colleen Marie
Carter, Karen Elizabeth
Carter, Timothy James
Carver, Robert Maxwell
Casey, Cleve Ernest
Casey, Cleve Kelvin
Chardon, Vernon Frederick
Charlton, Robyn
Cheers, Thomas Clement
Chessher, Russell Clive
Chopping, Lyle Owen
Clarke, Graham Stanley
Clarke, Leeonie Eleanore
Clarke, Michael John
Clarke, Vincent Matt
Clough, John Trevor
Cocks, Shane William
Coleman, Alan Stephen
Colvin, Edward Binny
Copeland, Jeffrey David
Cornish, Geoffrey William
Cosgrove, Shannon Lee
Court, Melanie Rae
Craig, Thomas William
Craige, Donald Stanley
Cross, Sharon
Cullen, Michael David
Curtis, Colin Richard
D'Mech, Robert William
Dacey, James Alan
Dartnell, Catherine Mary
Davies, Rodney Michael
Davies, Theresa Pamela
Davis, Kelvin Lindsay W.

Davis, Trevor Owen William
Daw, Neil Leslie
Day, Roger Mervyn
Delander, Timothy Philip
Dennien, Gayle Fay
Densley, Dennis Bertie
Dickman, Kristina Jane
Dodd, Michael Howard
Donnelly, Susanne Annette
Donohue, Fiona Louise
Dukes, Malcolm George
Eckhardt, Warren David
Edwards, Sandra Jane
Egart, Timothy David Robert
Ehrlich, Lucas Bevan
Eising, Jilliene Sue
Elfenbein, Bruce William
Ellerton, Jeffrey Lawrence
Elliott, Jamie William Robert
Elliott, Kay Frances
Evans, Raymond Anthony
Fairlie, Peter Gordon
Fallon, Graham James
Farrell, Richard Seymour Sonic
Fett, John Henry
Finch, Phillip John
Fisher, Mark Allan
Fisher, Michael James
Fleming, Ann
Fleming, Gregory Michael
Fletcher, Peter Charles
Flynn, Russell Leonard
Foster, Fiona Sarah
Foster, Jason Paul
Fowler, Craig Leslie
Fox, Allan John
Fox, David Charles
Fox, David Gerard
Franks, Brian William
Fraser, Fayline Agnes
Fullerton, Jason Ray
Fullerton, Ray Kenneth
Fulwood, Robert John

Furner, Adrienne Mary
Gadsby, Justin Stuart
Ganas, Peter George
Gangemi, Sonia Leigh
Ganzer, Jacqueline Denise
Ganzer, Terence Christopher
Gardiner, Leslie
Gardner, Christine
Gavin, Wendy
Geddes, John Edward
Geeson, David George
Genrich, Simon Christopher
Genrich, Tracey Diane
Gentle, Maxine Claire
Germain, Deborah Kay
Getsom, Anni
Gibson, Warren Lance
Gierke, Margaret Beth
Gillam, Charles Young
Gleeson, Peter Michael
Golle, Paul David
Goltz, Margaret Mary
Gordon, Colin William
Gordon, Linda Anne
Gotje, Barry John
Gourley, Stephen Charles
Graham, Eric Russell
Granter, James Mark
Green, Chris Allen
Green, Peter Robert
Greer, Ronald James
Greig, Reginald Keith
Grieshaber, Harold Percival
Grieshaber, Robert Noel
Grieve, Albert
Griffin, William Thomas
Haddon, David Leslie
Haining, Julia Patricia
Hall, Peter Brenton
Hall, Robert Selwyn
Hamilton, Brian Colin
Hannan, Edmund Maurice
Hanrahan, Edmond Joseph

Hansberry, Anne-Marie
Hansford, Edward Paul
Harbrow, Marcus Victor
Harms, Dennis Gregory
Harris, John Stanley
Harvey, Kevin Graham
Harvey, Peter Edward
Haskett, Cameron James
Heatley, Michael John
Henderson, Brian Robert
Henderson, Tracy Fay
Heye, Gary Anthony
Hickman, David John
Hills, Anthony Raymond
Hills, Christopher Douglas
Hills, Gail Mary
Hindle, Bryan Norman
Hines, Ronald James
Hitchcock, Kent Hilton
Hoffman, Shelley Marie
Hoffmann, Andrew John
Hoffmann, Graeme John
Hogg, Benjamin Peter
Hohn, Denise Carol-Ann
Holloway, Kirsty Lee
Holt, Robert Henry
Hoogkamp, Robertus Willem
Hoolihan, Leonie Jane
Horton, John Oliver
Hudson, Julia Clare
Hughes, Carissa Margaret
Hughes, Robyn Lenore
Humphries, Wayne Harry
Hunt, Arthur David
Hunt, Bradley John
Hurle, Jeffery Allan
Hurst, Peter John
Hutchings, Nicholas
Jackel, Barrie John
Jakobi, Shane Steven
James, Angela Maree
James, Leslie William
Janicki, George Matthew

Janicki, Lynne Patricia
Jarrett, Leonard William
Jensen, Brian John
Jensen, Ronald Arthur
John, Trevor Stanley
Johnes, Timothy Simon
Johnson, Donald Bilson
Johnson, Leslie William
Johnston, David Allen
Johnston, Paul Joseph
Jones, Barry Ronald
Jones, Kenneth John
Jones, Ronald Grahame
Jordan, Geoffrey Colin
Joy, Brett Terrance
Judd, Alfred Cecil John
Judd, Jason Paul Wesley
Juillerat, Rodney James
Kay, Anthony John
Keane, Susan Margaret
Keating, Colin Laurence
Kershaw, Tim
Kiernan, James Robert
King, Jodie Ann
Klingner, Phillip Roy
Knihinicki, Peter John
Kowalski, Richard William
Krause, Edward John
Kreis, Linda Jane
Kreis, Paul Douglas
Krueger, Dieter Gerhard
Kuster, Anthony William
Lambert, Graham James
Lammas, Richard John
Lane, Simone Marie
Lange, William Pryde
Langford, Bruce David
Langford, Robert Steven
Lawarowicz, Gerard Peter
Lawry, Kerryn Ann
Laws, Michael Anthony
Lawson, Gordon Leslie
Lawson, Michael John

Leaman, Janelle Karoline
Leben, Irene Frances
Lee, Noel Malcolm
Lee, Rebecca Jane
Lenton, Keith
Leschke, Ronald Alfred
Leske, Allen Robert
Liebke, Anthony John
Lindsay, Amanda Jane
Littleton, Fiona Louise
Livingstone, Karen Jean
Lloyd, David John
Lomas, Michael John
Lord, Brendon
Lowe, Ian Graham
Lowe, Warwick
Lowis, Alfred George
Loy, Natasha Ann
Lucht, Tracey Ann
Lucke, Gavin Douglas
Lyons, Jeffrey James
Lyons, Richard Mark
Macdonald, Greg Keith
Macdonald, Helen Louise
Macfarlane, Robert Donald
  Armstrong
Mackay, Kay Ann
Madden, Ian Colin
Mallinson, Tenny Carol
  Rosemary
Malpress, John
Marsh, Barry David
Marshall, Gordon Clive
Marson, Lorena
Martin, Christina Luise
Martion, Janice Maree
Massey, Andrew Nelson
May, Garry John
McAllister, Robert Andrew
  John
McAllister, Scott Andrew
McBride, Christopher John
McCafferty, John Paul

McCafferty, John Tony
McCafferty, Kenneth Aubrey
McCafferty, Rodney James
McCarthy, Therese Mary
McDougall, Lyle Kevin
McGuiness, Geoffrey Keith
McIlwain, Lorinda Anne
McInnes, Noel Donald
McKinnon, Terence
McLean, Ian Ross
McNicol, Arnold Keith
Meadows, Robert
Medlin, Lorienne Margaret
Medlin, Raymond Stanley
Menzel, Karen Joy
Merchant, Warren Ashley
Michelmore, John Raymond
Mietzel, Wayne Allan
Miles, Bruce Norman
Miles, Michael Bernard Jeffrey
Miller, Amanda Jane
Miller, Jason Robert McLean
Mills, Glenda Dorothy
Milsom, Graham John
Missen, Brian Henry
Mitchell, Dale Stanley
Mizzi, John Joseph
Moloney, Ian Noel
Moloney, Tania Mary
Morgan, Brian Stanley
Morgan, Craig
Moro, Robert John
Morrison, Edmund Joseph
Morrison, John Bernard
Mules, Richard Douglas
Mulley, Eric Neville
Murphy, Terrence John
Murray, Bruce Hamwood
Myers, Edward Barnet
Nash, Ian John
Neal, Trevor George
Nevin, Stephen Francis
Newmark-Jones, Lee Anthony
Nicholson, Vanessa Lee

Nickols, Adrian Victor
Nicol, Edwin
O'Brien, Denis John
O'Donnell, Brett Michael
O'Reilly, Laura Louise
O'Reilly, Sandra Maree
Oats, Robert Bruce
Orange, Owen Percy
Ormos, Michael Stephen
Osborne, John Edwards
Oscar, Alan Lynton
Owen, Alan James
Padget, Coral
Pattison, Stephen Daniel
Pavy, Carolyn Nina
Paxton, Maxine Lee
Pegg, Stanley Joseph
Perkins, Terence Arthur
Persson, Jane Lisa
Peters, Elson Edward
Peterson, Allan Douglas
Pfau, Wulf Heinrich Kurt
Philipson, Carolyn Sharee
Plant, Laurinda Jayne
Plasto, Julie Maree
Plymin, Kenneth Stuart
Postle, Neil Robert
Powell, Lance Arnold
Powell, William James
Probst, Alfred Heinrich
Purvor, Reginald Charles
Quinn, Maree Veronica
Quinn, Michael Gerard
Quirey, Tammy Michelle
Rasmussen, Neville Charles
Rattray, Jan Cyril
Reeves, Noel David
Reilly, Shaun Lance
Relph, David Colville
Rennie, Amanda Susan
Rennie, Graham Alexander
Rentell, Anthony Robert
Reuter, Bernard Allan
Reynolds, Mark Gregory

Richardson, Deon Robert
Rienecker, Juanita Louise
Riley, Lynette Maree
Ritchie, Vanessa Jane
Roberts, Stuart Norman
Rodger, Maree Elizabeth
Rodgers, Stephen John
Roff, Carol William John
Roseler, Paul
Rosengreen, Graham Allison
Rosengreen, Kaye Maree
Ross, Walter William
Rowan, Allan Mark
Rowland, Peter Wilfred
Rowles, Gary Bruce
Ruge, Dennis John
Rummell, Jodie Marie
Rummell, Peta Jayne
Sanders, Raymond John
Saunders, Hugh
Sawyer, Cherith Joy
Schmidt, Kenneth Leroy
Schoeffler, Thomas Luke
Schuller, David Paul
Scott, William Henry
Scurr, Robert Kevin
Seaton, Robert Graham
Sebbens, John Graham
Seiler, Stephen Frederick
Sharp, Michael William
Shaw, Raymond Charles
Sheen, Paul Leo
Shephard, Craig Royston
Sheward, Wendy Nicole
Shilvock, Alan Joseph William
Short, Gregory William
Sieders, Eite
Sieders, Glen Gary
Sieders, Shane Eite
Simpson, Kevin John
Sims, Russel Brian
Sims, Trudy Leigh
Skinner, Keith Raymond

Skinner, Suzanne Maree
Sloan, Karen Jill
Smart, Leo John
Smith, Anthony Michael
Smith, Cathryn Lenice
Smith, Dexter Arthur
Smith, Peter Stephan
Smith, Tonette Trisha
Smithers, Dior Dana Lois
Smithers, Lock Andrew John
Spence, Raymond Victor
Spencer, Bryan Christopher
Spencer, John William George
Spencer, William George
Spinks, Rodney Peter
Spyrou, Caron lee
Squire, Anthony Noel
Stedman, Peter Harry
Stevens, Victor Stanley
Stokes, Kenneth Arthur
Stone, Paul William
Stower, Steven Gary
Sullivan, Geoffrey James
Summers, Barry William
Summers, Philip James
Sutton, Helen Fay
Sutton, Sandra Isabel
Swain, Melissa Ruth
Tait, Heidi Amanda
Taylor, Debbie Lashell
Taylor, Gregory Ross
Teichmann, Alan George
Thomas, Denis Edward
Thomas, Kelly Louise
Thomas, Russell Dean
Thornell, Colin Henry
Thornton, Tony Stephen
Thrupp, Jacqueline Janet
Thrush, Phillip Arthur
Thurecht, Rabecca Amy
Thurgood, John Robert
Tighe, Dean Allen
Tilbrooke, Robert Rae

Timm, Shane David
Tinmouth, Craig Noel
Toms, Peter James
Totani, Lino
Travers, Ian Leslie
Trbusic, Ivan
Treichel, Paul William
Trenorden, Steven Robert
Trevanion, Arthur John
Underwood, Ian Charles
Ungerer, Audrey Noela
Vanderboot, Alex Andre
Vella, Raymond Leonard
Velt, Colin William
Verbrugge, Peter Andrew
Vidler, Ashley Martin
Wagland, Alfred John
Walker, Darryl Lindsay
Walker, Tracey Kay
Wallace, Norman Stanley
Walter, Carl Bevan
Warcon, Calvin Paul
Warcon, Leroy Charles
Warcon, Phillip Gerald
Ward, Anthony John
Ward, Jennifer Esther
Ward, Sally Jane
Warren, Damien James
Warren, Lucinda Jane
Warren, Stephen Alexander
Watt, Rodney Craig
Watts, Trevor Leonard
Weber, Wendell Paul
Weil, Paul Stanley
Welke, Ronald Bert

Welling, Terry Dale
Wells, Michael John
Wessling, Shane Warren
Weston, Ian Gilbert
Whaley, Melinda Jane
Whitla, Michael Francis
Wieden, Murray David
Wilce, John Phillip
Wilde, Jody Ande
Wilds, Brian John
Wilkes, Paul James
Wilkie, Raymond John
Will, Brian Conrad
Williams, Leslie Michael
Williams, Malcom James
Williams, Paula Maree
Williamson, Michael James
Wilson, Craig Darren
Wilson, John Sydney Vincent
Wilson, John William
Wilson, Margo Elizabeth
Wilson, Suzanne Maree
Withington, John Basil
Wittmaack, Mark Kenneth
Wolff, Micheal Christopher
Worden, Gregory Neil
Wright, John Michael
Wrigley, Natasha Jane
Yates, Christopher Thomas
Yelland, Victoria Louise
Young, Barry William
Young, Crayston Webster
Young, Tracy Louise
Zischke, Neil Leslie

McCafferty's Terminals across the Continent

Adelaide Terminal: 101 Franklin Street, Adelaide, SA 5000. Phone (08) 212 5066. Fax (08) 212 5166.

Alice Springs Terminal: Shop 3, 91 Gregory Terrace, Alice Springs, NT 0870. Phone (089) 52 3952. Fax (089) 52 3674.

Brisbane Terminal: Brisbane Transit Centre, Roma Street, Brisbane, Q. 4003. Phone (07) 236 3033. Fax (07) 236 1039.

Brisbane, West End: Duncan St. Workshop, Parcels and Freight. Phone (07) 846 5711.Fax (07) 846 1752.

Cairns Terminal: Trinity Wharf Centre, Wharf Street, Cairns, Q. 4870. Phone (070) 51 5899. Fax (070) 31 2609.

Coolangatta Terminal: Golden Gateway Travel, Boundary Street, Tweed Heads, NSW 2485. Phone (075) 36 5177. Fax (075) 36 9146.

Darwin Terminal: Transit Centre, 69 Mitchell Street, Darwin, NT 0800. Phone (089) 41 0911. Fax (089) 41 0928.

Emerald Terminal: 115 Clermont Street, Emerald, Q. 4720. Phone (079) 82 2755 or 82 2035. Fax (079) 82 3319.

Gatton Terminal: 47 Railway Street, Gatton, Q. 4343. Phone (074) 62 1267. Fax (074) 62 4352.

Melbourne Terminal: Spencer Street Coach Terminal, Melbourne, Vic. 3000. Phone (03) 670 2533. Fax (03) 670 3165.

Mt Isa Terminal: Campbell's Coaches, 29 Barkly Highway, Mt Isa, Q. 4825. Phone (077) 43 3685. Fax (077) 43 6903.

Rockhampton Terminal: Cnr Brown and Linnett Streets, Nth Rockhampton, Q. 4701. Phone (079) 27 2844. Fax (079) 27 9076.

Surfers Paradise Terminal: Counter 1, Surfers Paradise Bus Station, Beach Road, Surfers Paradise Q. 4217. Phone (075) 38 2700 or 39 0410. Fax (075) 38 5103.

Sydney Terminal: 179 Darlinghurst Road, Kings Cross, NSW 2011. Phone (02) 361 5125. Fax (02) 360 1282.

Toowoomba Terminal: 28-30 Neil Street, Toowoomba, Q. 4350. Phone (076) 38 1199. Fax (076) 32 5457 (Administration); (076) 38 3815 (Marketing).

Toowoomba Travel Office: Cnr Russell and Neil Streets, Toowoomba, Q. 4350. Phone (076) 39 4455. Fax (076) 32 0409.

Townsville Terminal: Townsville Transit Centre, Cnr Palmer and Plume Streets, South Townsville, Q. 4810. Phone (077) 72 5100. Fax (077) 21 1864.

Index

Index

Index